For Jessica,

good luck with
your Masters degree

TO BE A
trial
lawyer

TO BE A

trial
lawyer

Second Edition

F. LEE BAILEY

John Wiley & Sons, Inc.

New York • Chichester • Brisbane • Toronto • Singapore

Copyright © 1985, 1994 by F. Lee Bailey
Published by John Wiley & Sons, Inc.

Library of Congress Cataloging-in-Publication Data:

Bailey, F. Lee (Francis Lee), 1933–
    To be a trial lawyer / by F. Lee Bailey. — 2nd ed.
        p.   cm.
    Includes bibliographical references.
    ISBN 0-471-07256-7 (pbk. : acid-free paper)
    ISBN 0-471-11920-2 (special edition)
    1. Trial practice—United States.   2. Law—Vocational guidance—
United States.   I. Title.
    KF8915.B343   1994
    347.73'7'023—dc20
    [347.03077023]   94-14857

Printed in the United States of America

10 9 8 7 6 5 4 3 2 1

To the future trial lawyers of America.

Acknowledgments

There are many people to thank for their help. Harvey Hamilton, Jr. of North Carolina, who taught me how to try a lawsuit; Edward Bennett Williams, who was an early inspiration; my distinguished colleagues of the trial bar—Mark and Roz Kadish, Roger Zuckerman, and Ken Fishman, who offered helpful critiques; Professor Alan Dershowitz of Harvard for his thoughtful Foreword; Professor Bill Alfred and Rusty Miller of Harvard for their editing insights; and Linda Bailey, Karen Stout, and my irreplaceable Edna Adams for their toil on the manuscript.

Foreword

A lawyer's education is far too important to be left entirely to law schools. No school, regardless of how good it may be, is capable of teaching the potential lawyer all there is to know about the profession (and business) of law. Having said that, it is important to add that a lawyer's education is also too important to be left entirely to practicing lawyers. An excellent legal education requires a balance of classroom, courtroom, and office experience. This is especially true of the education of trial lawyers. For generations, law schools have not succeeded in their mission to educate trial lawyers. The law school at which I teach—Harvard—bears some of the responsibility. Back in the nineteenth century, its dean, Christopher Columbus Langdell, developed the appellate-case method of law teaching. Most law schools still employ this method of teaching substantive law, legal doctrine, legal theory, and procedure. Emphasis is placed on appellate decisions—that is, opinions rendered by courts of appeals, primarily on issues of law. That is understandable, since American law is largely judge-made, and our appeals courts are the primary makers of law. (Legislatures, of course, enact statutes, but statutes generally are very broad in application and rarely resolve specific disputes.)

What American law schools often do not teach—at least do not teach well enough—are the basic skills of advocacy: how to prepare a case, how to examine a witness, how to argue before a jury, how to write a brief, and how to argue before appellate judges. One of the understandable reasons why law professors don't emphasize these skills is that many of them simply do not have experience or expertise in them. Law professors are selected, at least at many schools, not because of their skills as practicing lawyers, but because of their reputations as legal scholars and teachers. (In fact, many law professors would probably make excellent advocates, since classroom teaching bears some striking resemblances to courtroom advocacy; law teaching is not one of those professions where "those who can, do, while those who can't, teach.")

For whatever reasons, it remains true that an honors graduate of an elite law school can enter upon the practice of law without the slightest inkling of what it takes to be a successful advocate. Nor, until now, has there been a single good book to which the student could be directed in order to enhance—really establish—these fundamental skills of advocacy. For the most part, students have been told to go out into the world and observe those who are thought to possess these skills. The problem is that most students don't have the foggiest notion of how to recognize a skilled advocate when he or she sees one. Advocacy is not a skill which is always apparent, especially in the brief observations that most students are able to make of practicing lawyers. Accordingly, students occasionally confuse articulateness with advocacy. Though articulateness may be a prerequisite to effective advocacy, it is not a substitute for it. Students, and indeed clients, often confuse smoothness, sartorial splendor, good looks, and charm with effective advocacy. Again, these fortunate attributes may certainly help a lawyer persuade a jury (or even a judge). But, in my experience, some of the worst advocates I have ever seen have been smooth, charming, good-looking—and stupid. Speaking of stupidity, law students also frequently confuse intelligence with effective advocacy. Again, a high degree of intelligence is certainly important for effective advocacy but it is by no means a substitute. I have heard some of the smartest people I know make some of the least effective arguments before judges and juries. Effective advocacy is one of the most difficult attributes to identify in a potential or practicing lawyer. It may take years to develop and hone that skill—really collection of skills—into the finished product of which the advocate is justly proud.

F. Lee Bailey's extraordinary book takes a giant step toward filling this vacuum in legal education. Bailey is, first and foremost, a consummate advocate. I have observed him in court. I have worked with him. And I have seen his work product. Nor is he one of the great advocates who claims that the skills of advocacy are a deep dark secret, like some fraternal ritual. Bailey is willing to share his skills and encourage others to develop them. He has few magic formulas. Developing skills of advocacy, Bailey argues, is a life-long project. Sure there are hints, shortcuts, blind alleys to be avoided, and other handy tools of the trade to be picked up, but the key is hard work, and Bailey tells his reader exactly where to devote his or her energies in order to maximize the return.

No law school graduate should regard his or her legal education as complete unless he or she has begun to develop skills of advocacy. The skills taught in this book are advocacy skills of a trial lawyer. But every lawyer, at bottom, is an advocate. Law is an adversarial profession. And the skills necessary to make a good trial lawyer are also helpful in making an effective office advocate, negotiation advocate, or consumer advocate. I strongly commend this book to all potential trial lawyers and, indeed, to all lawyers who hope to improve their skills of advocacy.

ALAN M. DERSHOWITZ
Professor of Law—Harvard Law School and author of *Reversal of Fortune,* 1986, *Taking Liberties,* 1988, *The Best Defense, Chutzpah,* 1991, *Contrary to Popular Opinion,* 1992, and *The Abuse Excuse,* 1994

Contents

Introduction

W hen, at the age of twenty, I decided that I wanted to be a trial lawyer—and not a writer, as I had planned when I majored in English at Harvard—I went looking for a book to guide me in preparing for my new vocation. I never found such a book, and in fact, I have not seen one yet.

During the past thirty years I have given various groups more than 2000 lectures, most of them about some aspect of the legal system. At universities and law schools, a question-and-answer period or a reception often follows the lecture, and at virtually every event, someone has asked, "How do you go about preparing yourself to be a trial lawyer?" I usually mention a few books that offer some insight to the profession, but none really attempts to answer the question in depth.

This book is an effort to furnish those answers. It is directed primarily at young men and women who are considering *advocacy*—the business of trying lawsuits before judges and juries—as a professional career. Among them there are those who simply do not possess the innate characteristics of personality, philosophy, endurance, drive, speed, and wit to be comfortable in this line of work, and this book will serve them best by persuading them to seek their fortunes elsewhere. Not everyone is suited to the demands of this calling, any more than everyone is suited to become a jet aircraft test pilot. To those who *do* find that they have the necessary ingredients, guidance will be offered as to how best to hone and ripen those talents and skills.

The book should also be helpful to parents and educational counselors who undertake to advise their charges in selecting a career. By the time a youngster is in his or her late teens, a parent should have a pretty good idea where his or her strong suits lie. Very little in life is more important than being happy and comfortable in one's work, and correct career decisions are vital to achieving that goal.

Finally, these pages should provide a checklist of sorts for clients confronting important trials. As a rule, laymen have too little help when selecting a trial lawyer to handle their critical problems. Some of the most miserable people I have known have come to me while a long-awaited trial was in progress, wringing their hands because they have come to realize that their advocate is inept, or ill-prepared, or unable to grasp what he is supposed to be doing. Their feeling is similar to that of one who is conscious during vital surgery and finds to his horror that the surgeon is not up to the task before him. Unfortunately, it is much too late, in either case, to start changing personnel.

If you should read this book and find that the business of advocacy is not for you, pass it along to a friend who seems to be a more likely candidate. If you *do* decide to embark upon this important and honorable career, keep the book with you as you progress. It is not meant to be digested at one sitting, or even two. Much of what it contains is subtle, and needs to be examined repeatedly as you mature, grow, and progress if you are to benefit most from the ideas, suggestions, rules, and principles herein. If you begin with the necessary elements, you will grow in each area of personality and character that a good trial lawyer must possess.

If you start right and work hard, your life will be demanding but exhilarating, often difficult but usually rewarding, and a source of lasting confidence and personal satisfaction. As the years go on, and goals of professional recognition and financial security are attained, most healthy human beings look about to see what benefit they have delivered to others. Good trial lawyers who reach this rung of the ladder of life usually have solid grounds for contentment, for they are the guardians and the managers of society's most important gift to its constituency: justice without violence.

This new edition contains two new chapters, Chapter 14 on "Computers and Their Use in the Law," and Chapter 15 on "Juries."

F. LEE BAILEY

1

What Trial Lawyers Do

To understand best the functions of a trial lawyer, or advocate, or litigator, let us view the practice of law as a pyramid. At the base of the pyramid are the clients and their lawyers, practitioners of many different specialties. These lawyers draw contracts, wills, trusts, and other instruments; they fill out income taxes and file them; they draft patents on new devices and inventions, or draw up copyrights and file claims upon them with the government; they bring claims for personal harms (called *torts*) against third parties; they draft insurance policies, which are then sold to consumers; and they pass new laws, rules, and regulations to govern the lives of the public. These are the people who create things legal, and a great many of these things are put into operation and come to rest as completed legal acts. When a

1

contract has been fully performed, or the provisions of a will carried out, or a claim paid at face value, the matter is concluded without leaving the base of the pyramid.

The next level of activity is carried on by lawyers who are "interpreters." Often there is some question over what the language in a document, regulation, or statute really means. Sometimes the lawyer who drafted the document is asked to advise how certain language should be construed. Often some *other* lawyer is asked to do the interpretation, particularly where the language under consideration appears in some law passed by the Congress or a state legislature. If the interpreter's advice and opinion are accepted by all the interested parties then the matter comes to rest. Since not all legal things that are *created* require *interpretation,* our pyramid is narrowing as we ascend.

When the interpretation of legal language is not accepted by all concerned, or when the parties are unable to agree on the *facts* to which that language applies, we have the elements of a *dispute.* At this point the service of lawyers who *negotiate* is required. Many negotiators are trial lawyers, but many more are not. Negotiators seek to sort out and resolve factual disputes, and frequently find that the dispute is principally the product of poor communication between the parties. If this is the case, a negotiated agreement is normally easy to reach.

But when there is an actual dispute of fact, or a sharp disagreement over what the controlling legal language means, negotiation becomes more difficult.

Suppose for instance that V, the vendor of some curtain rods, *claims* that he called C, a customer for those curtain rods, and informed C that the rods would have to be made of aluminum rather than brass, as originally specified in the contract of sale; and that C said, "Okay, I will accept that change, aluminum will be just fine." C claims, however, that no such conversation ever took place, and that aluminum rods are totally unacceptable. Now the negotiator is confronted with a *factual* dispute to resolve.

Or, suppose that the contract of sale called for prompt delivery of the curtain rods. C claims that he understood "prompt" to mean within thirty days. V thought that ninety days would satisfy the "prompt" requirement, and made delivery on the eighty-fifth day. C says that this is far too late for the rods to be useful to his project, and refuses to pay. Here the negotiator has a *legal* dispute—a question of what certain legal language ought to mean—to resolve in the negotiations.

For the first time in our pyramid scheme of the operation of the legal system, the use of *evidence* is required. Later in this book a great deal will be said about evidence, for evidence is the cornerstone of all trials. But for now it is enough to understand that evidence is most simply defined as *information that a judge will permit a jury to hear.* A trial judge, then, in addition to being a referee between the lawyers, and an instructor who tells the jury what law or rules to apply to the facts they find to be true, is also a filter. From all the information the lawyers offer him, he *filters out* what the jury may learn about and what they may use to decide the *facts.* In our example, a jury would have to decide whether V or C was telling the truth about the phone call substituting aluminum for brass. Or the jury might have to decide whether ninety days, under all the circumstances surrounding the contract, satisfied the "prompt" requirement.

While the *negotiator* cannot actually be sure what a judge might do with information offered to him as evidence, if he is trained, experienced, and skilled at his craft, he will try to *predict* what that judge will do should a lawsuit be instituted and brought to trial. The negotiator's first step will be to make an inquiry—to reach back to the base of the pyramid, where the sales contract was originally formed—and obtain all of the information he can find. After he has collected information from every source and has decided what part of the information might qualify as evidence, he has a basis to sit down with the parties and discuss the negotiations further.

Assume that the negotiator has found that V's telephone bill shows a call to C's number on the very day V says the conversation with C about the aluminum curtain rods took place. This does not necessarily show that V and C had a conversation, for V might have spoken only with C's secretary; however, suppose the phone bill also shows that the conversation was twenty-three minutes long. This fact tends to show that V had a serious talk with *someone* in C's office, and there is a logical inference that it was C. The negotiator will explain that the phone bill would be admissible in court, and that this piece of *evidence*—information that a trial judge *would* allow a jury to see—seems to *corroborate* V's story that there was a talk about aluminum rods. He will now attempt to persuade C to make an offer in settlement of the dispute.

As for the second question, however, assume that the negotiator has learned that it is a standard practice in the curtain rod industry to make delivery about thirty days after an order is placed. This fact tends to tilt the scales in C's favor regarding the proper meaning of the word "prompt." The negotiator will bring this point to V's attention and urge him to reduce the value of his claim for payment against C and compromise the matter. By exploring with the parties the strengths and weaknesses of their respective positions, the negotiator may be able to bring them together to a point where settlement is reached, and the dispute is ended.

There is a strong tradition in our legal system that favors compromising—often called "settling out of court"—claims between private parties or claims between a party and a government, state or federal. Negotiators perform a valuable service to parties in dispute simply by keeping them out of court. Trials take a long time to reach after a dispute arises, and are costly.

Even if the dispute cannot be settled by compromise and a lawsuit *is* filed, except in rare cases negotiation never ends. It continues right up to and during the trial, and through the process of appeal, if there is one. It is apparent, then, that although not all negotiators need be trial lawyers, all trial lawyers *should* be capable negotiators if their clients are to be well served.

When negotiation fails, the last step is a lawsuit. In a civil lawsuit, the complaining party or plaintiff files a written statement in the proper court briefly describing the claim and the relief being sought. Usually the relief sought is for money damages, but not always. Sometimes the court is asked to order someone to do something, such as vacate an apartment for non-payment of rent. In a criminal lawsuit, a government agency called the prosecution files with the court an indictment or an information describing what the accused party has done wrong. In both cases the defending party or defendant is served with a copy of the complaint that has been filed in court, and, as the Irish say, "The fight is on."

Lawsuits are often filed by lawyers who do not specialize in doing the actual trial itself, but who are knowledgeable in what is called *pretrial procedure*. While this works fairly well much of the time, it causes some problems. It is somewhat like having a general practitioner make the opening incision in the abdomen before turning an operation over to a surgeon, or like having an inexperienced pilot begin the takeoff roll in a sophisticated airplane before turning the controls over to the captain. Generally, it is better to let the one who is going to have to wage the battle plan it and start it, because that person is really the only one who can judge the ultimate significance of every pretrial move.

The fact is, however, many lawyers begin lawsuits that they never expect will go to trial; and indeed, about 90 percent of all lawsuits, civil and criminal, are settled or compromised before the trial begins. The lawsuit is used as a coercive force to cause a settlement, and is not given the thorough preparation an ultimate trial requires. If a settlement is reached, this may not matter much; but often, at the time the lawsuit is begun, it is impossible to predict whether a case will settle or eventually go to trial. It is not uncommon, therefore, for a practitioner to pay little heed to detailed preparation before, during, and after the filing of the lawsuit; to let it drag on toward trial with the expectation of a satisfactory settlement offer from the other side; and to find out on the very eve of a scheduled trial that there will be no settlement and that he is going to be called upon to "go to the mat." He then finds himself scurrying about in search of a trial lawyer who is willing to take over at the last minute and attempt to play "catch-up" while trying the case.

If there *is* a trial, it is to be hoped that a trial lawyer will finally be in command of the controversy. I say "to be hoped" because too many lawyers who do not have the experience or skill to do a professional job at handling a lawsuit will march into court nonetheless and "give it a whirl." There is little to prevent this, because our law has been far too slow to designate and certify specialists.

If you are a doctor who is other than a general practitioner, you choose early on the medical specialty you wish to pursue and concentrate on it. The training is long and rigorous, and the standards are high. The status of a "board certified" brain surgeon, psychiatrist, or cardiologist denotes a high level of skill and experience, carefully tested, and a solid protection for the public. Most people know that if you have a special medical problem, your doctor will recommend a specialist. A hospital will not extend staff privileges to a surgeon unless he truly is one.

Alas, courts offer the public no such protection. The unsuspecting client is led to believe that unless a lawyer is actually a specialist in trials, the judge would not allow him to try the case. Maybe things should be that way, but they are not. The fact is, with very few restrictions, any general practitioner of the law can walk into court and conduct a trial. Judges may cringe at the ineptitude lawyers display at times, but, sadly, they seldom *do* anything about it. It is little wonder that many clients finish a trial bitterly disappointed not only with the results, but also with the poor service they have received.

I hope to live to see the day when the true trial lawyers of this country will have the initiative to band together, create examinations, establish minimum experience and skill standards, and cause a rule or law to be passed that will keep incompetents out of the courtroom. The public deserves no less.

Considering this sorry state of affairs, you *could* very well put this book aside right now and say, "Well, if anyone who wants to pretend he's a trial lawyer can get away with that, why should I make any special effort to train myself?"

But if you have the ingredients to be a true trial lawyer, that notion will never cross your mind. You will have realized that life has a way of sorting itself out even when formal regulation is not present. Somehow top-grade trial lawyers wind up with the important cases. Everyone can don a football uniform, but not all make the team. Among those who do, the one with the greatest combination of skills is likely to be the quarterback.

Putting it differently, to try lawsuits without being trained and skilled makes no more sense than deciding to be a gunfighter without having thoroughly developed a fast draw and a firm resolve to shoot straight and first. Such careers tend to be short.

In any event, as we approach the trial, we are coming to the very upper section of our pyramid. This part of the legal system is dominated by the *trial lawyers,* who, by what they produce, will set the standard that guides the negotiators, the interpreters, and the original draftsmen.

It makes no difference with which legal specialty the original case dealt. It might be a contract, a will, a patent, a tax, or a personal injury that is in dispute, or a charge of criminal wrongdoing. Whatever area of law is involved, the trial lawyer will have to bone up on it thoroughly; and because he probably was able to cram for exams in law school, this need presents little difficulty. Deep concentration and an airtight memory will get the job done.

After a complete investigation of the facts, a careful study of any expert testimony that may be involved, and the conclusion of the court pretrial rulings, the central theater is ready. Although no acting as such is involved, a trial lawyer is in many senses producer, director, and lead player in a drama where the stakes are very real.

Unlike his counterparts in true theater, the trial lawyer participates in picking his audience, usually consisting of six or twelve people. He then has a chance to tell them what he is going to prove; to call forth the witnesses, documents, and other pieces of evidence that the trial judge will permit the jury to hear and view; to cross-examine, limit, and contest his opponent's evidence, and to give his final summation, explaining what has been shown and attempting to persuade the jury to find in favor of his client. His opponent has a similar opportunity, and then the jury gets the case to decide, having been first instructed by the trial judge concerning the laws and rules that they are to apply to the facts they find to be true.

At this stage of the trial, the jury retires to a private room. For the first time in the trial there is no court stenographer present, taking down every word that is said. What the jurors say and do behind closed doors is forever lost to history, for the law will never permit them to describe those moments for any legal purpose (unless of course there is some gross misconduct in the jury room, such as one juror threatening another). During the deliberations, a very important thing is happening. The facts are being settled and cast in stone. Whatever witnesses the jury chooses to believe, those witnesses are deemed by law to be truthful just because the jury has believed them—even if the witnesses have been lying through their teeth. Whatever *inferences* the jury chooses to believe the law likewise treats as true, simply because the jury chose to believe them. (An inference, for legal purposes, is a fact that may be presumed from another fact that has been established. If a witness testifies that one morning he looked out at a fresh covering of snow and saw footprints leading to and from his front porch, and saw a bottle of milk on the porch, a jury would be allowed to *infer* from the facts shown that a milkman had delivered the milk—even though no one had seen a milkman. This is called *circumstantial* evidence. If a witness had seen the milkman come, that would be *direct* evidence.)

To illustrate a jury in action, let's go back to the case of the curtain rods. There has been a trial. V the vendor and C the customer have both testified, and V has put his telephone record in evidence. Both lawyers have made their final summations, or arguments, and the judge has instructed the jury. In the course of these instructions, he has told the jury that delivery of the curtain rods within ninety, not thirty, days will satisfy the requirement of *promptness* in the contract. C's only defense, therefore, is his claim that he never got the phone call from V and never authorized the change from brass to aluminum.

Unfortunately for C, the jury does not believe him. They think V made a better witness, and they believe the telephone record to be significant. After all, they reason, who else could V have talked to for twenty-three minutes except C? C has admitted that the only other person in that office is his secretary, and she has testified that she does not remember V's call, but that certainly she never talked to V for an extended period of time on the day in question. They return their verdict in favor of V, and C has to pay for curtain rods that are of no use to him.

Well, you might say, C can appeal! Yes, he can, but in a very limited way. He *cannot* appeal on the ground that the jury was wrong, for they have acted and, so long as they acted within their powers, their acts are final. No one *knows* why they did what they did, and there is no way to do anything about it.

All C can appeal is what the *trial judge* did, not what the jury did. Everything the judge did is on the official record, and a higher court—perhaps more than one higher court, if the case is important enough—can scrutinize the judge's decisions and correct his mistake, in what is called a *reversal,* by ordering a new trial. In this case, for instance, an appeals court might say that the trial judge was wrong when he told the jury that ninety days was prompt enough to satisfy the contract. Having made that determination, the higher court would reverse the case and "remand" it to the trial judge for a second trial, with directions to give a different kind of instruction on promptness to the second jury. Or, if the trial judge had allowed in evidence some evidence harmful to C that was erroneous, or kept from the jury some evidence in favor of C that was erroneous, these mistakes might also be grounds for a new trial. The appellate court, however, can virtually *never* rule that the *jury* was wrong to believe V and disbelieve C, and order a new trial for *that* reason. Whatever the jury did is final, and that's that.

The question you ought to be asking at about this time, if you really would like to be a trial lawyer, is this: Has justice been done in this case?

Let us go a little further. It happens that TJ, the trial judge who presided at the trial of V against C, was a very good and fair trial judge. C has appealed and lost, because in order to win his appeal C failed to show that, as a result of something the judge did, the trial was unfair. This still does not answer the question: Has justice been done in this case?

Assume that we have an advantage that no jury ever has, but that all would love to have, in every case that goes to trial: We are a fly on the wall, seeing and hearing everything that really goes on. As that fly we saw and heard the following:

After V and C made a contract for the manufacture and delivery of the curtain rods, C's secretary, CS, had a vacation due her. She had no real plans, but a day or two before the vacation was to begin she got a call from V, who had been smitten by her appearance—she was a striking woman—when she visited C's office. V explained that, although married, he was separated and in the process of divorce, and would like to meet her socially and get to know her better. CS, herself recently divorced, had thought V attractive and charming when he came to C's office, and she mentioned in the course of this conversation that she was about to take a week off. V immediately offered to take her out on his yacht for a friendly cruise. CS accepted, and they went off for four days of bliss.

When V returned to his manufacturing plant, he discovered to his horror that more than half of C's order had been manufactured, and that aluminum had been used instead of brass. V's company was in financial trouble—indeed, he had rented the yacht—and it simply could not sustain the loss that would occur if the mistake made by V's manufacturing foreman in using the wrong material had to be absorbed.

V called CS at C's office to explain the problem; C was in his private office at the time, talking with another contractor. CS knew, and told V, that aluminum rods were not what was wanted. CS thought she might help V—C had refused her a raise a month before, and she did not like him anyway—after which V might take her yachting again. She suggested to V that he deliver the aluminum rods and simply say that C had agreed. Privately, she thought little harm would be done. She did not know that the owners of the seaside hotel C was decorating had *insisted* on brass rods, because of the tendency of aluminum to corrode in salt air. When it later developed that V was using that very phone conversation with her as evidence to blame C, CS did not dare say anything except: "I don't remember any call."

On the strength of the testimony of V and CS, the jury found the wrong facts to be true and disbelieved C, the only truthful witness in the case. Ironically, for purposes of this litigation *wrong* became *right*. Justice was not done. As a result, V and CS believe that the law is not difficult to manipulate, and they may try it again. C is embittered in all probability, because he knows he has been dealt an injustice and that there is nothing he can do about it.

Why was justice not done? Because a jury made a mistake. Why did that jury make that mistake? Because C did not have a very good lawyer. Here are some of the mistakes TLC (C's trial lawyer) made.

First, his investigation was not thorough, starting with his own client. In the face of V's claim that a very important phone call took place that effectively modified the contract, C swore adamantly that there had been no such conversation. Did TLC believe his client? We do not know. Some lawyers do not like to press their clients too hard on a credibility question of this sort. They are afraid that the client may admit he is lying, in which case TLC, being an ethical lawyer, will have to inform C that he cannot allow him to testify. Therefore, he must tell C that he has no favorable evidence, and accordingly no factual defense. Consequently, reliance on the legal definition of "prompt" remains as his only hope of winning.

Many lawyers, just like TLC, avoid confronting their clients and forcing the truth out of them for fear that the client, having learned the consequences of telling the truth when it is adverse to him, will go to another lawyer. But a good trial lawyer will never settle for less than the truth from his client, even when the truth hurts. There is little professional pride to be derived from selling a false story to a jury, even if one wins the case and earns a fee in the process.

As a sad example of what can happen when a trial lawyer follows a practice like that used by TLC, consider the case of Mary Katherine Hampton. In the early sixties, Mary's boyfriend, a rampant murderer then awaiting execution in Florida, told the authorities that Mary had killed two people in Louisiana. On the strength of his story, Louisiana indicted Mary for the two murders. In each case, she pleaded guilty to murder in the second degree, which carries life, rather than death, as the punishment. She was sentenced to two life terms.

In 1964 a Pulitzer-prize-winning reporter named Gene Miller, of the Miami *Herald,* looked into the case and discovered that on the very days the two murders had been committed, Mary Katherine Hampton had been *in jail* in Clearwater, Florida. Being in jail can be about the best alibi in the world for any accusation of criminal wrongdoing—except one occurring in that jail. Miller brought these facts to my attention and asked me to get her out, for obviously an injustice had been done.

I brought a lawsuit claiming that her pleas of guilty were the product of mistake, and asking that she be allowed to withdraw them and proceed to trial. With the Clearwater jail records, a trial would have been a shoo-in for the defense. At the hearing that resulted from bringing the lawsuit, I called both of the lawyers who had represented her to the stand. Both said that they *had never asked her* if she was guilty. They *assumed* that she was. As a result, they did no investigation and did not discover that she had what most trial lawyers would consider a perfect alibi. Mary, who had little education and was not terribly bright, had been very concerned about being electrocuted for murder in the first degree. (In Louisiana, at the time, electrocutions were accomplished by an antiquated portable electric chair, which occasionally did not work right on the first try, in which case a second shot of current would be administered.) At the urging of her lawyers, pleading guilty to a lesser degree of murder seemed the right thing to do. The embarrassment to her counsel, and to the law generally, as a result of the publicity surrounding this incident, was profound. Fortunately, the Louisiana attorney-general persuaded the governor to pardon Mary, and the lawsuit was dropped.

Clearly, TLC *should* have pressed C hard for the truth, even subjecting him to a polygraph test if necessary. (No matter what you have heard, polygraph or lie detector testing, when done by a true expert, is a very valuable tool to a trial lawyer, principally because it is quite accurate when a matter as simple as the one in our example needs to be tested.) Once TLC had been convinced that C was telling him the truth, he would have begun to apply his logical, analytical, and investigative skills. Phone records are generally accurate. *Someone* had called C's number from V's office on the day in question and talked for twenty-three minutes. Because V had offered his telephone bill in his own behalf, TLC had the right to get the full record from the telephone company. The full record would have shown that the call began at 10:52 A.M. and ended at 11:15 A.M. Both C's and CS's appointment books would have shown that from 10:30 A.M. to 11:45 A.M., C had an appointment in his office with X, a contractor. X's diary would have reflected a similar appointment, and X would have been able to testify in C's behalf that he was with C for the entire period, during which time C took no calls—certainly none that took twenty-three minutes.

By applying logic, TLC would have reasoned that the *only* person who could have received that call and had a lengthy conversation was CS. But why?

C would have told TLC that CS had recently asked for a raise and been refused; that their relationship was somewhat strained; and that shortly before the phone call in question CS had gone on vacation. Investigation would have shown that V was absent from his office during the same days that CS was on vacation. Further investigation would have revealed that V had rented a yacht during the period. TLC would then have taken depositions from the owner of the yacht, from those who worked in the marina where the yacht was docked, and from the person who cleaned up the yacht after it was returned. (A *deposition* is a statement taken under oath before trial that is recorded—

each question and each answer—with lawyers for both sides present.)

Following these depositions, and before the depositions of V and CS were taken, V's trial lawyer would have had a hard talk with his client and dismissed the suit before a perjury charge was brought by the district attorney. C would not have had to pay for curtain rods he did not order, or pay the costs of trial. The *best* service a trial lawyer can render to a client is to be so thoroughly prepared that the other side throws in the towel without a fight.

I hope that at this point the *importance* of the role of the trial lawyer has begun to sink in. He is the last resort, the last hope for justice. If he is skilled, talented, thorough, and ethical, justice has a pretty good chance. If he is not and his opponent is, he may lose a case he should have won.

Important as a trial lawyer's efforts may be to his client, they are also of great importance to the system as a whole. Remember our pyramid? We said that trial lawyers function at the top of that pyramid, resolving the cases that could not be resolved by interpretation or negotiation. We also said that 90 percent of all cases where a lawsuit is brought are negotiated to a settlement before the jury returns a verdict (and some are settled even after that). What do you suppose these settlements are based upon?

Settlements usually involve a number of factors and considerations, but paramount are almost always these questions: What will be the result if I don't settle and I go to trial? What will a jury decide after hearing my evidence and that of the other side? What are the risks? Suppose I am not believed, even though I know I am telling the truth?

It is the trial lawyers who, by the examples set when their cases do go the distance, determine the standards that guide others in achieving their compromises. Stated more graphically, the results of their labors flow back down through the pyramid to influence the judgment of those who are trying to resolve cases short of a lawsuit or a trial.

Because this is true, it is necessary that we recruit, train, and field the very best talent for the trial bar. People should have confidence that when push comes to shove, justice has an excellent chance of prevailing. Attorneys below the apex of the pyramid should have consistently good examples of trial results to guide them in their interpretations and negotiations. That is why, if you have sincere interest and real potential, you should plunge on. This country has a lot of lawyers—some say too many lawyers—but it has never had enough good trial lawyers, and they are sorely needed.

2

What Kind of People Are Trial Lawyers?

Of all the questions put to me during a lecture series, one of the most frequent is this: What kind of person makes a good trial lawyer?

The answer is simple. Top-flight trial lawyers are extraordinary people who possess a whole panoply of special abilities. I do not mean they were born with them. Apart from a basic good intelligence quotient, very little about a trial lawyer is hereditary. The skills that count in a courtroom are whittled into shape, then honed and polished. They take practice, and lots of it. They take confidence, discipline, and determination. There is no free ride involved anywhere along the line. If there is a good trial lawyer anywhere in the Anglo-American justice system who did not work hard to *become* what he is, I have not met him or heard of him.

The principal problem with the training of trial lawyers is that they start too late—usually after graduating from law school. The ideal time to start the process is in undergraduate school, where people are apt to be enlarging their horizons at a rapid rate.

Undergraduates often say: I think I would like to be a trial lawyer. Should I major in government, political science, accounting, or business? My answer is always the same. If you want to be a good trial lawyer, learn to read, write, and speak the King's English, and do it *now*. English should be your major. Beyond that, a solid, broad-based liberal arts education is best, with emphasis on philosophy, history, and psychology. There are good, sound reasons behind these recommendations.

The ability to handle language effectively is the trial lawyer's lifeblood. All of his skills surface through his written or spoken words, or his ability to read rapidly and comprehend what others have written. The advocate with a solid command of the language has a leg up on any opponent who is less talented, for the language of persuasion is his only tool. In the law we have substituted rhetoric for the sword, and if we were more successful and enjoyed more public confidence, more people would be content to use our courts to resolve their disputes instead of trying to settle them themselves, often with disastrous consequences.

Philosophy? A large part of our business is philosophy, for we are in charge of what will happen to men and women who have problems. Philosophy deals not so much with the way things are as with the way they ought to be. As attorney general Robert Kennedy once said: "Others say 'Why?' I say, 'Why not?'" It is an important part of a trial lawyer's function to have a personal philosophy to guide him in wielding his immense power, and to command philosophical principles sufficiently to urge new rules and precedents on courts that are both appealing and humane.

History? As every law student very quickly learns in his first few weeks of enrollment, law is taught by teaching history. Before he graduates, a law student will have read hundreds and hundreds of *cases,* each reflecting an appellate court decision on a question of settling or interpreting law. (Remember our "promptness" appeal, in which it was decided that, legally, ninety days is within the meaning of "prompt" in the curtain rod industry?) The American method of legal education is called, quite accurately, the *casebook* method. Each case is a piece of legal history.

Psychology? This is the study of human behavior, and that subject will be of daily concern to a trial lawyer for all of his days. He must know human behavior well enough to be able to *predict* it with some degree of accuracy. His predictions will involve judges, witnesses, jurors, clients, and opposing parties. What will each do when confronted with this dilemma, or this problem, or that frustration? An understanding of the principles that govern most normal human behavior, together with a wealth of experience, which will continue to accumulate throughout a trial lawyer's entire career, are essential tools of the business. And if one chooses to specialize in criminal law, an understanding of *abnormal* human behavior will be essential as well.

Perhaps the cardinal personality trait of a good trial lawyer is that of easy self-reliance, a willingness to act swiftly based on one's own counsel, with little or no time to consult with or be advised by others. In other words, this is not a business where one can "check with Dad" or some other adviser before making a decision.

Lawyers frequently attempt to make their points and accomplish their persuasion by using analogies. In trying to understand the special qualities of a capable trial lawyer, a very good analogy can be drawn from flying.

It was my good fortune to be given a flying education by the United States Navy and Marine Corps that money could never buy. Jet fighters were comparatively new when I entered flight training, at the age of nineteen, and all of us in the program thought them tremendously exciting. They were. They were also tremendously demanding, and those of us who survived to become naval aviators learned several rules quite thoroughly. They are the following:

> **Rule 1:** An airplane is a wondrous instrument of motion, and if in your thinking and handling of the controls you stay ahead of it, it will take you from place to place safely and very well.

> **Rule 2:** If you get behind in thinking and handling an airplane, it will surely kill you.

Rule 3: If most of the time you are trying hard just to stay even as you control an airplane, at some point it will get ahead of you—now apply Rule 2.

The point, of course, is that thinking ahead and *anticipating* what may happen next are vital elements of success in many human endeavors. Flying is one of them. Trying lawsuits is another. This may explain why a great many of the leaders of our current trial bar are also pilots. The two professions have the following in common:

1. Pilots understand early on that they must make decisions, often rapidly, *and* make those decisions correctly. So do trial lawyers.

2. Pilots learn that to be in charge of an airplane successfully, they must not be in the *habit* of obedience to others (except for military pilots working as a group). Trial lawyers must do the same.

3. Pilots know that in order to do what they do on a regular basis they must develop a strong self-confidence, and not agonize over every demand that confronts them. This is also true of trial lawyers.

4. Pilots must be prepared to decide and move with great speed, and to avoid mistakes even when rushed. Trial lawyers must meet the same requirement.

5. Pilots, being human, *do* make mistakes from time to time. They know that not all flying mistakes are necessarily fatal, provided that they can learn to (a) recognize that a mistake has been made, (b) analyze its nature and what it will take to correct it, (c) take corrective action swiftly and decisively, and (d) not panic or freeze at the controls in the interim. Every good trial lawyer frequently goes through this same syndrome.

If you should interpret this analogy as a subtle invitation to go and learn to fly, let me delete the subtlety—go *do* it!

I do not mean that you should become a qualified airline captain before trying to become a trial lawyer. That is not necessary. But you could sign up for a student pilot course, which will at least get you through your "solo" flight, when the instructor steps out of the airplane for the first time and says, "Take her around," which means take off and land by yourself. This is the point at which many students start wishing for terra firma, and, as one wag put it, the more *firma* the less *terra*.

Nonetheless, although most people who first solo an airplane are saying to themselves, "How the hell did I ever get myself *into* this situation?" they do solo successfully, and they find out, once the experience is behind them, that they have become a different person—more relaxed, more confident, buoyant with self-pride, and shining with accomplishment. These qualities are also ingredients of a good trial lawyer.

In order to make hard decisions rapidly, confidently, and correctly, trial lawyers must develop strong skills in analysis and logic; they must have the ability to understand the nature of a problem or issue, and to reason out the various solutions or options which present themselves. For undergraduate students who wish to become advocates, any courses or extracurricular activities that require this sort of intellectual exercise will prove helpful.

A simple example is the game of chess. The number of different problems chess presents to a player is almost infinite. A successful chess player must be able to foresee all the possible consequences of particular moves, and then choose the best one. Normally the player who can perceive these options and possibilities with the greatest accuracy and clarity will win.

Moreover, chess presents an opportunity to learn another very valuable skill—that of intelligent sacrifice to win a long-range benefit. A chess player is going to lose pawns, knights, bishops, and rooks in almost every game against an evenly matched opponent. He may lose his queen, but if the king is saved, he wins the game.

Trial lawyers must do the same thing, constantly. Every time one introduces some evidence in a case, there may be a price attached, for a great many things that a judge might not permit a jury to hear can *become* admissible in evidence because of what a lawyer does.

As an example, let us assume that D, a defendant in a criminal case of assault and battery, wishes to show the unlikelihood that he was the aggressor by calling witnesses to establish that he has a very peaceable nature; that he is not the kind of person who is likely to initiate violence in a dispute. To show this, he may call witnesses who know of his *reputation* as a passive sort of person.

By presenting this type of evidence, D's lawyer has opened the door to contradictory evidence that would *not* have been admissible had he left the subject alone. As a general rule, in criminal cases the prosecution is not allowed to show that one committed a specific offense—such as hitting someone, in this case—by showing that the same person behaved the same way in the past.

When the door is opened by the defendant himself, however, the rule changes dramatically. By trying to show that he is a peaceable man by reputation, the defendant legally invites the prosecutor to attempt to establish the contrary. Now the prosecutor may call witnesses, if he can find any, who will testify that *they* have heard that the defendant is a man of violence, with a reputation for using his fists or a weapon at the slightest provocation. More than a few criminal trial lawyers have been badly wounded by such a development in a case, simply by ignoring the principles of chess.

Just as a chess player asks himself, "Should I sacrifice this bishop to get a good chance to take my opponent's rook for an advantage in the long run?" a trial lawyer must go through the same exercise constantly. "Will my witnesses showing a reputation for peacefulness be strong enough to offset those that the prosecution may call to show a tendency for violence? At the end of the case, will I have done my client more harm than good by taking this chance?" Decisions such as this one are difficult and sometimes must be made rather quickly.

Because of this "quickness" factor, one who wishes to use the game of chess to develop his skills as a trial lawyer should avoid playing the "long" version of that game.

Chess players sometimes sit and study the board for a very long time before deciding what move to make. They examine every option and every possible consequence in great detail. This sort of training is fine for learning *strategy,* but not very good for learning *tactics.*

Unlikely as it may be to compare chess and the trial of a lawsuit to warfare, it is useful for an understanding of the difference between strategy and tactics. When a military force sets out to do battle against an opponent, the wisest and most senior admirals and generals sit around in a planning room and decide how best to use their fighting men and equipment to defeat the enemy. The placement of ships, tanks, troops, artillery, and aircraft, and how and when they are to attack, must be coordinated well in advance of any actual battle. All of these strategy decisions take into account predictions of what the enemy can do, and is likely to do, once the battle begins. Such planning is very much like what a trial lawyer and his staff do when they are laying out a case for trial—always trying to anticipate what the opposition will do.

Tactics are basically adjustments made to the master plan once the action starts. Battlefield commanders often find that the enemy is not reacting as everyone thought he should or would, and that a quick change is necessary. The leader of a squadron of attack bomber aircraft might find, for instance, that an attack on an enemy airfield is not going well because the airfield is more heavily defended than anyone involved in the *strategic* planning had anticipated. He realizes that if he continues his attack, he may lose all of his aircraft without neutralizing the enemy's ability to use that airfield for its own counterattacks, thereby jeopardizing a fleet of his own ships just offshore.

He knows from his pre-battle briefing, however, that the enemy ammunition and fuel supply depots are only a few miles away, and observes that they do not appear to be as well defended as everyone had expected when the strategy was formed. He therefore makes a rapid *tactical* decision to shift his bomber squadron firepower to the new, more opportune target. After all, airplanes without ammunition and fuel do not represent much of a threat to anyone. He radios his aircraft to interrupt their attack on the airfield and turn instead to the ammunition and fuel depots. He destroys them, saves most of his planes, and puts the enemy out of business.

To use the game of chess to teach the intellect a sense of tactics, a time factor must be introduced. Therefore, if you are going this route, agree with your opponent on a time limit during which each one must make his moves, and play the game with a stopwatch. The time allowed can vary, down to as little as a minute or thirty seconds. Mistakes will no doubt increase in number as the decision time is reduced, but the opponent's mistakes will increase as well.

After you have become used to the discipline that you *must* decide your next move on the chess board quickly, take on some players who are very good, but have little practice at the speedy version of the game. You will find that their mistakes outnumber your own by a substantial margin, simply because they are not in the habit of making these quick decisions. Until they attain that aptitude, you should trounce them with some regularity.

Something very similar happens when a lawyer who is careful and methodical finds himself in a courtroom faced with a skilled trial lawyer. Once the methodical attorney's strategy is upset by an unexpected development, he will begin to flounder, because he has not trained himself to adapt swiftly to changing circumstances. Without time to think things through, he falls behind. If he were a pilot flying in bad weather, he would crash. To succeed as a trial lawyer, you must train yourself not to crash very often.

So far, we have said that a good trial lawyer must possess confidence, discipline, swift and accurate decision-making abilities, and the intellect to be good at analysis and logic. But there is more. Lots of people are well qualified in these departments who even so ought to find something to do with their lives other than try lawsuits.

A trial lawyer must be a creature of *resourcefulness, initiative,* and *imagination.* He must not be straitjacketed by convention. The greatest enemy of progress is the person who says: "We're going to do things this way because we've always done them this way." When you hear writers and public figures despair over people they call "bureaucrats," this is the kind of mentality about which they are complaining. If it were a controlling principle of life, little change would ever take place.

A resourceful person is one who imagines that he has a better solution to a problem than the ones currently being used and who has the initiative to give it a try. Not every new method or idea will work; without initiative it will never be attempted. Being innovative and imaginative can cause false starts and mistakes, but historically, personalities with these qualities make the best trial lawyers. I can think of two examples in my own experience that help to illustrate the point.

When I was twenty, and in the final phase of naval flight training, I was as anxious as any of my colleagues to finish up and get my Navy Wings of Gold. The final hurdle before that happy event required eight landings on an aircraft carrier in a Grumman Hellcat, a big, heavy, powerful World War II fighter plane.

To land on a carrier, one needs to approach the flight deck at an air speed just above the point of stall, when an airplane slows so much that it stalls and falls like a rock. As the deck of the carrier passes under the airplane, the pilot pulls back on the throttle and the plane slams onto the deck. A hook hanging from the tail catches one of nine cables stretched across the deck and stops the airplane.

As the pilot approaches the carrier landing deck, he is continuously given advisory signals (or so it was done back in the fifties) by the "LSO," or landing signal officer. At the final moment in the approach, the LSO gives one of two signals: either a "cut," which means to chop the power and land, or a "waveoff," which means, "Get the hell out of here, you're endangering the ship—if you have enough fuel, go around and we'll give it another try; if not, ditch in the water and a helicopter will pick you up if you survive." Either signal is *absolutely mandatory,* no exceptions.

But aircraft carriers are expensive, and only those considered qualified to attempt their eight landings were allowed to go there. To qualify it was necessary to do FCLP—field carrier landing practice—which means landing repeatedly on a carrier "deck" painted on the runway back at the airfield.

I was not doing well at FCLP. The LSO, who was an irascible sort, kept giving me signals telling me I was too fast, and then giving me a waveoff. Finally he said on his radio that if I did not slow up properly, I would not be going to the carrier for a while.

I did not react gracefully. As a strong-willed young man, I was convinced that my speed was tolerable, even though he might not be satisfied with it. I said to myself, "I will show this cranky old sonofabitch who can fly slow and who cannot!" On the next pass, I came staggering up the "groove" toward the painted deck well below the recommended speed, with the Hellcat literally hanging on the wash from its own propeller, a somewhat dangerous condition. I had no doubt that the LSO would be satisfied with this tricky performance and signal a cut.

I learned then and there a strong lesson about failing to anticipate the enemy properly. The LSO knew that I was *too* slow, and decided to teach me a lesson. As my left hand was ready to chop the throttle, he gave me a *waveoff*, which I had never expected. I jammed the throttle forward hard and the engine roared. I was only twenty feet above the runway at this point, when suddenly the worst happened. The plane was so slow that its controls had very little air flowing over their surfaces, not enough to combat the tremendous torque, or twisting power, of the engine. I slapped the stick hard to the right, but the airplane rolled to the left, out of control.

I had followed a mandatory signal that never should have been given in a practice situation, and was about to die for my disciplined reaction to that signal. The dreaded "torque roll" was a legendary pilot killer, and I was about to join in a very unlucky list. Had I abandoned reason and blindly followed what had been burned into my brain as a "must" situation, a fatal crash was inevitable.

Fortunately, the instinct to survive is a strong one. I realized quickly that, although in wartime it might be necessary to cash in one's own chips of life to save the ship and its men, and thus the battle, and thus the war, this was only a *pretend* aircraft carrier painted on some asphalt. The only one at risk was me, since I had seen the LSO running like hell to get away from what he now knew would be a fiery crash. I considered that rejecting his signal might land me in Portsmouth Naval Prison for a long stretch, but somehow that seemed to be an acceptable alternative to the crash.

I yanked the throttle back, thereby getting rid of the awful torque that was causing me to roll, kicked the right rudder hard to try to pick up the left wing, and slammed onto the runway on the left wheel. I managed to get the rollout under control, and taxied back to the ramp with legs of jelly. A few minutes later the LSO met me in the flight shack, looking very pale. We agreed that no one had much to gain by raising hell about the incident, and that if the situation had been real I would have been better off to try to land on the deck than to crash on it upside down. The next day I went to the carrier, made eight uneventful landings, and was designated a naval aviator.

I mention this incident not to suggest that what I did was wrong or right under the circumstances, but to point up the need to do your own thinking when a crisis is at hand and no one else can solve or even address the problem. Right or wrong, I am here writing this book, something that cadavers have never done with much success.

The second incident occurred when I had been a member of the bar of Massachusetts just one year, almost to the day. I was asked to help free a Cleveland doctor named Sam Sheppard from prison. Sheppard was serving life for the alleged murder of his wife on July 4, 1954—just a month or two after I had been unwisely practicing torque rolls in a Grumman Hellcat. I met him in November 1961, after reading *The Sheppard Murder Case* by Paul Holmes (I recommend this book to any prospective advocate), which persuaded me that he was innocent.

As soon as I accepted the case and the press took notice, older colleagues began giving me hedged congratulations. They said, in effect: "That's a great case, lots of publicity; but get a good fee from the family, 'cause you can never get him out."

"But I think he may be innocent," I would reply. "He deserves to get out!"

"Maybe so," they would say, "but he's had over ten appeals and lost them all. Many think he didn't do it, but that's too bad. He's there for good."

Had I been a good listener, receptive to the sincere and well-meant advice of older and wiser men, Sam Sheppard might still be in prison, or on parole. I simply could not accept the notion that a man could be held in prison for something he had not done, and plunged ahead. After a couple of false starts, I finally studied the case and all of its immense records until I knew it cold, then proceeded to declare war on the state of Ohio with a federal petition for a writ of habeas corpus—an ancient and powerful remedy for unjust imprisonment.

A courageous federal judge from Dayton finally freed Sam in July 1964, calling his trial a "mockery of justice." After a trip to the United States Supreme Court, which agreed, we went back to trial. The second jury wasted little time in concluding that Dr. Sheppard had *not* killed his wife, and set him free.

Had I been willing to listen to sound advice instead of rebelling against "the way things are, and have always been," you probably would not be reading this book. An immovable object—and the Sheppard conviction was viewed by Ohio as just that—will yield only to an irresistible force, which sometimes means just butting your head against a wall in every new way you can think of, until it finally gives.

Even if you should find that you have these qualities—or the potential to acquire them, which is just as good—still more is necessary if you are to be a successful trial lawyer.

You must be a "real" person, and a "people" person as well.

A "real" person is one with a good comprehension of what life on this earth is all about, and who is what he seems to be. The former comes from seeing and understanding what confronts you from day to day, as opposed to fantasizing about things and getting your fantasies mixed up with reality. Fantasies are fine, and every healthy person has them, but they should be understood as fantasies and not as the way things are. If you fall out of a boat and fantasize that you are secure in a warm bed, chances are good that you will drown. If you realize that you are in the water but do not panic, even though there is some real danger of drowning, you will probably make your way to safety—even if you have never learned to swim.

A "people" person is one who is comfortable with other people, getting along with them and allowing them some elbow room of their own without resenting the concessions that may have to be made. Some people would rather deal with things, such as computers, laboratory instruments, a craft such as woodworking, or a vehicle. Others prefer to live in a world where imagination can act as a shield from the harsher side of reality. Some artists, though by no means all, would fall into this category.

A trial lawyer works with people every day: clients, witnesses, other lawyers, judges and their court personnel, people of every kind and description. It helps to learn early on that people vary greatly within the parameters of what is considered to be "normal" human conduct and that one must be flexible to a substantial degree to get along successfully with almost all of them.

Especially, a trial lawyer must be adept at dealing with jurors, for they hold his and his client's fate in their hands. Jurors are mostly ordinary people who, although individuals all, are going to have to act collectively to accomplish a result. (Most verdicts must be unanimous—that is, all the jurors must agree, or else there will be a "hung" jury or mistrial—although this requirement is gradually being eased in many states.)

Jurors are in part the product of their communities, and a skilled trial lawyer must be able to understand community values as they bear upon his case. One would not present a case in New York City, for example, in the same manner as in Butte, Montana. The people who become jurors are raised differently and think differently.

This is *not* to say that a trial lawyer ought to be a person of many faces, because good ones have but one face and do not try to change it. True actors adopt many different faces successfully and persuade us that the face is the person. Anthony Hopkins, for example, convinced us that he *was* the hunchback of Notre Dame, and in another drama that he was the premier of Israel. John Wayne was a good actor, and an American folk hero, but he was always John Wayne. Acting roles were written to fit him, whereas Anthony Hopkins fit himself into roles that were written before he was born. Good trial lawyers are actors in the John Wayne sense.

Although the face doesn't change, expressions, mannerisms, and concessions to local custom do. If one comes riding into town as a know-it-all and attempts to make the judges, jurors, and opposing counsel do things the way *he* thinks they ought to be done, he will be in for some sad lessons. It is the ability to adapt to circumstances—to adjust one's methods in a way that makes others comfortable and trusting, without compromising one's ideals and objectives—that marks a professional trial lawyer. It is always possible to suggest to an entrenched judge that he ought to consider a new way of approaching a problem without offending him in the process. There are few situations in life that cannot be improved with a little courtesy; and good trial lawyers, however strong their egos, are courtly and courteous people.

If meeting and relating to new people—strangers, as they are called in rural communities—makes you feel awkward, self-conscious, and uncomfortable, do not despair. This is not uncommon in those who are normal in every respect. But if the feeling persists despite your best efforts to overcome it, give some more thought to your desire to try lawsuits. You might be better off doing something else—and doing it very well—where contact with others is minimal. Trial lawyers must really span the spectrum as "people" persons. If you need others, like to be part of group decisions, and lean on others in times of difficulty, this trade is not for you. The business of looking only to yourself for decisions in times of severe tension requires a creature who is not overcome by fears of being alone, and is self-sufficient to a large degree. but that same person must be warm-hearted, considerate, and understanding of those who see things differently, or he will lack the human compatibility to be happy as a trial lawyer. If he *prefers* isolation, he ought not to apply.

If up to this point you feel that you measure up to the standards I am suggesting—or will be able to as you grow—there is a final hurdle, which is more important than all of the other qualities: a very high personal standard of *ethics* and *integrity.*

A *lawful* person simply obeys the letter of the law in the technical sense. If something is unlawful, he will avoid doing it. If something is lawful but still very mean, he may do it anyway. He will promise to sell you a piece of land, and later tell you that he has changed his mind and that you forgot to get his promise in writing. A lawful lawyer might note that his opponent's time to meet a certain court deadline is running out, allow the date to pass, and then insist on a default judgment. An *ethical* lawyer, whose ethics can usually be measured by the length and breadth of his integrity, has matured to the point where he realizes that life is too short to be governed by petty habits.

No matter how many laws we may pass to regulate human conduct and protect the rights of an individual, no one has ever found a way to legislate someone into being a good person. Good trial lawyers are good people, purely and simply. They will fight hard for their clients' rights in a fair manner, but without being sneaky, engaging in sharp practices, or hitting below the belt.

This is a profession where perhaps more than in any other, one's *word must be good at all times.* Trial lawyers are constantly making promises and representations to courts, juries, and other lawyers. If they are not to be trusted, they cannot effectively function.

Trial lawyers have tremendous power, which can easily become abusive unless it is balanced and checked by an equally great sense of responsibility and personal integrity. All of us have the *power* to start a lawsuit against someone on the flimsiest excuse, to tie up his assets, cause him great anxiety and legal expense, and generally make him miserable with little if any justification. I wish I could say that this is a rare occurrence, but sadly it is not. Many who call themselves lawyers will do just that, usually to squeeze a few settlement dollars from one who cannot afford the time or inconvenience of going to trial. The actions of these people do much to explain why America generally regards its legal community with suspicion and little affection.

Then there are those who become confused into thinking that law is some sort of national sport. This attitude is pumped up very often, unfortunately, by the news media, whose accounts of actual trials are superficial and focus wholly on who "won" and who "lost," even though they have little understanding of the true meaning of those terms. Vince Lombardi, the great football coach of the Green Bay Packers, once said, "Winning is not the important thing; it is the *only* thing." That may be true in football, but not in the handling of lawsuits.

As in football, in every lawsuit that goes to a conclusion one side must lose. But unlike football, in a lawsuit usually one of the parties deserves to lose and should lose if all the truth comes out and the correct rules of law are applied. The fact that a litigant *deserves* to be heard, to present his evidence, and to have his day in court does not mean that he deserves to win, any more than V deserved to win the curtain rod case in the last chapter. Lawyers who cause victory by manipulating and bending the rules serve no one, not even themselves, however sweet the taste of victory may seem.

This is especially true of some prosecutors, who believe in going all out to convict anyone they have brought to trial, even though they may have to use false testimony to do it. I can think of no more disgraceful accomplishment than jailing a fellow citizen on false evidence just to attain credit for having "won" something, and yet it goes on every day.

These lawyers have never heard—or never believed—the worthy old maxim that is engraved in granite above the pillars of some federal courthouses: THE UNITED STATES WINS EVERY TIME JUSTICE IS DONE TO ONE OF ITS CITIZENS.

If you have difficulty understanding this principle, or for some reason do not believe it, please take your earthly labor to some other profession: We do not need it and do not want it.

3

A Command of
the Language

If you are an undergraduate and have not yet committed to a major study course, do not choose any subject *other* than English unless you are persuaded to do so for very good reasons. Accept the fact that no matter how many English courses you take, there will be more that you should have taken. English in every form—literature, writing, elocution, grammar, and syntax—should be your first concern. Sign up for a course in speed reading if one is available.

The use of language is a trial lawyer's daily fare and, if he is good at it, a daily joy as well. Only those who have refined and polished their ability to handle words in any and every form can know the delight that such a faculty offers. Among the many talents that can boost one's self-confidence, none surpasses the

31

ability to spellbind an audience. Only entertainers, political figures, lecturers, and trial lawyers experience the surge of adrenaline that comes from speaking well.

Although some people are natural-born talkers, most who excel at speaking didn't start out that way. Language is extremely complex, and the English language in particular. It is full of contradictions and anomalies that seem to make no sense in the initial stages but eventually are absorbed into an individual's habits and techniques until they cease to puzzle.

Like fingerprints, no two speakers or writers—message *transmitters*—are identical. Likewise, there is no "best" speaker or writer, only those whom we recognize as excellent, or outstanding, or superb. By the same token, there are many different ways to *receive* messages from others—a double exercise called *reading* (or listening) and *comprehension.* A reader must first recognize the word (or, if he reads in phrases as speed readers do, the thought or concept) that is before him; then he must comprehend or understand the message. "Reading comprehension," one of the principal segments in most intelligence and aptitude tests, is a speed measurement of one's ability to read a set of facts and then answer questions about them.

I mentioned above the value of a speed reading course. Many are available, taught in several different ways, but all have the same objective: to increase dramatically one's ability to scan a text while drawing the main facts from it and remembering them.

Speed reading is *not* comfortable, especially at first. One method of teaching involves an opaque plate that descends from top to bottom along the page at a preset rate, covering line after line in sequence. If you don't keep up with the machine, you miss part of the text. Just as in the beginning phase of most endeavors where speed is a factor, an individual must *push* himself to better and better performance.

Most people are rather lazy readers, lumbering along through the text before them. If you now can read 400 words per minute, while retaining good comprehension of the material, you would be considered a fairly fast reader. During my naval flight training, speed reading was a mandatory course. I entered with a normal *concentrated* rate of just over 400 words per minute, and three weeks later was going at a clip of 1600 words per minute, not a very unusual accomplishment.

Like lifting weights, speed reading is a discipline one must stay with to preserve. Weight lifters who abandon their daily routines soon watch their muscle turn to flab. Speed readers who do not practice constantly lose some of their quickness, but not all of it. I now read at a rate of about 500 words per minute for text that I wish to understand in detail and remember, jumping to 1000 words per minute to scan text that is less important.

If it is your aim to be a lawyer in *any* branch of the profession, reading will be very important to you. Law school curricula all demand a tremendous amount of reading on a daily basis. Students who complain that the reading requirements of their law courses are suffocating them are normally those who don't read very fast.

Moreover, the reading assigned to law students is of a most singular nature. The appellate court cases that make up the bulk of law school training may vary in length from a few pages to more than fifty. The lesson to be learned from studying a case is buried somewhere in those pages. It is called the *holding* of the case, and a student is graded on his ability to locate, understand, and remember this holding. In the longer decisions, trying to find the holding is hard work. To operate efficiently, a student must scan through the language in the decision until he comes to the holding; then he reduces his speed and carefully absorbs the critical language. He must then increase his speed to scan once again through the end of the case, to make sure that there is no additional important language to be learned.

Should you take a speed reading course and on graduation turn to something other than law, your time will have been well spent. For despite the special relationship between speed reading techniques and the scan-then-slow requirement for reading law cases, there is almost no business or profession where the ability to read and comprehend written material swiftly does not offer one distinct advantages.

If you take such a course, have the discipline and determination to *finish* it, and to put your technique to work when you are done. You need not force yourself along at uncomfortable speeds if you are reading for pure enjoyment, such as a juicy piece of fiction. But for all of your homework assignments, newspapers and magazines, and all of the other layers of print on paper that come your way, keep the pressure on and the speed up. After six months to a year, your habit will take a fairly permanent set, and the discomfort will gradually subside.

As important as it is to take in *written* messages from others rapidly and with a good level of comprehension, it may be still more important for a prospective trial lawyer to be adept at receiving and understanding *oral* messages. These are much more fleeting, cannot be immediately re-examined without asking the speaker to repeat himself, and generally communicate more than written messages.

By the way, to start your mastery of language off on the right foot, discipline yourself to use words with *precision*. Many people abuse the word "verbal" because they don't appreciate its meaning; that is, they use it to indicate an "oral," or *spoken* but *not written,* contract. The word "verbal" means only that *words* were used in the described communication. It is imprecise because it lends no clue as to whether those words were written or spoken, when normally that distinction is important.

Trial lawyers spend a large part of their lives listening to jurors, clients, and witnesses, and to the statements, rulings, and assertions of judges and other counsel. Hearing and comprehending these oral communications is an essential function. To do this with maximum efficiency, it is necessary to keep one's eyes on the speaker, for there are many clues to what is *really* being communicated beyond the words themselves.

As I will state with more emphasis when we take up the basics of cross-examination, I am not an admirer of prolific note-takers who are acting as lead trial counsel. People who are busy writing while someone else is speaking simply *miss* too much. The *unarticulated* communications that accompany the spoken word are numerous; often they are vital to grasping all of what the speaker has on his mind. This phenomenon is sometimes called "body English." It consists mainly of small movements and subconscious gestures and reactions. The eyes of the speaker deserve the most attention, for they tend to communicate first.

Some people cannot look at you when they are addressing you, which indicates that there is a problem of some sort. It may be that the speaker is bashful or shy, or is uncomfortable speaking to you in front of others. It could also be that he feels badly because of what he is saying. Or it might be that he is lying, and cannot look at you with a straight face.

The eyes also embellish the words being spoken with a signal of the speaker's mood. Eyes can flash or become cold with anger, or they can twinkle with mirth or glow with affection. People whose heads are buried in a notepad will not see these things, and thereby miss an important part of the communication.

There are still other kinds of signals. A male witness is continually brushing lint from his trousers and jacket, when there is no lint to begin with, or a female is crossing and uncrossing her legs constantly. This kind of nervous activity *usually* indicates that the witness is becoming anxious or upset about something; it is a clue to an experienced trial lawyer that he may be probing near fertile ground—an area the witness would like to avoid.

Few cases in the files of a professional trial lawyer do not warrant the presence of an assistant at the counsel table to attend to the note-taking. Indeed, if our trial-lawyer training programs were structured properly, there would *always* be a trainee present to give just this kind of help, for there is no better place to learn trial technique than in the courtroom itself.

In any event, though any student is going to have to take a lot of notes between his freshman and final years ("body English" during lectures is not so essential or informative as in the courtroom), it is a good idea to practice thoroughly and constantly the business of giving complete visual and aural attention to anyone who is speaking. This, like speed reading, is a discipline few come to college with. It must be learned and then constantly practiced until it, too, becomes a habit.

To put the matter simply, learn to *pay attention*—very close attention—when a person is speaking to you. Communication between human beings, particularly oral communication, is a complex process. Unless you have had some very specialized training in your past, you have not mastered it yet and will not for some time. But it will not be very long, if you work at it, before you realize that you are getting more from what people say than you used to, and much more than those around you are getting.

Another vital function of the trial lawyer involves transmitting written messages, usually to courts and other lawyers. (I can think of no occasion where a written message is created for submission to a jury.) This is why I have urged you to take courses in writing—and not just one.

First, you should realize that there are very important differences between good written messages and good oral messages. For the moment, just accept the two rules that follow; in time, you will fully understand their validity and import:

> ***Rule 1:*** A well-written message does not work well when it is *read* to a live audience.

> ***Rule 2:*** A well-spoken message does not work well when it is reduced to writing and then *read* by someone as a substitute for a written message.

Some people who can speak beautifully and persuasively are not very adept at creating polished writings. By the same token, there are those who can write very well indeed but who never succeed as fluent, polished speakers. Your burden, if you want to become a first-rate trial lawyer, is to practice and *master* both.

The reasons for the differences between these types of communications are, if carefully analyzed, not very difficult to understand. Writings are structured to reach an audience the eye cannot see at the time. It may be a general audience, such as when a President addresses the country. He will design the substance and text of his messages for some kind of median listener, as close as he can get to an "average" voter. He will accommodate the very bright and the slow of wit if he can, but the target remains the median person. Even if he reads his written message on television, he has no live audience whose reaction can give him an ongoing assessment of the efficacy of what he is saying. In the same sense, a trial lawyer who is writing a brief to submit to a judge in support of some legal contention is deprived of the opportunity to watch that judge's response to what he is transmitting.

Written messages are more carefully conceived and thought out, in general, than oral messages. The opportunity to edit, revise, and rewrite is present, as well as the chance to submit what one has written to others for review and comment, whereas spoken messages are usually a "one-shot" affair.

Additionally, in writing, complex words may be used more safely. A reader who is not clear on the precise meaning of a given word has several choices: he can look it up in a dictionary, ask someone nearby for the meaning, or make a note to check it later. One sitting in an audience has no such opportunity. Unless he is a student in a lecture hall, he may have no chance even to write the word down, and probably won't remember it.

A reader can go back over a piece of text that was unclear to him at first blush, and perhaps comprehend on the second or third try what the writer is trying to say. A listener has no such option. For this reason, a good speaker trying to get a difficult point across may express the same thought several times, in similar but slightly different language. This technique, called *message redundancy,* is used to some degree by all accomplished speakers. To use that same degree of redundancy in a written message can annoy the reader, and at worst may be taken as an insult to his intelligence.

In conceiving and structuring a written message, pay attention to the old triumvirate, *unity, coherence,* and *emphasis.* Before you set pen to paper, decide what it is that you want to say. What is the central thought that is to be transferred from your brain to that of the intended target? In all probability, using the most bare-bones rhetoric available, it may require only a few sentences, or a paragraph or two, to state this thought. But a bare-bones presentation is not the objective. The objective is to *sell* the thought to the target reader, through what is called *persuasion.*

Therefore, something more is required than the naked expression of an idea. It must be attractively wrapped, and presented with a certain degree of finesse. Words that fit together smoothly and invite attention in an appealing way must be assembled. They must lead logically to a central point. In what might be termed a "preconditioning" exercise, you will come at your reader from several different preliminary directions before presenting the focal point of the message. Often several different lead-in paragraphs, each illustrating a different perspective on the central issue, will be used. This is called "covering the bases," an analogy from baseball.

Assuming that you have developed in your undergraduate years a good writing style, with an acceptable degree of simplicity and clarity, together with an easy flow of words, be prepared for a threat to that style when you embark upon formal legal training. If you follow the guidelines offered you by your professors, your style will gradually become corrupted into something quite different from the original.

The language of the law has many requirements that are antithetical to good English. Paramount among these is a *precision* of language going far beyond that of ordinary good communication, and relying upon a *redundancy* of statement and expression that would make an English professor gasp in horror.

This is unfortunate, but as of this writing, no one has found a better way. Those of us who create legal documents defining important individual rights are obsessed with seeing that they are susceptible to one, and only one, interpretation. Unless a document is considered to be legally airtight, it is very likely to be attacked by anyone with an adverse interest in the property it moves or controls.

Thus, if we were friends, I might say to you: "I have a house lot there next to my own home. I like you so well that I am going to sell it to you for one thousand dollars. Then you can build yourself a home and be my neighbor."

The thought and intent of that communication seem simple enough, but by the time a real estate lawyer has finished drawing the necessary documents of sale, you will have trouble finding the original basic expression of an agreement to sell. The word "sell" will have become something like "sell, assign, transfer, grant and deed over in fee simple . . ." The word "you" may now be "to Jones, his heirs, assigns, legatees and beneficiaries . . ." The effort, of course, is to overstate, using every conceivable applicable word, what the parties are doing, so that later there can be no claim of mistake or ambiguity.

Although you as a trial lawyer will have little to do with creating such tedious and stilted language, you must be able to comprehend it and to know why this peculiar dialect was used when the transaction under litigation was created. And you will have to be competent in writing briefs and legal memoranda to other counsel and trial and appellate judges, expressing your points of view and the factual and legal arguments supporting them.

Legal language is in essence a dialect, and one must learn and work with it. During your early days at law school, friends who are not fellow students may notice distinct changes in your manner of writing letters and other messages that have nothing to do with school. This is normal, and you should not be alarmed.

Do not, however, become submerged in this new world of language. You are being corrupted, to be sure, but you must be resurrected later on, or you will lose your ability to communicate effectively to non-lawyers with what you write. The simple and fluent style you bring to formal legal training must be preserved, and you must retain your ability to shift back to it when appropriate.

There is a tendency for students who are rapidly learning lots of new words to reach for them instinctively as their writing talents grow. Student papers often tend to be stuffy and pedantic, loaded with "fifty-cent" words, when some well-placed twenty-five-cent words would reach more people and have more punch.

I do not criticize this process, for it is part of growing into a mastery of language. After learning the words, a wise writer will use them more sparingly. A budding table tennis player learns to use a fierce chop or a hard slam mostly by trying those shots, and missing the table a lot. As he perfects the two techniques, he will use them less frequently and more effectively. The same can be said for a maturing writer who is smitten with complex and rarefied words.

I do not mean to suggest by all of this that lawyers are necessarily writers of such ponderous prose that they cannot appreciate a well-turned phrase. Indeed, although most judicial decisions are anything but light reading, our casebooks contain a few phrases that have survived purely on their merits as good language. Judge Learned Hand and Supreme Court Justices Benjamin Cardozo and Oliver Wendell Holmes were frequent contributors to this somewhat limited inventory.

Effective legal writing involves a basic sequence, and an order of sorts. The first task in a brief is to *state the issue*. What needs to be decided here, to move this case along to a conclusion? What are the parties really arguing about? The ability to analyze a disputed set of claims and to describe the issue in clear and simple terms will be rewarded in law school with good grades, and in practice before courts with more tangible benefits.

Step two requires a *brief summary* of the position you are taking. It is simply an introductory step to alert the recipient of your written message to your position.

The third step is a *description of the facts* available. Before a trial, this description is apt to be a statement of what you contend the facts to be. When the trial is complete, the facts will have been decided by a jury, and, whether you agree with them or not, you will be stuck with them. It is important that your description be both fair and accurate—no matter how much it may hurt, if you believe that the jury was mistaken—else you may forfeit the trust of the court. Judges do not like to be forced to comb through a trial record because opposing counsel offer wildly differing accounts of what that record contains.

The fourth and critical step in writing a legal brief is termed *the argument,* and it is here that the writer must shine. Why should the judges vote your way? How will the result affect the parties, and will it be fair? Is your client asking for something he truly deserves? Because the decision you seek from the judges will be used as a precedent for other courts deciding similar cases, will the outcome you seek create "good" law from a social point of view?

All of these questions must be considered as you assemble your words and phrases in an argument. Ducking a tough question will not get you by an intelligent judge—and most of them *are* intelligent. And even if it might, you can expect that your opponent will club you with your own omission, either in his reply brief or in the oral argument of the appeal.

Young lawyers tend to load their written messages with colorful adjectives and lofty phrases, describing each position they wish to assert, for instance, as "clearly" correct. There are places for such rhetorical techniques, but not many places.

Judges have to read an enormous quantity of written rhetoric submitted by lawyers. They develop a healthy disrespect for redundancy, verbosity, and "Fourth of July" language generally. You will do them, your client, and yourself an immense favor in most cases by cleaving right to the point, saying what you have to say with as much clarity and directness as you can muster, and little else. Long, windy legal briefs are often handed to a judge's law clerk with the instructions, "Boil this mess down to its essence, so I can see in a few minutes what the hell he is trying to say."

Now, most law schools turn out a fair number of good legal writers, particularly those who have ranked sufficiently high in their class to be invited to join the law review, a sort of legal digest which most schools publish. When it comes to legal *speakers,* they do far less well. If you wish to emerge from law school able to deliver an oral message and deliver it well, you had best bring a large part of that skill along with you as a freshman. Although the Chief Justice of the United States Supreme Court and many others have bemoaned the inability of most lawyers to deliver a convincing oral presentation, as of this writing the law schools have not addressed themselves to that deficiency with any real intensity.

Put another way, for every good legal speaker, there are probably fifty to one hundred good legal writers. Legal writers don't necessarily have to be good speakers. Trial lawyers *must* be.

A trial lawyer's speaking obligations are awesome. The important things he says will all be captured verbatim—*haec verba,* or "word for word"—by a court stenographer. Be prepared to be embarrassed more than a few times following your first few court appearances when you read transcripts of what you have said, for surely you will be. Don't be discouraged, however, because this happens to everyone; it is part of learning, of "cleaning up your act."

The spoken word, once uttered, cannot be taken back. True, you can mutter a red-faced apology and ask someone to disregard what you said as mistaken, but this is a most awkward experience and one which a trial lawyer cannot frequently afford. Your speaking role will be a continuing "one-shot" affair, with no turning back or equivocating. In your choice and delivery of phrases and sentences, you must be as surefooted as a mountain goat on a steep trail only inches wide.

Once you are "on camera," there will be no chance to review and edit what you say to make it come out better next time. There will be no chance to consult with others, looking for a better way to express a thought. There will be no retakes, such as actors enjoy and often need. There will be no erasure of the words and utterances you have committed to history. If you goof, so be it. You and your client will be stuck with what you have done at all times, for better or for worse.

By now you may have some inkling that among the skills a trial lawyer must possess, to me speaking is the truly *important* one. You are correct. Indeed, I will go further. To paraphrase the Vince Lombardi philosophy we looked at in the last chapter: The ability to speak effectively, for a top-flight trial lawyer, is not the important thing; it is the *only* thing. You may be able to live with less than stellar performance in the written language, but unless you decide emphatically that you *will* master the spoken word, accept the fact that history may never record your deeds and accomplishments. Of all the trial lawyers you have learned about to date, and all that you will learn about as you progress, few if any had less than a mastery of the spoken message.

I now have good news and bad news. The bad news is, if I may be repetitive (and in this case redundancy is justified), that the ability to speak with excellence is the *sine qua non* of excellence in advocacy; and the road to that lofty pinnacle is steep and demanding.

The good news is that if you force yourself to climb there, you will find very little company. You will meet and know many others in the field of trial advocacy who are good, even better than good, but they will be unable to attain that summit because they did not have the energy, discipline, drive, and determination to constantly rework, reshape, hone, and polish their speaking abilities and techniques.

If you are an otherwise competent trial lawyer and a superb speaker, you will stay out in front of the pack. You will have more business than you can handle. You will be offered the best cases, with the finest fees. Clients will seek you out and pay you more than they would pay your less fortunate colleagues, for clients like to hear their cases stated in the finest language available. Judges will appreciate you, and listen to your words with a subconscious disposition to be convinced. Jurors will give you their full and unbroken attention—and with jurors, that is sometimes half the battle.

I would like to say that these pages contain all the answers necessary to make you an outstanding speaker. If I could honestly make such a claim, I would expand this chapter into a book of its own and retire on the proceeds, making many people very happy in the process. But I cannot.

When it comes to public speaking and delivery, each person must develop a style that suits his own personality. It would be a grave mistake for me or any other public speaker to say to an aspirant: "Based upon my *experience,* here is the way you *must* do things if you are to be a successful speaker."

I have heard, sometimes with awe, public speakers of markedly different styles and techniques. All, however, share common elements, which I will try to isolate and explain during the balance of this chapter.

The first requirement is that you learn to be *comfortable* while you are talking. This may not come easily. People who can be very articulate in private conversation and enormously entertaining in an informal group often choke up when called to the podium to address an audience. To become comfortable, you must acquire several kinds of *confidence.*

First, you must be confident about yourself. Get a good night's sleep the evening before your address, and take pains to be dressed and groomed as meticulously as you can. Check your appearance in a full-length mirror before you leave your quarters, and convince yourself that you are as pleasing to the eye as you can be, and that you will be viewed as a person of good taste. A good appearance will give you an edge with most any audience.

Second, you must be confident about your subject matter. If you are presenting an informative lecture on some topic, make sure *you* believe what you have to say is in fact informative. It may help to try out a summary of your points on a thoughtful friend, simply to test your own judgment. Your presentation should be well organized and logical, and should include periodic high points that will snap your audience to attention throughout the delivery. Some humor will usually help, particularly if it is self-directed. There are very few people who do not instinctively like humility in another, particularly one in a superior position; as a speaker, you will be both physically and psychologically in a superior position.

Third, be confident about your manner of delivery. If your knees feel rubbery, if you are afraid that your throat is going to suddenly go so dry that no sound will come out, or if you have a sudden impulse to feign a coronary seizure so that you can duck the frightening experience confronting you—relax. These feelings bother all speakers from time to time, especially when they are inexperienced.

Remember, this audience came to hear *you.* Some of them are eagerly receptive to what you will say; some are frankly skeptical. Some are fully prepared to be bored. Pay no attention to the fact that every audience will have some negative people in it.

Don't speak to a blurred "sea of faces," for if this is your perception of the folks before you, you will have difficulty becoming comfortable with them. Scan the group until you find a pleasant face, one that seems receptive. Talk to that face for a few seconds, then scan some more and find another one. Keep this shift going as you warm up, using natural facial expressions and gestures as you speak to enlarge your base of communications.

Plan ahead of time some quotable phrases to use as you approach each highlight of your talk. When you come to one of these, begin it by looking directly at one of the friendly faces you have already located; then shift your gaze to another friendly face elsewhere in the audience, and come down on the punch line with some emphasis.

Just as in good writing, the opening of a good speech should have a "narrative hook," something that will tickle the listener's imagination. Perhaps a better analogy is that of a springboard or launch pad. You need a good jump start, an attention-grabber. You might say something like this: "Yesterday, the President of the United States told an audience in St. Louis that this country is in dire need of a strong deficit in the national budget in order to defeat inflation. If you will listen carefully and follow closely what I am about to tell you, you will soon understand that he is wrong, horribly wrong; that he does not understand the problem, let alone the answer, and that if his ideas are adopted, he will wreck the economy of this nation in less than twelve months!"

Fourth, you must *become* confident of your audience. Although they may be strangers, you should have learned all that you could about the composition of your audience before taking the lectern. You will often have to modify your delivery *and* your rhetoric to suit the listeners before you. As you progress, always looking from individual to individual, you will get feedback from the faces looking up at you that will offer guidance. If more than one looks a little perplexed at something you have said, paraphrase it and say it again. A certain amount of redundancy is perfectly acceptable, and often appropriate if your central theme is to get across.

Many audiences have trouble spots. People whisper to each other, or move around audibly, or in some other fashion generate background noise. Pinpoint the source as quickly as you can and address your next few words directly at the offending party, or at the person sitting next to him. This usually suffices to shut down the distraction.

Different audiences respond to different kinds of delivery and rhetoric. I once had to address a highly radicalized undergraduate student body at the University of Pennsylvania at ten in the morning, then fly my Lear Jet to Terre Haute, Indiana, to give a dinner speech to the Wabash Valley Speaking Club, an arch-conservative group if ever there was one. Although the theme and the messages were the same in both places, I daresay that if one of the Penn students had attended the dinner speech he would have recognized very few of the words uttered there!

Now we come to the cruncher, the one that is going to cause you to consider burning this book. You are going to learn to speak *without notes!*

Written materials are a crutch to a public speaker. The worst speakers write out their full texts in large print (or have someone do it for them), and simply read those written words. You can see them turning the pages, glancing up from time to time for effect, but making good eye contact with almost no one. And although the speech writer may have tried to formulate words in a fashion that will simulate good oral communication, none that I have known have ever made it. The syntax and punctuation on a printed page don't belong in an oral message—period.

Somewhat better are the speakers who come to the podium with stacks of cue cards. These too are crutches, though somewhat less severe. The speaker spends more of his time looking at his audience, and may even pick up some of their feedback, but he is nonetheless distracting himself continually by glancing down at his cards. His train of thought *and* his fluency of delivery both suffer in the process. He will not control the speech as he should, or constantly adjust it to accommodate his audience's reaction, for control will be in the cards, constantly yanking his attention in one direction and then another. Speakers of this ilk are apt to punctuate their talks with a lot of *um*s and *ah*s; those two utterances have no place in a good speech.

The least offensive of the crutch people are those who come to the lectern with only an outline, something to guide them along and assure that no points are missed. Still, an outline is distracting too, and often acts as a lock-in. A good speaker will often sense a particular stratum of interest in his audience after he gets going, and will alter and adjust the structure of his speech accordingly. Because it keeps steering one back to the original plan, thought out and conceived before there was an audience to work with, an outline can act as a shackle.

Crippled people are often marvelous, and can do incredible things despite their handicaps. I have known and admired many, but I have never met one who *chose* to be crippled. Don't you choose it as a way of carrying on when you don't have to. Train your legs to walk with a good stride, and throw away all the braces and crutches. When you are sitting around the cocktail lounge regaling some friends with a unique experience, you don't have any of these things. You *just talk!* If you are a good talker, you don't have to elevate this form of communication very much to turn it into a stirring address.

I do not mean to suggest that you will suddenly cast all your crutches aside and hold forth unassisted. Like an infant leaving the bottle and the diapers, you are going to have to be *weaned* little by little. And you are going to have to wean yourself!

Assume that you are going to give a talk about a new statute that Congress has passed, affecting all Americans and creating an abrupt change in individual rights. Make up an outline to organize your subject matter.

You might start by reviewing the state of the law in the area in question *before* the new statute went into effect. You would then discuss the ways in which the old law was thought to be deficient, and what cures Congress was seeking to effect when it passed the new one. A history of the hearings held prior to enactment might be touched upon, and then a good, solid boiled-down analysis of what the new statute seems to say.

Finally, you will want to tell the audience what scholars and other legal writers have to say about the potential for the new law, how its aims may be frustrated by ambiguity in its language that may tempt judges to interpret it in differing ways, and whether this law will be able to withstand constitutional scrutiny by the federal judiciary.

In conclusion, you will want to give a personal observation, pro, con, or neutral, about the law. Your ending should be strong and thought-provoking, something like this: "On balance and after studying this statute at some length, it is my own feeling that in the long run it is going to benefit a great many more people than it hurts."

Once you are satisfied with your outline, make up some "fact and phrase" cards. Each one will contain either a brief note of some important fact to be covered in the presentation, or a carefully thought out phrase calculated to drive the point home. When this task is complete, you are ready to *really* go to work on your speech.

Now shuffle the cards. How long does it take you to put them back in order without peeking at the numbers? How much of the card do you have to glance at (don't read—glance!) before you can recite what is on the rest of the card without seeing it?

Commandeer the help of a patient friend, and give him the outline and the cards. Have him read from the outline—only a phrase at a time—and then tell him where that phrase appears, and what notes precede and follow it.

Then have him cue you on the fact and phrase cards by giving you the number or the first few words. You give him the rest of the information on the card, as well as that on the cards numbered immediately before and after that one. Keep at it until you can perform these tasks without a slip.

Next, tell your friend what your talk will be about and how you are going to handle it. Try to persuade him of your point of view as you go along, and gauge his reaction. When you are through, ask for his comments. What is weak and what is strong about your presentation? What needs patching and filling, or deletion?

Now go ahead, and in normal one-on-one relaxed fashion, present your talk to him. Tape record it as you do. If you have access to videotape equipment, use it. You will find videotape to be most informative.

When you have finished, watch and critique the videotape. Then bring another friend in to see the tape, or to listen to it if audio equipment is the best you can procure. See what *that* person has to say after observing only the finished product. Now go back and make some final adjustments, polish the whole thing up until it fairly shimmers, and have at it.

Until your confidence builds, you may wish to take your outline and cards to the lectern, just in case you suddenly draw a blank (which happens to the best every now and then). But set them so that you cannot read them without consciously reaching for them and moving them. See if you can get through the entire delivery without consulting even one crutch. If not, go as far as you can and resolve to do better on the next occasion.

Do not be horrified by the notion that you are going to have to go through this entire procedure every time you are scheduled to give a speech. This is a weaning process, remember? As time goes on you will find that less and less formal written preparation is necessary. You will simply go through these same processes in your head, and if the topic of your address is something you are familiar with, you will do this mental work in the last thirty minutes before you begin to speak.

I wish I could say that you cannot truly succeed as a trial lawyer unless you can give a good speech without notes, but in honesty I cannot. There are many who use some notes and are quite good. I suspect this is because very few of their competitors have graduated to the point where *they* don't use notes, so there is a lack of incentive.

Do not, please, content yourself with a decision to be less than the best if you decide to enter this branch of the profession. In a field where it is possible to lead the pack simply by applying yourself a little harder during your training, it is a shame indeed when aspiring barristers aim short of the mark. If people try to convince you that it is inordinately difficult to free yourself from "word supports," don't believe them. It may seem that way at first, but most things worth accomplishing don't come easily.

One useful device, which gets you into the habit of talking without reference to written materials, is to pretend that you are being graded on your ordinary daily conversation. The average person is sloppy with his English when speaking informally, and therefore must make a conscious effort to clean up his rhetoric whenever he has an audience.

You have no doubt known people who speak beautifully all of the time, even when discussing matters of little significance. Many of this sort can be found in university English departments. They have simply trained themselves to take pride in the structure and composition of their natural speech patterns, and to do so without conscious effort. If this seems difficult, I assure you that it is not, if you are determined to get tough with yourself.

Your problem may be that you have encrusted too many years of bad habits onto your natural ability, and these must be whittled away. What you will be attempting is a revamp and polish job; after all, you already know the language, and if you're not too bashful to carry a pocket dictionary around and make sure to monitor your vocabulary and your usage of words, the change will come rather quickly.

Once you have reached this plateau, you will have taken a giant step toward being able to handle yourself without notes before an audience. The extent to which you can develop this talent will be limited principally by another human faculty, which we are going to consider when you turn this page: the memory.

4

The Memory

Many of the "doers" of this world contend that the human animal develops and uses only a small part of its faculties from crib to grave. I am inclined to subscribe to this notion, having observed that in most people the level of function is well below the limit of potential. To learn and understand one's limits is an important step toward success in this life. People who try to push themselves beyond their limits are apt to overtax their physical systems and wind up collapsing in their forties. Lawyers who attempt to become litigation specialists, but are not really equipped for the constant pressures of that undertaking, are good examples.

One faculty that literally loafs along through most of life, however, is the memory. It is very seldom fully taxed. If you feel that your memory is being overburdened (and students with an intensive curriculum often get this feeling), the chances are that it was not developed as completely as it might have been when you were younger. This is not to suggest that everyone on earth is capable of demonstrating a computer-like storage bin for facts, figures, names, dates, and other details. Psychologists are pretty well agreed that memory can be indexed to intelligence in a general sense; and the brighter a person is, the better the chances that he has a good memory potential.

I doubt that you would be contemplating a career in the law, or attending a college or a university, if you were not confident of having a pretty good intelligence. If you do, it is probable that you have a good memory too, a good portion of which is seldom used because you have not stretched it enough. If you don't eat for a few days, your stomach will shrink and cause you to feel full after a small meal; if you eat heartily on a regular basis, your daily capacity enlarges, as many a prominent paunch demonstrates.

As is true about the rest of your system, you will expand the capacity and efficiency of your memory only by working it intensely and on a regular basis. Once again, this is hard work. But the beauty of this effort is that, as with learning to speak comfortably and efficiently, once you have reached a certain level of performance, it is not very difficult to stay there.

What is memory? How does it work? No one really has very good answers to these questions. With the age of computers upon us, we are gaining some insights, at least, because computers electronically duplicate many memory functions and perform them more exactly than humans can. Marvelous as computers are, the human mind is far better; you need to consider a few hints about what you ought to be doing to improve *your* memory, and what exercises will help you to stretch its capacity from a little to a lot. A trial lawyer's memory is an invaluable tool, and you ought to whip yours into the best shape you can if you hope to excel at trying lawsuits.

Why is it important for a trial lawyer to have a strong and flexible memory? For a whole host of reasons. Without it, the ability to articulate effectively is very limited. A good deal of what a trial lawyer does involves reacting, very swiftly, to something that is placed before him with little warning. It may be the response of a juror or a witness, or a question from a trial or appellate judge. There is not sufficient time to go hunting through notes or other reference material before making the next move. When your opponent says "I object" to a question you have asked or a statement you have made, you are going to have to come up with your reasons *right away.* The rules of evidence are of little value to you in the give and take of a heated trial unless you have them firmly in your memory and can produce them orally even as you begin your responses.

Imagine yourself cross-examining a witness during a trial. There he sits, having told his story, parts of which you are convinced are simply untrue. Much of cross-examination, as we will see in chapter 11, involves prior statements by the testifying witness, and speed is very important to a good cross-examiner. If you have to have his prior statements before you in your hand and search through them for the precise phrase you wish to confront the witness with, you are leaving him an excellent opportunity to think up suitable answers.

If, on the other hand, you are able to reach into your memory and immediately challenge his last answer—with a response like "Didn't you tell Detective Jones on May 18, 1981, that the man you saw running from the building at dark was wearing a *T-shirt,* not an *overcoat*—and sir, I refer you to page two of your statement on that date!"—you will be far more effective.

Being able to come up with precise recall of such details has many advantages. First, it convinces the witness that you are more than ready for him, and that he had better be careful. Second, it preserves the flow of cross-examination, which is very important to its efficacy. To interrupt the questioning and search through a document looking for the passage you need wreaks havoc on the process.

I have said earlier that many trial lawyers went through law school as crammers—they were able at the last minute to stuff their heads with an immense amount of material, and to lay it out a day or two later in the form of answers to examination questions. In the business of trying lawsuits, cramming becomes a daily routine. The better you can cram, the more effectively you will be able to handle the material that is your ammunition.

As in speed reading, there are courses you can take to drill your memory and improve it. Many of the tricks taught in short-course memory schools involve the technique of association. In order to remember the name of a person, for instance, you try to associate that name with an image of some sort, one that can be easily recalled. Take a lady named "Beverly" as an example. You might examine her face and figure until you find something that strikes you as "beveled." It could be a nose, a chin, a brow, or some other part of the body. You then make a mental note to think of that bodily part whenever the person is seen again, or her last name is mentioned, and to remember that it has a "beveled" look. The name "Beverly" will pop into mind quite easily.

Remembering numbers often involves an association between the numbers themselves. The simplest would be a telephone number, with area code, that was listed as 123-456-7890. With all the numbers in sequence, you would only need to remember the first one, and that the rest followed. You could then resurrect the entire number from memory at any time, even though you had made no effort to memorize all ten digits independently. Real telephone numbers are much more subtle and difficult, but even so internal associations can be developed in many of them.

In most people there is a profound difference between memory as *recall* and memory as *recognition*. Although they are different forms of the same phenomenon, the latter is far less demanding than the former. To be able to come up with a fact, name, or number without a hint of some sort is more difficult than to select the correct information from a list of suggested data. A handy example is the multiple choice form of examination; here, following each question, several possible answers are offered, and the examinee is invited to choose one of them, having been forewarned that only one is correct. Many people can score correctly on this kind of question (sometimes merely by eliminating three answers seen to be incorrect!) who could not *remember* the answer in the strict sense; that is, without an assist they would have been unable to produce the answer strictly from recall. Trial lawyers, most of the time, have a far greater demand for recall memory than for recognition memory. Although occasionally cues are available, such occasions are apt to be the exception rather than the rule. Under normal circumstances a lawyer in the middle of a trial will need to pull facts and figures from his recollection without much help if he is going to keep a healthy pace as he works. I would therefore recommend, if you do attend memory technique courses, that you concentrate on working with pure recall as much as you can.

To stretch your ability to recall things, file things in your memory daily that you plan to recall at some later time. If you are a student, you will be forced to undergo this exercise, for a student's whole performance is judged by his ability to recall what he has learned and to work with that material in answering examination questions. But quite apart from what is forced upon you as a memory exercise, there is much more that you can do. Some of it is fun, some of it will serve you well in a number of ways, and some will make life more pleasant. All of it will probably help you make better grades on your examinations, and that isn't all bad.

To go about the business of stretching your memory in an orderly fashion, you are going to have to use systems, and I propose to suggest some. I wish to make clear at this juncture that I have never taken a memory course as such, so these systems are my own. Indeed, they go back to the days when I used to be suspected of cheating on a regular basis in grade school arithmetic classes: I would turn in test papers with no working computations shown, only answers in the answer column. Even though my answers didn't seem to match up very well with those of the students in adjacent seats, my own seat used to be changed with some degree of regularity.

Drawing from the format of today's small memory machines—microcomputers—let's attempt to set up the things you wish to remember in "files," just as though you were keeping a sheaf of papers in a manila folder in a file drawer; except that this file will be with you at all times. If you are reading this book at the start of a semester, the first file we will want to set up will be your schedule of classes, so that you will always know what your formal time commitments are without having to lug a printed schedule around in your wallet or purse. Assume that for the fall semester you have the following classes on a weekly basis:

MONDAY	0900	English
	1100	Spanish
	1400	Humanities

TUESDAY	1000	Humanities
	1100	Elocution
	1500	Philosophy
WEDNESDAY	0900	English
	1000	Psychology
	1100	Art
THURSDAY	1000	Spanish
	1100	English
	1400	Literature
FRIDAY	0900	English
	1000	Philosophy
	1100	Art

Now, set this book aside for a moment. You have seen your schedule, and it has passed into your memory, but it probably didn't stick there very well. Take a piece of paper and see to what extent you can resurrect from your memory what you just read. Not very much, you say. That is quite normal. Let us therefore create a file, and pack away this information so that you can pull it out whenever you need it.

First, we will name the file CLASS SCHEDULE. Simple enough. Next, we will break it into five words, each word beginning with the first letter of the day of the week concerned—the days of the week are already *in* your memory, and thus the file, and have been for many years. The words are, using the first letter of each of the classes you are taking:

MESH

THEP

WEPA

TSEL

FEPA

Notice that the first word is a common one, and easy enough to associate with the activity word concerned. Monday is the beginning of the week, dreaded by many, and on that day you are going to have to shrug off the effects of carousing all weekend and MESH with the program—that is, get back to the business of going to school. You will probably be sluggish on Monday, so on Tuesday you will need to THEP out and get cracking (pretend you lisp for this one). For Wednesday, depending on your inclination, you can go two ways (and as many more as you can think up): You can either look on this midweek day with sorrow (so far from a weekend in either direction) or view yourself as your own EPA (we should all be our own Environmental Protection Agency anyway) and determine that on Wednesday you will be *Working* for your EPA. If you go this route, Friday becomes simplified by association, because on Friday (FEPA) you will be through with your classes at noon, and you will be conjuring up some *Fun* for your EPA for the weekend. This leaves only Thursday, which is the day (TSEL) on which you must *sell* yourself to your professors, in order to deserve all the fun you expect starting on Friday.

So, you now know that you are to MESH on Monday, THEP out on Tuesday, WEPA on Wednesday, TSEL yourself on Thursday, and FEPA on Friday. If you did not elect the Environmental Protection Agency association for Wednesday and Friday, then just remember that you are a weeper (sorrow) on Wednesday, and a Fun weeper (tears of joy) at the close of classes Friday. Go back and forth over these five words a few times until you have them in your memory. After a few minutes, they will be embedded, just as certain commands can be embedded in a computer.

We now have a letter code for each day of classes to tell us the order of the classes, which leaves two problems: Some of the letters stand for more than one kind of class (English and Elocution, Philosophy and Psychology), so we need a couple of further associations to resolve the ambiguity; and we need a trick to remember the hours when these classes are given.

As for the ambiguities, the simplest road is the best one. E always stands for English except for one occasion: On Tuesday you must THEP out to avoid an *electrocution* (Elocution), and that is the only time you must do that. On Wednesday, whether you are a weeper or working for your EPA, you will have to be "psyched up" (Psychology) to get through the day properly; P otherwise stands for Philosophy.

The time question we will address in a different fashion. Put into your memory the fact that all classes begin at 0900 (always, by the way, use the military or twenty-four-hour clock for memory work—it saves the annoying A.M./P.M. ambiguity) and go in one hour increments after that. If you begin at 0900 and are consecutive, you have no problem—your code word all by itself will tell you where to go and when.

But when there are breaks in the schedule—blank hours—you need a way to remember which hours are blank. Try using the word "Pop" to indicate a blank hour in your code word. WEPA and FEPA are fine as they are, for they have no blank hours to contend with. MESH now becomes ME-Pop-S-Pop-H, THEP becomes T-Pop-HE-Pop-Pop-Pop-P, and TSEL becomes T-Pop-SE-Pop-Pop-L. Go over the "Pop" sequence a few times to remember them for the three days that they are needed. If at this point in the exercise you are "Too pooped to 'Pop,'" devise some other memory code for the blank hours, but do it, don't let it slide. In any event, you should now have your class schedule where it belongs.

The next exercise you might try is also appropriate to the beginning of a semester. Determine that you are going to memorize the names of everyone in your English class; if the class is a large one, let's use twenty-five people in that class. Get their names from a directory or a class list, and try to ascertain which states they are from. Prepare a written list of last names in alphabetical order, and note the groupings: How many "A" people, how many "B" people, and so on.

Now, begin to match names to faces. Take the three most attractive of the opposite sex. Find something about their features or their home states to associate with the face. A blonde named Mildred from California would be an easy one, for instance. Why? Because California turns out blondes as if it had a "mill" where they were made, that's why.

Try a man named Bobby from Alabama. Think of him as "BobbyBama." The manner in which you make your association is not important. What is important is that you do make an association of some kind, one that will stick in your memory like peanut butter to the roof of your mouth. Once you have the easy ones out of the way, begin to work on those that are less remarkable, and thus more difficult to remember. Stay with it, and before very long you will have twenty-five identities filed away. Title the file ENGLISH CLASS PERSONS and store it.

Next, pick out the people you like the best and get their telephone numbers. There are many different ways to remember groups of numbers. Some people just like to say them over and over again until they stick. This method of remembering by rote is okay if it works for you, but it has one glaring disadvantage: Should you forget one of the digits, or, as is more likely, transpose two of the digits, you will have no tricks of association to get them back again—to resurrect them, as we have called it. Better systems allow for these associative clues so that you can "reconstruct" the missing digits.

Twenty-eight years ago, the Federal Aviation Administration issued me a license to fly airplanes, #1287353. How was I to remember this number? As a young airman, I had been taught that there were some old pilots, and some bold pilots, but very few old, bold pilots. I therefore resolved that as a pilot, I should always be getting younger. I would start at 128, then become 73, then 53. The first number, 128, was easy: That was the number of the largest, fastest highway in Massachusetts at the time, where most of us with brand new driver's licenses were wont to sneak away and "fly" when we thought the police were not looking. Those two simple associations were enough. I am not called upon to recite my pilot license number more than once every couple of years, but it always comes up, because it is in the file!

Another example. A very, very special woman (she has become Mrs. F. Lee Bailey) I know from the Midwest had this telephone number: 567-9843 (sorry, friend, no area code). A pretty woman should have numbers in a pretty sequence, and she does—3456789—but the phone company jumbled it so that not too many people could remember it. To confuse memories, they pulled the 567 out of the middle, transposed the double numbers on either end and reversed their order. That is, when they took out the 567, we were left with 34——89. By transposing, we have 98——43. Simple? It is, if you think about it.

What do these little gimmicks have to do with the kind of memory capacity you will need as a trial lawyer? A great deal. It is not the purpose of this chapter to teach you how to remember the exact wording of a witness's prior statements, or the four leading Supreme Court cases on search and seizure. The purpose here is to get you into the habit of filing things away in your head, not in a filing cabinet. You can't take a filing cabinet with you to the courtroom, and even if you could, no judge would allow you the time to rummage through it every time a question was asked or an answer given. If you will but exercise that wonderful storage bin between your ears, it will become larger and more valuable to you—and give you a solid edge over your opponents.

Take memory courses, if they are available, but most of all, just keep pushing yourself all the time to remember more and more. If you push, you'll get there.

5

An Introduction to Evidence

In the last chapter I mentioned that every trial lawyer must have rules of evidence carefully filed in his memory, because during a trial there is rarely time to look them up. You will learn the rules themselves in law school, not from this book. My undertaking in this chapter is merely to introduce you to a concept, and to teach you to begin to think like a trial lawyer.

Before dealing with evidence itself, it will be helpful to spend a few moments discussing another concept: proof. You have undoubtedly challenged some friend or colleague in the past with the assertion, "You can't prove that!" Although different people mean different things by this phrase, what is generally meant is something like, "You can't show that so clearly that everyone will know it to be true."

If you try lawsuits for a living, you will literally live in the world of so-called proof. It is perhaps best to understand right here that most cases are decided on something less than strict proof. If something is so clear that it is really "proven," it probably won't even be in contention during the trial.

Let me give an easy example. Let's say that in a criminal case, it is charged that D, the defendant, killed V, the victim, within the state of New York. This is something the prosecutor will have to prove in his case, because unless the crime (or some important part of the crime) occurred within New York State, the New York court will have no jurisdiction: That is, it will have no power to hear and decide the case.

Assume that it is clear from the evidence that V was shot on Fifth Avenue near the Empire State Building in Manhattan. Will the prosecutor have to prove that Manhattan is within the state of New York? Will the defense lawyer be allowed to contend that Manhattan is not in the state of New York? Of course not, for such an exercise is a foolish waste of the time of the court. The fact at issue—is Manhattan in New York State?—is so notoriously true that the trial judge will take Judicial Notice of that fact and bar the lawyers from arguing about it. Once this has been done, the jury will be told that the fact at issue "has been proven as a matter of law," and they are not to worry about it further. This process, then, has resulted in "proof."

In that same case, the prosecutor also has to prove that V is dead, and that V died as a result of the gunshot wounds in his body when it was subjected to an autopsy by the medical examiner. As to the fact that V is dead, the defense lawyer will almost always *stipulate* that he is. He will probably also stipulate that the cause of death was the gunshot wounds, and not some other cause. In an exceptional case it might be possible to show that V was already dead at the time the bullets entered his body, but such a case would be rare indeed.

What is a stipulation? It is an agreement between the lawyers that something is true and need not be proven; that is, the jury may find without hearing any evidence that V is dead, and that the cause of death was gunshot wounds. Normally a trial judge will "accept" the stipulations of the lawyers, and from that point on no one will be allowed to contest them—that part of the trial is over, just as is the part where *Judicial Notice* was taken.

So far the lawyers haven't had to do much, have they? The whole proceeding has not been very exciting. True. But a lot of time has been saved, and now the lawyers can get down to brass tacks, to the thing this case is really all about. Was it D who shot V or did someone else do it? That will be the sole remaining issue at the trial, since everything else necessary to convict D has been "proven" without calling a single witness.

This issue—did D do the shooting or didn't he?—will form the battleground. Now follow carefully the procedure the law uses to resolve this issue.

In a lawsuit, someone must have what we call erroneously—as I will show in a moment—the *burden of proof.* That is, the burden of going forward with evidence to show that his version of the facts in dispute (who shot V) is the correct one. In baseball or football, both sides have the burden of scoring, and the side that scores the most is judged the winner. A team can only satisfy that burden when it has the ball (or is at bat), and this opportunity shifts back and forth during the game according to its rules.

In a lawsuit, the lawyer who started the whole thing by filing his complaint (or in a criminal case, his indictment or information) has the burden of proof, and he starts with the football, so to speak. He uses evidence, rather than running backs and blockers, to try to reach his goal line of "proof."

The defending lawyer tries first to stop that evidence from being used, and thus to keep the ball from being moved against his. Failing that, he must prevent his opponent from reaching the defense goal line and wait until he gets the ball, then run it back as far as he can. If he makes the opposing goal line, he wins. If the ball winds up somewhere between the goal lines when the trial ends, the jury has to determine whether it is close enough to one goal or the other to decide the case. Otherwise, they may disagree, causing a *hung jury,* and the case has to be tried all over again.

In this fashion the trial against D proceeds. The prosecutor has the burden of proof, and as such must go forward first. He makes an opening statement to the jury, describing his intention of showing that D did the shooting, and the sort of evidence he is going to use. Then he calls his first witness.

In this case he would probably begin by calling the police officer who was called to the scene, to describe what he found, how the body was positioned on the street, where there appeared to be bullet wounds in the body, and to identify photographs taken at the time by a police photographer. Next, the prosecutor will call the medical examiner who did the autopsy, to describe where the bullets entered the body and at what angle, and which one or more of them caused death. Then he will call a firearms identification expert (often called a ballistics expert, which is not quite correct) to testify to the caliber of the bullets and, if the weapon that did the killing has been found, to confirm that the bullets match the weapon and could only have come from it. As a final part of his preliminary case, the prosecutor might call someone from the Bureau of Firearms Registration to testify that, according to official records, the serial number of the weapon that killed V is registered to D, or to some other person. Most of this testimony probably won't be very hotly disputed by D's lawyer.

Then comes the rub. All that has been shown so far is fine, but none of it shows that D is the person who pulled the trigger. This fact the prosecutor may try to show in one of several ways.

First, he may call an eyewitness who says that he saw D raise his pistol and shoot V. Another eyewitness may corroborate the first one. This would be *direct* evidence, and if the jury believes these witnesses, they would be inclined to convict D unless he can show a pretty good justification for shooting V.

Second, the prosecutor might call as a witness a police officer to whom D confessed the shooting, even though no one saw D pull the trigger. This too is direct evidence, because if the jury believes that D made such a confession, and that his confession was true, they will find him guilty.

Third, the prosecutor might produce a witness who says that he was around the corner from the scene of the crime when he heard a loud noise like a gunshot, that he ran to the scene at once, arriving no more than five seconds after the noise, and saw D standing over V's fallen body holding a pistol. This would be called *circumstantial* evidence, since no one saw D shoot V. Indeed it is possible that V was trying to commit suicide and that the weapon went off while D was trying to get it away from him. Possible, but very unlikely. The prosecutor might then call another witness to say that he had observed D and V in a heated argument in a bar a block away a few minutes before the shooting, and the possibility of an attempted suicide by V goes out the window. The prosecutor might then rest his case, and hand the football to D's lawyer.

D's lawyer now has several choices. He too can rest his case, and try to persuade the jury that the prosecutor's witnesses are not to be believed, that they have lied about what they saw because they were friendly to V, or are enemies of D and want to see him in jail. Or, D's lawyer can come forward and try to move the ball in the other direction. He might call witnesses of his own to say that they were present at the time, that it was someone else who shot V, and that D merely picked up the pistol after the shooting was over. Or D himself might testify that V threatened him with the weapon, and that in trying to wrestle it away from V it went off accidentally. (If there is more than one bullet wound, this will be hard to sell to a jury.) Or D's lawyer might call a psychiatrist to say that, having examined D, he believes that at the time of the shooting D was insane, and actually thought he was shooting the devil himself, and that God had instructed him to do it.

Both lawyers then make arguments to the jury saying which witnesses ought to be believed, with the party bearing the burden of proof—in this case, the prosecution—normally having the last chance to argue. Then the judge instructs the jury on the law of the case and how it should be applied to the facts they find to be true, and they go off to deliberate.

In a typical jurisdiction, the jury would have a number of choices. They could find that D killed V, and that he had planned to do so in advance—usually called *premeditation*—and that he was therefore guilty of first degree murder. Or they might find that D and V were having a fight, and that during the fight D decided to kill V and did so. That would be second degree murder. Or they might find that D intended to shoot V only to wound him, without intending to kill him, which would be manslaughter.

Then again, the jury might disbelieve the prosecution witnesses, and find D not guilty; or they might find that D acted in self-defense, or that the shooting was an accident, and still find D not guilty; or they might believe D's psychiatrist, and find D not guilty by reason of insanity.

But there is another possibility. It might be that after a lengthy discussion the jurors agree that they don't know who to believe. All the witnesses stood up under cross-examination pretty well, and any one or more might be telling the truth. The jurors just can't decide. In that case they would look to the judge's instructions and be reminded that the prosecutor had the burden of proof. When it cannot be decided who was telling the truth, there has been no proof; but still, someone has to win and someone has to lose. In this case the prosecutor loses, because he had the burden and failed to "carry it." When the jury is not persuaded by either side, the loser is the person who carried the *risk of nonpersuasion*. Remember that term, and whenever you hear "burden of proof," substitute in your own mind "risk of nonpersuasion," for that is what the burden really is. The judge has told the jury that if they are not persuaded by the evidence that D is guilty, they must acquit him, and this is what they have done.

In arriving at this point, the jury has observed another important rule used in trials. They have applied a standard of proof that must be met before the risk of nonpersuasion has been satisfied. In this, a criminal case, the jury must be convinced *beyond a reasonable doubt* that D is guilty before they can convict him. In a civil case, perhaps one brought by V's heirs against D to collect money damages, the standard of proof would be a *preponderance of the credible evidence*.

To understand these concepts better, imagine the familiar symbol of the scales of justice. Imagine that during the course of the trial the lawyers are each putting pieces of evidence in their respective sides of the scale, and that only evidence that is "credible," or believable, has any weight. At the end of the trial, the jury looks at the scales. If the party who had the risk of nonpersuasion (the one who started the lawsuit) has put enough "weighty" evidence into the dish on his side to tip that side down, he will have furnished a "preponderance"—the greater weight—of the evidence, and he deserves to win.

But in a criminal case, the prosecutor must have more than a preponderance. He must tip the scales so far down that there is not enough weight in D's side to create even a doubt, with a reason behind it, about D's guilt. Then D can be convicted. Criminal lawyers like to think of a preponderance of the evidence as being 51 percent or more of the weight of the evidence produced during the trial. No one has ever put a figure on the percentage of the weight needed to satisfy the "reasonable doubt" standard, but it is generally agreed that it is far more than 51 percent, a much more difficult burden. The reasoning behind this dual standard is simple: We should be much more careful about taking a person's life or liberty than about taking his property, which is all that a civil judgment can usually do.

Now, and in this framework, let's get back to the subject of evidence. As I said earlier, basically evidence is information that a trial judge will permit a jury to hear. For the judge to decide whether a jury may hear a certain piece of information, he must ask himself two questions: first, Is this information relevant to the case on trial? and, second, Is this information admissible? Each question requires a separate analysis.

The question of relevance is the primary screen that excludes information from a jury's consideration. No matter what other attributes that information may have, unless it has some bearing on the questions to be decided at the trial, it will not be used. As a glaring example of lack of relevance, suppose the prosecutor in our shooting case wanted to introduce evidence that the Los Angeles Dodgers had won the most recent World Series. That information may be entirely correct, and of great fascination to sports fans, but it is of no value in helping a jury to determine whether D shot V, or under what circumstances, or why. It has no logical relevance to the shooting in question, nothing that we could call a rational connection between the two events. This is one test of relevance—logic.

There is a second kind of relevance, called *legal relevance,* that requires the application of a somewhat different test, but for the moment it is enough to understand that the threshold question to apply to each piece of information offered for consideration in a legal case is: Is this fact relevant?

The question of admissibility is far more complex, and is basically what the rules of evidence are all about: "All information relevant to an issue on trial will be admissible in evidence unless it is excluded by one or more of the rules of evidence." In many senses this is true, and is a useful rule to work with in trying to explain to a layman this complex but critical segment of trial law.

Admissibility is a concept that is best thought of as a filter of sorts: What we don't want a jury to hear, we filter out. We want juries to decide important cases on important information, information that has a real pertinence to the decision at hand. It is a basic function of the rules of evidence to operate this filter, and to assure that the information used to decide legal cases is pertinent.

In this context, there are two basic reasons for excluding information from a trial and thus denying it the status of evidence. The first is one you are probably already familiar with: the *hearsay* rule. The other general category of reasons to disqualify information is called *policy*.

Legally, "hearsay" generally refers to second-hand information. If in our shooting case the prosecutor had called a witness, W, to testify that another witness, W-2, had told W that W-2 saw D shoot V, there would be a loud objection by D's defense lawyer, for reasons that I'm sure are obvious: We don't want a second-hand version of this event, we want to hear it from the person who saw the action himself. D would object on the ground that W's testimony was to be mere hearsay, because if W-2's story is offered in evidence through W, it fails each of three tests that define legal hearsay:

1. W-2's statement was made out of court.
2. W-2's statement was not made under oath.
3. W-2's statement was not subject to cross-examination by D's lawyer.

D's objection will be sustained, unless the prosecutor can think of an exception to the hearsay rule that would allow W to testify to what he was told. In this case, if it could be shown that W-2 had died prior to trial, many jurisdictions would permit W to relate what W-2 had told him. If it could further be shown that at the time W-2 made his statement to W he *knew* and *believed* that he was about to die, then almost every jurisdiction would allow W to testify about the statement. Such a statement would be labeled a *dying declaration,* which in the eyes of the law restores to it some of the reliability that ordinary hearsay lacks, since it is presumed that a person won't tell an important lie when he is about to meet his maker. The statement of a deceased person, particularly a dying declaration, is a recognized exception to the general rule barring hearsay. In addition to these exceptions, there are others that the prosecutor might invoke to get W's testimony about W-2's statement around the hearsay rule.

(It would be a good idea to point out at this juncture that when I use the term *jurisdiction* I am referring to a sovereign entity with the power to convene and operate a court, as well as the power to render binding judgments. American lawyers have essentially fifty-three jurisdictions to contend with: the fifty states, the District of Columbia, the federal courts, and the military courts. Don't let that large number frighten you, however; if you are equipped to try a lawsuit in one of the fifty-three, it takes very little to adapt to the others.)

I have described two exceptions to the hearsay rule for one principal purpose: to show that in the trial of a lawsuit, a lawyer who wants certain information to reach the jury will try to think of some rule or other to justify its receipt as evidence, to get it over the hurdle of admissibility. The opposing lawyer, of course, will be trying just as hard to find grounds to keep the information out of the trial and to persuade the trial judge that the grounds for excluding the information are more weighty than the grounds for admitting it into evidence.

There is a second major ground for excluding information from a trial even when that information is both relevant and reliable, and that ground is policy. No matter how much a jury might like to hear such information, and no matter how much it might help them to decide the case, the law simply will not let them have it. We will take a look at several of these rules to give you a basic familiarity with the reasons behind them.

The first group of policy rules are generally termed *privileges,* since they confer upon the individual a right not to have certain information used against him, even though it may be both relevant and reliable. Perhaps the best-known privilege is the constitutional right not to incriminate oneself, often referred to as "taking the fifth." In addition, no person in a criminal case can be called to testify against himself. That is a privilege parallel to and in addition to the Fifth Amendment right against self-incrimination.

Let's stop for a moment and examine these two privileges, because they are a very important part of our law. They do, of course, make the trial of our lawsuits—especially criminal lawsuits—grossly inefficient.

If you were assigned the task of designing a system whereby courts could determine very quickly who was responsible for wrongful conduct, and what the extent of that responsibility was, you would probably think: "Let's take the best suspect we have, put him on the witness stand, and question him. Then, after we have his story, we can check it out to see if it is true. If he is lying, he probably committed the crime." Simple enough, and quite logical. But under United States law, that is precisely what the government may *not* do. Because of these twin privileges—the right not to incriminate oneself and the right not to be called as a witness by the prosecution against oneself—the government must go an entirely different route to prove a criminal case.

In a civil case a party to the lawsuit can be called to the witness stand by his opponent, but he retains the right to assert his Fifth Amendment privilege and refuse to answer questions if those answers will incriminate him for criminal wrongdoing in any fashion. This right can be taken away in certain circumstances, however.

First, if you have been either acquitted or convicted, the government may be able to force you to answer questions because you no longer risk prosecution based upon your answers; that is, the case against you is *over*, which the law refers to as *res judicata*, meaning "the thing has been decided." Or, if the jurisdiction concerned has a law providing for such an action, the government can ask a court to confer a *grant of immunity* on you, after which you can be forced to answer questions or be sent to jail for contempt. If you do answer, your testimony cannot be used to prosecute you for any crime you talk about, but it can be used to prosecute others. You have probably heard of cases where the government, having discovered two or more culprits engaged in criminal conduct, immunizes one from prosecution in order to use his testimony against the other.

The next most common privilege that the law confers on the individual concerns the relationship between attorney and client. Without the opportunity to confide fully in one's lawyer, a client has little hope of receiving the correct advice. This is no different from seeking treatment for an injury or illness from a doctor; if you hope to receive proper treatment, you have to tell him what hurts, and when, and in what fashion, and you have to be truthful when giving the doctor this "history," as it is called.

Lawyers must be given a truthful history, too, or their advice may be predicated on false facts. But if it were possible for the government to call a lawyer to the witness stand and compel him to repeat what a client had told him in confidence, that client's trust and confidence in dealing with his lawyer would be destroyed. Therefore, any communication between attorney and client is *privileged* at the option of the client; if the client claims the privilege, no judge will permit the lawyer to be questioned about what has been communicated orally, in writing, or by sign or signal between himself and his client. However, sometimes the client will want those communications to be disclosed for his own benefit, in which case he may *waive* or give up his privilege. Once a judge is satisfied that this waiver is a knowing, understanding, and voluntary act on the part of the client, he will rule that a waiver has taken place and permit the lawyer to testify. As a rule, though, a waiver cannot be retracted—once it is done, it cannot be taken back. Waivers of this sort should therefore be considered carefully before they are given.

Other privileges upheld in most jurisdictions are those between doctor and patient, and penitent and priest (or other clergymen). Similarly, private conversations between husband and wife during the marriage are usually protected.

In addition to privileged material, certain other kinds of information, although relevant and reliable, are excluded from use as evidence because of policy. The rule against illegal search and seizure is one good example, and the rules barring confessions that are wrongfully procured are another.

The Fourth Amendment to the United States Constitution bars unreasonable searches and seizures, and prescribes certain ways in which searches and seizures can be accomplished lawfully. If the police ignore these restrictions and break down the door of your home or apartment to see what they can find, they will not be allowed to use anything they discover against you in a criminal case, principally because they have violated your constitutional rights.

By the same token, if the police question you as a suspect in a crime, and they beat you until you make a statement admitting that you committed the crime, your statement—even if completely true—will be excluded from evidence as "involuntary."

Or, if you have been arrested and are in police custody, you may not be questioned at all until you have been advised of your rights: the right to remain silent, to have a lawyer present if you want one (and even if you can't afford one), and the right to know that anything you say may be used against you in a court of law. If you give a statement before these rights are explained to you, that statement will not be received in evidence against you at a later trial, the reason being that the average citizen has little understanding of such technicalities, and unless they are explained to him, they are of little use to him in his efforts to protect himself.

To summarize, evidence is any information that is relevant, reliable, and does not conflict with a specific policy in the law. You may now be understanding why this is an extremely important field to a trial lawyer, one he must master very thoroughly if he is to do his job correctly. You may also begin to comprehend why it is that jury verdicts don't always reflect the truth as a fly on the wall might have seen it unfold: The jury is simply prevented, usually for policy reasons, from hearing some information that, if received, would have given them a completely different view of the case.

Two more things need to be said about the concept of evidence before we discuss how you should prepare yourself for learning this vast and complex subject.

First, what happens when two rules of evidence appear to conflict, as they often do? The fact is, a great deal of information that is admissible on one ground is generally excludable on another. For example, suppose in our shooting case the prosecutor wanted to offer photos of V's nude body on the autopsy table, so that the jurors could see for themselves the nature and location of the gunshot wounds. Photographs, if relevant and properly identified, are usually admissible. But D's lawyer objects! He claims that the jury ought not to be able to see these particular photos, because they are very gory, and could "inflame" and outrage the jury so as to blur their objectivity and incline them to prejudice against D.

The trial judge now has to perform a balancing act. Out of the presence of the jury, he examines the photographs to answer for himself this question: "Which weighs more in the circumstances of this case, the probative value of these photos, or their probable prejudicial effect?"

Probative value means information that is valuable to prove something important to the issues in the lawsuit; in this case, the nature and location of the gunshot wounds.

Probable prejudicial effect means the likelihood that a jury looking at the photos will become so upset that they will want to see someone, anyone, punished for this horrible deed. In this case, the only one they have the power to punish is D, since he is the only one on trial.

Let's assume that after examining the photos the judge finds them particularly repugnant. Assume also that he believes that the facts of V's shooting as described by the police officer at the scene and the medical examiner in their testimony are not going to be disputed to any great degree by D's lawyer. If that is his view, he will rule that the jury may not see the photos, because their probable prejudicial effect outweighs their probative value. Disputes of this kind are common in a trial, and the lawyer who is best prepared, fastest on his feet, and most persuasive in his arguments is likely to win more than his share of these courtroom skirmishes.

The second situation to consider is what is called *curative admissibility*. Very frequently, information not initially admitted into evidence because of some defect of reliability or policy will be "cured" by an event that takes place as the trial progresses. To illustrate, let's go back to our hearsay problem with W and W-2. W-2's statement has been excluded as hearsay. But now, while cross-examining W, D's lawyer asks this question: "Isn't it a fact, W, that while you were at the scene immediately after the shooting, W-2 told you that he had seen X, not D, do the shooting at V?"

Because D's lawyer has "opened the door" to the conversation between W and W-2 by asking this question, W will now be allowed to recite the conversation that up to this time had been barred. The hearsay defect has been cured, in effect, by the invitation from D's lawyer. Fundamentally, the principle active here is one that we all encounter many times during our lifetimes: "You can't have your cake and eat it too!"

Another example: With respect to the photographs that D's lawyer has successfully kept from the jury, suppose D takes the witness stand and claims that he was acting in self-defense; that V was assaulting him with a knife; and that he shot V once in the chest to save his own life. Now the prosecutor will once again offer the photos in evidence, for they show that V had no wounds in the chest, but four wounds in the back instead. In all probability, the trial judge will address the question anew, repeat the weighing process, and this time conclude that because of D's claim the probative value of the photos now has a *greater* weight than the possible prejudicial effect. The jury will now be permitted to view the photos, so that they may evaluate the truthfulness of D's story. The original obstacle to their admissibility—the result of the trial judge's first "balancing act"—has been cured by D's testimony, which made the location of the gunshot wounds a critical issue for the jury to decide.

Since I have said that I do not want or expect you to immerse yourself now in the constantly shifting sands of that vast desert called evidence, why burden you with the information set forth above? A fair question.

The reason is one I hope you will keep in mind through all your years of law school. It is that the whole foundation of justice as we like to think about it is inexorably intertwined with the concept of evidence. All of the rights you think you have can only be asserted or protected in a court of law, when all negotiation fails, and courts can act only upon the presentation of admissible evidence. Individual rights can be trampled in the most horrible fashion where there is a failure of evidence. Innocent people have gone to jail because the evidence against them was false, or because they lacked the evidence necessary to show their innocence. Citizens who have done nothing wrong at all have had to pay huge money judgments in civil cases—sometimes to the point of bankruptcy—because of a failure of evidence.

Every trial lawyer worthy of the title has to understand evidence instinctively. During a trial, there will be one battle after another to accept or reject information, and the lawyer called upon to argue these points must respond instantly, and with computerlike efficiency. His memory must quickly comb each of the rules that apply, and the curative rules set in motion by the developments in the case, select those arguments most helpful to him, and articulate them without hesitation, thinking just ahead of what he is saying.

That is a tall order. You may now appreciate my insistence on speaking well without notes, and on training your memory to store information and spit it out upon demand. The ability to handle evidentiary questions in a trial with assurance and spontaneity is one of the trademarks of a top-flight trial lawyer. When a trial judge perceives this ability, he will caution himself before ruling against a lawyer who consistently has good legal reasoning at his fingertips. Ideally, as a trial lawyer you will become what Boswell called Dr. Johnson: "a dangerous person to disagree with."

It is mandatory that you start thinking now about the world of evidence, and how important it will be to your professional life. You are not going to get nearly enough exposure to evidence in law school to have it under your command. The course that you will be taught will nearly gag you with its intricacies and contradictions. Most students get a few weeks into the evidence course and feel a sense of utter bewilderment. Young lawyers venturing into court for their first few trials regularly show a distinct weakness in handling evidentiary questions. To avoid that shortcoming, I want you to think and breathe evidence every day from now until your first case in court, and then forevermore. Until you have changed your thinking and reasoning habits to perceive life in terms of what the evidence will show, you will not be ready for the responsibility of trying an important lawsuit.

If you should feel ambitious during your prelaw years, don't feel bashful about sneaking into the law school bookstore and buying a textbook on evidence. The first time you read through it, you won't grasp or retain much. The second time, a little will stick. If you stay with it, some of what you are teaching yourself will begin to take hold. Your efforts will be handsomely repaid in two ways: First, when you do get to your course on evidence in law school, you will be miles ahead of the rest of the class and probably stay there. Second, you will get a lot more out of something I am going to ask you to do later in this book—going to court and watching trials in progress.

You may have noticed that in describing the kinds of qualifications that can permit mere information to rise to the status of evidence, there has been one glaring omission. We discussed *reliability* as one of the basic criteria, but said nothing about the trial judge rejecting information because it was *false!* This is because he is almost totally without power to exclude information he believes to be untrue. That is a jury's function—to determine the credibility of a witness—and a judge must leave the task in their hands. When he tests information for reliability, he does so on the assumption that what is offered is at least true, no matter how weak or second-hand it may appear to be.

The sad fact is, lying testimony or perjury, a serious but seldom punished crime, is perfectly admissible. If the jury believes a lying witness by mistake, as they did in our curtain rod case in Chapter 1, injustice will not be far away. And, as I have said before and will stress every time I get the chance, if the jury makes this kind of mistake, there is no remedy, no appeal, except in the rarest case. The injustice flowing from that mistake will permanently affect the party who is wronged by it. False testimony is as powerful as it is evil.

You have doubtless said or heard others say more than once in the past, "You can't prove that—it's just your word against mine!" What is usually meant by this challenge is, "Since I didn't put my statement to you in writing, I can always lie about it later on." Many people who believe this make horrendous mistakes predicated on what is no more than a time-honored fallacy.

With rare exception, the testimony of one witness against one or a dozen others who claim he is lying is more than sufficient to make out a case. If the jury believes that witness, as they are free to do, they can render a verdict saying, in effect, that *all* those telling a different story are lying, and must lose. Trials of this sort take place every day, and there are none of us who have been trying lawsuits for very long who haven't lost a few such cases.

As an extreme, and grimly humorous, example, consider the story of a young married woman I defended some years ago. She was accused of hiring a very bad man to kill her husband so she could collect fifteen thousand in insurance, of which she was to pay the killer five thousand. Before he could commit the grisly act, she had a change of heart and called him to cancel the contract. He refused, saying that they had an agreement, that he was going to carry out his end of the bargain, and that when it was done he would expect to be paid. With a layman's indignation she said: "You can't do that—I didn't sign anything!"

In any event, no matter how insistent your friends may be in asserting their right to lie in or out of court about important matters, you must give it up now and always if you want to be a lawyer. Your word must be as good as solid gold, to match the high degree of trust that society places in your hands.

There is no *right* to lie in a legal case, and never has been. But people have the *power* to tell lies, and often do. I have rarely seen a trial of consequence where one or more witnesses didn't lie on the witness stand. Sometimes they got caught, but not always. Sometimes the jury believed them, leaving justice totally frustrated.

As a trial lawyer, you are the best protection the public has against these corruptors, partly because of your instant-reflex knowledge of evidence, and partly because of another absolutely essential skill: the ability to cross-examine.

6

What Preparation Really Means

As you recall from Chapter 1, C the curtain rod customer lost his case because his lawyer had failed in the essential: adequate preparation. When you begin to go to court for a living, the most common shortcoming you will see in your colleagues and opponents will be just such lack of preparation.

Pretrial preparation has often been compared to a part of the iceberg that sank the *Titanic,* namely the part that was underwater (about 87 percent of the whole). You may not be able to see it from a distance, but you know damned well it's there. The trial itself is like the portion that sticks up out of the water for all to see.

Edward Bennett Williams, one of America's greatest trial lawyers, and perhaps *the* greatest, was once commended on a brilliant courtroom tactic that had enabled him, his admirer said, to "pull a rabbit out of a hat." In response, Mr. Williams is said to have replied: "To have any chance at all of pulling a rabbit out of a hat in a trial, you have to come to court armed with fifty rabbits, fifty hats, and a lot of luck. If the luck is with you, you may get to use one rabbit and one hat."

Preparation is exhausting, painstaking, and occasionally heartbreaking work, but it is an absolute duty that a trial lawyer owes to his client. Years ago, it is said, great trial lawyers were basically great orators, who depended more on their rhetoric to win their cases than on a command of the facts. Dealing with juries far less educated and less sophisticated than those today, they would read from the Bible, the *Encyclopaedia Britannica,* and famous works of literature to sway their listeners.

Those days are gone. Ed Williams is often given credit for leading the "new breed" of trial lawyers, whose ace talent is preparation, not just good speechmaking. He demonstrated the success of his methods with a long string of stunning courtroom victories in the fifties and sixties, setting an example for the whole profession to follow.

The foundation of good preparation is good *investigation.* Unfortunately, good investigators are rarer than good trial lawyers, who are scarce enough. Law students get virtually no training in investigation, and thus have little notion whether the work an investigator turns in is excellent, good, mediocre, or incompetent. Therefore, you need training as an investigator if you want to be a trial lawyer, and you have to seek it yourself.

Melvin Belli, a top trial lawyer often called the "king of torts" for the many huge personal-injury awards he has won for his clients, once said: "If the investigator is good enough, most any trial lawyer will do." While I cannot subscribe to the latter part of his statement, his first point is well taken.

How do you describe a good investigator? How do you define a good trial lawyer? In venturing answers, I am tempted to retreat into the formulation of Mr. Justice Potter Stewart, formerly of the United States Supreme Court, who finally said, after grappling unsuccessfully with an attempt to define pornography: "I can't *define* it, but I *know* it when I *see* it."

But good investigators, like good trial lawyers, can be described. They are basically bright, sensitive, patient, and thorough people. And they like, and enjoy the company of, other people. They have to, for they spend a great deal of time just sitting and talking to people.

During a trial, many different forms of evidence are received. There may be writings (called *documentary* evidence); objects such as a murder weapon (called *real* evidence); audio and video recordings (*electronic* evidence); photographs (*photographic* evidence); scientific tests such as fingerprints, x-rays, electrocardiograms, electroencephalograms, firearms identification tests, handwriting comparisons, polygraph tests, and so forth (*scientific* evidence); and the testimony of witnesses (*testimonial* evidence). A good investigator will understand and be prepared to deal with all of the different kinds of evidence, but his long suit will be in the most volatile sort: testimonial evidence, which means people.

While any type of evidence may be in contest during a trial, in current times 90 percent of what is really litigated is testimony from those who take the witness stand. There is a good reason.

Consider, from an objective overview, what a trial lawyer is really trying to do when he conducts his courtroom scenario. First and principally, he is trying to recreate a piece of history, which has been growing more and more remote ever since it happened. In a rare case, he may have a piece of film to ease his burden. The shooting of Lee Harvey Oswald, for instance, was filmed and the film was used at trial to show the guilt of the defendant, Jack Ruby. When John Hinckley shot President Ronald Reagan in 1981, that event was recorded on film. In both cases the defense lawyers saw that one could hardly contest what the camera had captured, and therefore based their defense on the one claim that no camera can see: the mental condition of the assailant.

But these are rare cases. Normally there is no videotape camera present when an extraordinary event takes place. We have to recreate these occurrences with a much more fragile kind of evidence: the testimony of people who come to the witness stand to describe what they think they saw.

But people are not cameras, and their efforts to recreate moments from history are not nearly so faithful to the details of the original event as the camera can be. Before a human being can observe a "happening" as it takes place in his presence and then report his observations in a court of law, several obstacles, grounded in human failings, have to be hurdled. They are, in order: *perception, memory, articulation,* and *candor.*

If an eyewitness performed all of these functions to perfection, he could bring to a jury as accurate and objective a portrayal of what happened as a camera. But there never has been such a human being, and I don't expect to live to see the first one.

Let's examine these hurdles one by one. The first is perception. You have gone through life so far telling people, "I saw this," and "I saw that," when the verb "to see" is not what you meant at all. We "see" a great deal that never registers. Our true field of vision is about 180 degrees. In order to keep an active pilot's license, you must take a periodic medical examination that includes a test of your peripheral vision—your ability to stare straight ahead while still being able to see an object to the immediate left or right; out of the "corner of your eye," so to speak. We "see" through that entire range.

But "perception" is something else again. Our range of perception in degrees is rather narrow. In order to perceive something, you have to "look at" it. If you are looking at an object or scene, it may or may not form an imprint on your memory. If it does, you will be able to describe it in some fashion later on.

At this moment, for instance, you are perceiving this page of this book, translating the words you see into thoughts that are filed in your memory. Later today or tomorrow you should be able to recite what is said here in a general way to a friend. A year from now, if you follow through with what I hope to teach you, two things will happen: First, you will have a vague recollection of the thoughts you are now considering; and, second, you will reread this chapter, find that it makes a lot more sense, and get a great deal more out of it. That progression should improve on an annual basis until after you have tried a fair number of cases.

You are perceiving the words on this page because you are looking directly at them as you read along. You can see the entire page at all times; however, if you fix your gaze on the center of the page, you will not be able to read it, only to determine that it is there. To read the words, you must move the focus of your vision from left to right and down the page. That is what I meant when I said that the range of perception is a narrow one.

In dealing with witnesses, this is one of several phenomena that cause courts and lawyers severe problems. People often testify to things that they saw, but didn't actually perceive. Let me give a couple of classic examples.

I have said that healthy peripheral vision works over a range of about 180 degrees. Although you can't perceive things that happen off to the side of your central vision, you do notice them. A flash of light or sudden movement off to your extreme right will attract your attention, causing you to look at it, and then to perceive it. The trouble is, by the time you *do* perceive an important event to which you might later be called upon to testify, it has been "over" by a split second.

Take the case of a gunshot, or two vehicles colliding at an intersection. Unless for some reason you happen to be looking directly at the weapon or the vehicles at the moment of contact, the chances are that your attention will be drawn to the event by your sense of hearing, which is omnidirectional. Upon hearing a loud noise—especially one that is unexpected—you are apt to whirl and glance about until you locate visually the source of the noise. (This is why noises in the night are so unnerving, because you can't see the source.)

When your perception does finally locate the source of the noise, you are too late. The weapon has already been fired, or the vehicles are in the process of bouncing off one another. At this point, however, a psychological phenomenon comes into play that may later cause you to believe that you were actually staring at the central event before the noise occurred.

The strongest impulse known to man or beast is the impulse to survive. Anytime a human being believes that he is threatened, he will react with what is sometimes called the fight-flight-holding syndrome. These are three available remedies, one of which must be selected very quickly. To understand the syndrome, imagine that you have been startled by a gunshot. You turn rapidly and see a man standing twenty feet away with a pistol in his hand. At his feet is another man, writhing in agony. Although you didn't see it happen, you assume that the man holding the pistol just shot the one on the ground. You make this assumption because you must figure out *what* has happened and *why* in order to select the best of the three remedies. Your decision—really an *inference*—is forced on you by necessity. Depending on what you decide, and what your circumstances are, you may elect:

Fight: You too have a pistol, you are cornered, you are convinced that this assailant is a crazy man who will shoot you next if you don't get him first, so you attack with your weapon; or,

Flight: You are not concerned, you don't have a weapon (or are reluctant to use the one you have), and so to achieve personal safety you run like hell; or,

Holding: You have no weapon and no egress, so you freeze on the spot, hoping that you won't be noticed, or that if you are you won't be worth shooting; or you may decide that the quarrel was strictly between those two "other guys," and that if your conduct is innocuous you'll be all right.

The point is, no matter what choice you make, in recalling the event later you may easily confuse the inference you drew from the circumstances with what you *wish* you had seen, and report that you acted as you did because you actually *saw* the shot fired.

You are now a witness who believes that he saw something he didn't, and who has subconsciously and innocently made up details that in reality he missed. Does this cause problems? You bet. It also goes a long way to explain why eyewitnesses to a traumatic event usually differ wildly over the details. As good evidence of this, bear in mind that in the trial of Jack Ruby for shooting Lee Harvey Oswald, the witnesses gave sharply disparate accounts of the shooting, even though the entire event had been captured on motion picture film!

Our investigator, then, trying to get at the facts of this shooting, already has a substantial problem with the witness's perception: the difference between what he *really* perceived versus what he *believes* he perceived. And his problems are only beginning, for this is only the first of four major hurdles.

We must now confront the problems of memory, and they too are severe.

First, it is well established that memory fades with time, and at different rates. Ask yourself where you were last March 21; unless it was your birthday, or the birthday of someone you love, you probably can't tell me (unless you happen to be reading this chapter on March 22). But if I need to know where you were last Christmas morning, there is a much better chance that we can dig around in your recollection and come up with the right answer.

Second, if there is upcoming litigation with respect to an event you witnessed, you will be questioned repeatedly by others, some of whom may be very experienced interrogators, who have an interest in "assisting" your memory to favor their side of the case. Assume that you did see at least part of the shooting we were discussing a few pages back, and that you know there were three others on the scene. You recall that the assailant was wearing a blue sports jacket. You tell this to the investigator, who mentions that the other three witnesses are quite sure that the assailant was wearing a brown sweater.

You become concerned. The whole affair was very upsetting at the time, and perhaps you didn't observe correctly. Perhaps the lighting was not too bright. You take no comfort in the prospect of testifying in the case and being contradicted by three other witnesses. Pretty soon it becomes quite easy to recall a brown sweater, not a blue sports jacket, and you sign a statement that you saw a brown sweater. When you do testify at trial, you are puzzled to discover that only two of the other three are testifying, and that one says he saw a green business suit while the other claims to remember a gray overcoat.

As memory fades, it becomes more vulnerable to the power of suggestion, and that power is abundant in pretrial preparation, simply because all the questioners—the lawyers and the investigators—have an ax to grind. Impartial objectivity may be the business of judges and juries, but it is not the business of those who must take sides in the case. Therefore, even if one did perceive an event correctly, his story may be heavily distorted through this combination of fading memory and suggestibility by the time it reaches the courtroom.

But assuming that our witness *did* correctly perceive the event on trial, and did manage to remember it without undue fading or distortion, we must still confront the next problem: articulation.

In order to transfer information from one mind (the witness's) to other minds (those of the jurors), the images in the memory must be reduced to words, which are then spoken (transmitted) by the witness, heard (received) by the jurors, and transferred back to images again. Depending on the ability of the witness to use the King's English properly, and the ability of the jurors (or at least some of them) to understand what is said, there will be some slippage from one image to the other.

This process—transferring images through words—introduces several risks into our system of "recreating" a moment of history long gone. Suppose, for instance, that the only person who saw the shooting was a small child. Should we trust a youngster to give an accurate picture in words of what took place when the weapon fired? What if fantasies interfere with recollection? Should the child be allowed to testify? If the child is less than, say, twelve, the trial judge will hold a hearing out of the presence of the jury to determine whether this young witness is *competent* to testify. If so, the jury may be presented nonetheless with a rather flawed account of the event.

Or suppose that the witness is a Rhodes Scholar who majored in English at Oxford, and who is utterly incapable of expressing himself in what we might call "ordinary" language. He may have a totally accurate recollection, but unless he is willing to lower the plane of his conversation to a level jurors can comprehend, he may create only the fuzziest of images in their minds. In short, it is the job of the investigator, and later the trial lawyer, to get the witness to express himself with precision and clarity to the best of his ability, and often even *that* is not very good. A clear perception coupled with near perfect recollection may bring the witness to the stand with some images in mind that are faithful to the original happening, but difficulties in articulating those images can reduce an otherwise good reproduction to rubble.

The greatest enemy of all is the final one: candor. Assume that we have been exceptionally lucky, and that at the time of the shooting a person of good intelligence was on the scene, looking in precisely the right direction before and during the time that our victim was shot. That person has a clear recollection of the event, and a level of articulative skill that is entirely intelligible to the jurors. Also assume that the witness has a very strong reason to lie. Where are we now? In deep trouble.

If you have ever watched "Perry Mason," or most any other Hollywood trial lawyer, you may think that those who try to lie in court are stung with brilliant cross-examination, tearfully admit to the perjury they have tried to commit, and then tell the truth. If that were so, and if I could assure you that you have the patience and persistence to become a truly superb cross-examiner, you could always trap the liars. Unfortunately, such is not the case. A clever lying witness who carefully thinks out the details of his fabricated story has the edge on the cross-examiner every time. If he does get caught, and if his credibility does get effectively destroyed, it is usually because an investigator of skill and talent has been working on him for a long time prior to trial.

The task of the investigator—trying to sort out what really happened by talking to people who claim that they know—must take into account natural failings in each of these four areas. In our chapter on cross-examination, we will meet these same problems again; if, however, that is where they are confronted by counsel for the *first* time, the chances that justice will eventually be done are not very good.

A skilled investigator must have an inquisitive mind, steeped in human experience, to sort out all these difficulties and come up with a hypothesis of what a videotape would show had there been one in motion at the time of the event. His ability to relate to people, most of whom are rather apprehensive about being an "eyeball" witness to an event, must be excellent. His patience, and his ability to perceive what it will take to relax a witness to the point where the witness's best recollection can surface, will usually be the measure of his success. If he does have these talents, but is so anxious to please the lawyer who hired him that he is willing to bend and twist the witness's story with his interrogative skills, justice will suffer. A good investigator—one who is to be trusted to take his responsibilities seriously—must have the same ethical standards as a good trial lawyer. Deliberately inducing a witness to lie, or subtly showing him the way to lie with the implied promise of some reward, reduces our process to a mere sham. Unfortunately, there are investigators who are quite willing to corrupt their skills to achieve some near-term victory. More unfortunately, the worst of these that I have seen have worked for the United States government.

Louis Nizer, a celebrated trial lawyer, once said: "When trying to evaluate the credibility of the story a witness tells, always be mindful of the probabilities." This is good advice. Human experience is a factor in almost every judgment we make, and it is especially valuable in assessing the likelihood that a witness's version is true. Things tend to happen again as they have in the past, and if the account of an event is highly improbable, it deserves the closest scrutiny. How does the witness's account match up with the circumstances known to exist at the time? How does it mesh with the stories of other witnesses? How likely is it that things could have happened as this witness describes in his claimed perceptions? These and other questions touching on probability must be constantly in the investigator's mind, and yet at the same time he must be alert for the bizarre.

What is the bizarre? The improbable, that's what. The extraordinary event, the circumstance that appears to defy human experience. The law seems to get more than its share of these occurrences, and it usually doesn't handle them very well, simply because we are so in the habit of assessing "probabilities" that courts and juries are very reluctant to admit that the unlikely could take place.

As a striking example of the bizarre, and the extent to which it can mislead the legal process, consider the Vermont case of a man who was found dead in a river, his hands and feet tightly tied behind his back. Based on common experience, the prosecutor decided early on that this was no accidental death. The man had so many enemies, and had been such a bad person for most of his life, that the suspect list was a long one. Ultimately, a man was indicted and brought to trial on purely circumstantial evidence. He was acquitted. Later a second man was indicted for the same murder on a different theory. During that trial, the defense called as a witness one of the finest forensic pathologists this country has ever produced: Dr. Richard Ford, for many years the medical examiner for Suffolk County (Boston), Massachusetts. He took the stand and, when queried as to his opinion on the cause of death, replied: "Suicide." The prosecutor, after gagging a bit at the answer, rose to cross-examine. "I wonder, Doctor," he said, "if you would be good enough to explain to the jury how this 'suicide' managed to tie his hands and feet tightly behind his back before jumping into the river?"

"I thought you might ask that," replied Dr. Ford, "and I will explain the best way I can." He then produced from his briefcase a length of rope, and with a couple of flicks of the wrist and a sudden jerk on the rope fell to the ground, his hands and feet securely bound behind his back.

By the time the trial came to completion, it was apparent that the victim had been suicidal, and that he had made an elaborate effort in staging his own demise to see that the people he hated so much would suffer as suspects for what was intended to look like a premeditated murder.

A trained investigator will remain alert for any psychological imbalance in a witness's story. This is a purely subconscious phenomenon that arises from an internal bias. If the witness is a friend of the subject of the investigation, he will have a natural tendency to want to help, and his account of events is likely to be shaded in favor of the friend. Or it may be that the witness has suffered some past trauma that distorts his judgment. A woman who has been a rape victim, and who witnesses a man and a woman having a sexual encounter, may infer that the female partner is being raped at the slightest indication that her consent is less than obvious. One who has lost a friend or family member who was struck by a car, and who then witnesses an accident between a motor vehicle and a pedestrian, is very apt to perceive the event from a bias in favor of the pedestrian. A skilled questioner will probe carefully and gently for such distortion factors.

One of the most controversial arguments in the field of legal investigation centers around this question: Should an investigator attempt in each instance to take a written statement from a witness? Experts do not agree. Here are some of the reasons.

Laymen believe, as we discussed before, that any oral statements they make are easy to change or deny because of the it's-only-your-word-against-mine fallacy. They are much more apt to talk freely if there is no note paper or tape recorder confronting them. They may give all sorts of juicy details or biased opinions (which are invaluable for later cross-examination) if they believe that they are having an informal, off-the-record conversation with the investigator. Objects that make a record of oral statements can intimidate a witness, in short.

On the other hand, a written statement bearing a witness's signature is a handy device to have in hand when the witness seeks to vary his story on the stand. He may well claim that the investigator wrote out the statement, that the words it contains were the investigator's and not his own, or that he didn't read the statement carefully before he signed it.

Because of the frequency of this last excuse, most experienced investigators make at least one obvious mistake on each page of the statement and then allow the witness to discover, correct, and initial these mistakes as he goes through each page before signing. This technique usually disposes effectively of any witness's claim that he didn't examine the text before signing.

With some exceptions, I do not personally favor placing much emphasis on coaxing a witness into giving a written statement unless he makes it clear that he will be comfortable in doing so. There are several reasons for this view.

First, it is often necessary to interview a witness several times between initial contact and actual trial. If an investigator insists on reducing the first group of recollections a witness offers to a written statement, properly constructed, he may have "locked the witness in" to an uncomfortable and even counterproductive situation. Few people remember all the details of what they perceived during an initial interview, particularly when an investigator is new to the case and does not know what questions to ask. As the investigation moves along and more details become available from other sources, it is frequently appropriate to return to a witness for additional information or for clarification of his earlier statement. Here lies the problem.

A written statement is a *commitment,* and even though supplementing such a statement is perfectly legitimate if honestly done, most witnesses feel committed and are reluctant to say anything new that will contradict that statement, even though the new material—often the product of recollection triggered by details that the investigator has learned and explained during a secondary interview—is true and correct. To aggravate this situation, a good statement will have covered affirmatively all that a witness claims to have perceived, and all the *negatives* as well. In other words, a good statement will have many sentences in which a witness asserts that he *did not* notice a particular detail, if it occurred. This makes it difficult to turn around and contradict those negatives in a second writing by affirmatively remembering the missing detail.

Generally, I prefer an investigator who is intelligent, honest, and has sufficient memory to interview a witness freely and informally, then make his notes later. Before trial, the lawyers will probably take a written deposition of the witness, under oath, with every question and answer recorded; this pretty well locks in what the witness is going to be able to say at trial, no matter what written statements he may have given before the deposition was taken.

Nonetheless, it is important that the investigator maintain a good working rapport with each witness up to and throughout the trial. The dynamics of trial produce many frequent shifts in the evidence, and often questions never contemplated in the preparatory stages arise. To each proposition appearing in the evidence, the witness may be required to affirm, deny, or say, "I don't know." So long as the witness trusts the investigator, good communications will be maintained, and these day-to-day new "wrinkles" in the evidence can be discussed and ironed out.

Investigation is a continuing activity, from the onset of a case to its conclusion. One of the investigator's prime responsibilities is to ensure, insofar as is possible, that the trial lawyer gets no surprises while the trial is under way. This is why Mr. Williams spoke of the fifty hats and fifty rabbits. Put another way, you must take a look at everything in sight—two or three times if necessary—to make sure that nothing is missed.

All physical evidence should be viewed, studied, and noted. By physical evidence, I mean all that the eye can perceive, the hand can touch, the ear hear, the nose smell, or the tongue taste. The five senses are what witnesses use to arrive at the perceptions to which they will testify, and the investigator must duplicate the experiences to the extent that he can. It is embarrassing to conduct an interrogation that includes an elaborate description of the way things were at the scene of an event, only to visit that scene the following day and discover that they are quite different, and that the interview must be started over almost from scratch. Where feasible, a skilled investigator will learn firsthand of all physical evidence before beginning his witness interviews.

If the scene of the event is important to the litigation, a fairly detailed diagram should be made and placed in the file right at the outset of the investigation. Distances should be paced off in order to assist witnesses in their distance estimates (how far from the incident they were standing, and so on), which are normally atrociously inaccurate. It is also a good idea to take a series of sharply detailed photographs from a number of different angles. These will further help witnesses to locate themselves and to recall some of the details of what they perceived. In an important case, it is often worth the cost to order an overhead aerial photo to be taken from a helicopter, providing what is virtually a map of the area. The more aids of this sort the investigator has at his command when he conducts his witness interviews, the more detailed and accurate the witnesses are likely to be.

One should make it a practice to test the assertions of every important witness by conducting simple experiments. If a witness says that he perceived something in a certain place at the scene while he was in a certain location, determine either by resort to the diagram and photos, or by a personal visit, whether such a perception was in fact possible, or whether his ability to see would necessarily have been blocked in any way. By the same token, if a witness claims that he heard and understood a conversation between two people twenty feet away speaking in normal tones, stand twenty feet from him, say a few words, and allow him to demonstrate his ability to repeat them.

Other kinds of claims can be checked for feasibility. If in an accident case, a witness recounts having perceived both cars in a collision as they approached the intersection where the accident happened, and gives the speed of each and its distance from the intersection when first seen, work out the numbers carefully. Often, if the witness's estimates—normally rough approximations at best—are taken as true, it can be demonstrated that the cars could not have collided at all!

As with the other kinds of personal contact mentioned earlier in this book, it is wise during witness interviews to watch your subject as closely as you can without making him feel uncomfortable or self-conscious. It is important not only to assess the value, if any, of what a witness tells you, but also the manner in which he tells it. Is he credible? How will a judge or jury react to his testimony if it is used? Is he a nice person, one who sincerely wants to be of assistance? Is he the kind of person you might enjoy spending an evening with, or going on a vacation with? What is his probable intelligence level? How well does he express his thoughts? Is he careful in what he says?

You will review the answers to these questions many times before the witness is ever called to testify. Sometimes, when a witness is weak, a trial lawyer will elect not to use him, simply because he is so vulnerable on cross-examination that in the long run he will probably not be an asset to the case.

As I have said, you are going to learn the whole business of investigation pretty much on your own, simply because it does not appear in any law school curriculum. Law schools teach law, and do a pretty good job of it. But trial lawyers are "facters" as much as they are lawyers, and must be self-educated to a large degree. Investigative experience is not easy to attain, but most things that are not easy can still be done. I will offer some suggestions, which can probably be supplemented by many sources: family, student advisers, Dad's lawyer, and so on.

First, find the local court of general jurisdiction and make it your business to go watch some trials. Find out who the experienced trial judges are, and ask for an appointment with a member of their staff. Explain that you are considering a career in advocacy and would like to watch some interesting trials to get an idea of the process. You will find that most judicial staff members are agreeable people, who approve heartily of youthful interest in the trial bar. Each judge has a calendar, and his clerk or secretary will usually be willing to take a few minutes to explain what the different trials coming up are all about, and perhaps advise you which of the trial lawyers involved might be worth watching. Sit through a couple of trials. Criminal and personal-injury trials are apt to be the most informative for your purposes, since they usually involve traumatic events, and these are the ones that most sorely test the ability of the witnesses to recount their perceptions, for all of the reasons we have discussed.

Watch the witnesses as they are led through the procedure of giving evidence: first, telling their stories with the guidance of the "friendly" lawyer who called them to the stand; and second, undergoing cross-examination by the lawyer who opposes their testimony. As you listen, try to imagine how the witness was discovered, who interviewed him and refined his tale, and what his attitude is about the whole business of appearing to testify.

Trial lawyers are usually very busy people when a trial is in progress, but they are often warm people as well. When the court is in recess and everyone is standing around the hallway, introduce yourself to one of the lawyers—both, if possible—and tell him why you are there. Many of the good ones will have sons and daughters your own age, and will invite you to learn a little about the "inside" of the way they are handling their cases.

If your schedule permits, try to find work in a law firm, even if it is only as "gofer." The pay will probably be very modest, but if you can afford it, the experience will be well worth the sacrifice.

Although in the beginning you will probably do little more than deliver papers to the courthouse or to other lawyers, one day you will be asked to take on more significant tasks.

If you are not already a camera buff, ask for a camera for the next birthday or Christmas. Modern cameras are quite simple to operate because they are highly automated, and if you have the ability to do so you may soon be asked to do some of the firm's legal photography. Make sure that you produce excellent results, even if you have to use four rolls of film to produce a single important picture (which is what top professionals do—take hundreds of exposures looking for just one outstanding photo).

As opportunity allows, you may be permitted to sit in on witness interviews, or to drive the witnesses to and from their homes, or both. Watch how they are handled. What does the lawyer do while he asks his questions? Does he keep his eyes on the witness, or does he bury his head in his notes? No matter what *he* does, *you* keep your eyes on the person who is speaking, for you will be learning about communications, a subject of the most vital importance.

Be patient. Even if you feel you are brimming with natural talent, don't expect it to be discovered quickly. Lawyers are skeptics, well aware that only time can produce experience. Watching others, initially at least, is the best opportunity to learn.

As time goes on and it becomes apparent that you are earnest and sincere in your efforts to progress, you will find yourself getting more and more help. Lawyers love to talk about their cases, and if you are a good listener, the opportunities to absorb their experiences—at least in the retold version, which may be just that little bit embellished—are often worth whatever time it takes. This will acquaint you with the flavor of the advocate's daily life.

If you are fortunate enough to put in some time working with a law firm as an undergraduate, you will find yourself acclimating to the law school environment much more easily when you finally get there. The language and ideology peculiar to the practice of law will have already become part of your system, and you will feel much more comfortable during the transition into law school than many of your classmates.

Once you enter law school, your opportunities to learn more and do more meaningful things in the firm will accelerate about as fast as your initiative and performance allow. One of the first things a law student learns is legal research, and after a semester or two, you will be asked to prepare memoranda on some issue or another. More important, you may be asked to interview a witness or two in a preliminary fashion. In other words, you may get to do the screening that leads to deciding whether a person has perceived enough to make it worthwhile to interview him formally.

No matter what task is assigned you, do it, even if it is no more than getting lunch for one of the secretaries. A great deal of the day-to-day practice of law is anything but glamorous, and lawyers are ever alert to see who will do the least colorful tasks without dragging his feet or complaining.

If you can work for lawyers on any basis throughout college and law school, you will have taken giant steps toward being a trial lawyer, for over a period of time expertise tends to rub off on one who is genuinely enthusiastic to learn. What is lacking in your formal law school training—the practical and "people" part of the business—can only be learned where it is all going on, and that is an office with an active practice.

There are some other training situations in which you can learn to be an investigator, but I am deliberately omitting any discussion of them. If you want to be the best, then get the best education you can. Apart from law school, that can only be through association with a law office. In the last ten years I have not hired any lawyers unless they came to our office at least by the second year of law school. Many other lawyers have learned the wisdom of this practice, and if you seek them out hard enough and present yourself in your most favorable light, you will find one. Settle for nothing less.

7

Managing a Trial

66 The play's the thing," wrote Shakespeare in *Hamlet,* and so it is in court. A trial is a play, in some senses, and it is anything but a play in others. One who hopes to be an advocate will learn the distinction very quickly.

A play, whether it be serious drama or light comedy, is the brainchild of its creator. It is a product of the imagination, and before it opens the playwright can adjust it infinitely to make sure that it provides good theater. If a character doesn't work, he can be changed or eliminated. If a scene doesn't come off just right, the facts can be altered. The flexibility is almost total.

A trial is almost the opposite. The scenario is written by history, and the trial lawyer has very little room to change it. The facts are there, and they are real. The witnesses do not work from scripts devised by a screenwriter, but from their recollections. Rewriting scenes or lines is not considered ethical (lawyers who do it often wind up in jail), and one takes what one gets.

A good producer or director in the world of drama picks the best actor he can to play each role. If one actor doesn't work quite right, he tries another. In the law, there is no such luxury. Often the only witness to an event is a most undesirable person. He may have a criminal record, be an inveterate liar, or hold out for money for his testimony. Whatever he is, we are stuck with him. We may decide not to call him, but we can't write him out of the script. Sometime during the trial the jury will find out that he was on the scene, and wonder why he has not testified.

Although the drama of a trial is not the product of a creative mind, there are some options and alternatives that give the trial lawyer an opportunity to "manage" the show. The selection and the order of witnesses can be shuffled to a degree, and the tenor and tone of the presentation can be made to range from light to very intense. Basically, it is a question of what is appropriate. In a criminal case, laughter is an asset to the defense and bad news for the prosecution, for laughing juries do not ordinarily convict. Similarly, a plaintiff seeking substantial money damages wants his case to be taken very seriously by the jury, while the defense lawyer will favor as much levity as he can manage, for laughing juries seldom return large damage awards.

One of the most difficult and annoying aspects of a trial lawyer's life is uncertainty as to when the trial will take place. Except for high-powered, headline cases, courts do not do a very good job at setting firm trial dates and sticking with them. Judges would like to operate on a definite schedule, but this objective is often frustrated. An earlier trial may last much longer than anticipated, one of the lawyers may be engaged in another trial elsewhere, or a critical witness may be ill or out of the country, where he cannot be reached with a subpoena. Whatever the reason, it is not uncommon for a trial lawyer to bring his whole "act" to the courthouse, only to find at the last minute that a postponement cannot be avoided.

On the other hand, occasionally one learns with surprise that a trial date has been moved forward unexpectedly. If earlier cases suddenly settle short of final verdict, the judge's secretary may be on the phone telling counsel that a trial will start Monday,

not two weeks from Monday. Unless they are pretty well prepared, there is likely to be a mad scramble to find the necessary
witnesses. This business of living on the edge of uncertainty is an
unpleasant side of the practice with which trial lawyers simply
have to learn to cope.

For these and other reasons, the files of a case that is scheduled to be litigated should be very well organized. The master file
normally contains the information necessary to pull together the
elements of the trial on short notice, and should contain at a
minimum the following:

1. *Case Summary:* This is a brief narrative summary or
   overview of what the case is all about. Its purpose is to
   bring to mind in encapsulated form this particular litigation, for successful trial lawyers normally have a good
   many cases pending and several that are ready for trial.
   It is not unusual for a trial lawyer to be set for one trial,
   only to find that is has been continued (postponed) and a
   second case called instead. If there are specific problems
   in a given case, these should be outlined in footnotes to
   the case summary. At the end of the summary, there
   should be an indication of the current state of any settlement negotiations, or "plea-bargain" negotiations in a
   criminal case.

2. *Order of Evidence:* This page in the master file will be
   the most helpful in dealing with last-minute notices to
   get ready for trial. It sets forth, in the order of expected
   production, the witnesses and other evidence to be offered at trial. The identity of each witness, together with
   all of the means to get in touch with him, will be listed.
   (When interviewing a witness, always get his phone
   numbers at home and at work, as well as the numbers of
   a couple of family members or friends who are likely to
   be able to locate him if he should be vacationing or traveling.) A quick summary of what the witness will say,
   what documents or other evidence are to be introduced
   through his testimony, and the probable duration of his
   time on the witness stand, should be noted. One of the ju-
   nior lawyers, or perhaps a legal intern or secretary, can,
   by reference to this page, round them up quickly, see that

they are properly served with subpoenas, and schedule their appearances for a final pretrial interview.

3. *Legal Points:* The third section of the master file addresses any legal issues that need to be decided before the trial begins, together with a list of evidentiary problems that are expected to arise as the trial progresses. If any of these promises to be sticky, there should be memoranda covering each, with the relevant decisions and other legal authorities on which you intend to rely.

When the day for trial finally comes round, the preliminary matters remaining to be decided before a jury is picked will vary greatly from one jurisdiction to another. The federal courts and a number of the more progressive states have an extensive pretrial procedure, which attempts to settle every issue that can be eliminated before trial, to reduce the trial itself to a sharp focus. This procedure usually results in a *pretrial order,* in which counsel agree to all points that need not be disputed. Often the exhibits to be used will be marked and listed in chronological order, so that introducing them once the trial is under way will not delay the proceedings.

If a given jurisdiction has no provision for such a procedure, professional lawyers accomplish much the same thing on their own. Skilled attorneys will eliminate by stipulation every point that need not be litigated. This method not only saves valuable courtroom hours and costs, but allows the jury to understand very quickly what they will be called upon to decide, and to focus upon those questions alone. A lawyer who refuses to stipulate anything, and insists upon calling a witness to "prove up" every small element of his case, probably has some doubts about the strength of his presentation, and hopes to use quantity instead of quality to persuade the jury. A strong trial judge usually aborts such a plan once he learns that a stipulation has been offered, but some allow the lawyers to do nearly as they please.

Once the trial proceedings are under way, it is important that the "manager" keep things moving at a decent pace. Sitting in a jury box can be the most boring experience in the world when the proceedings drag. Frequent interruptions in the presentation, or long excursions into testimony that is neither terribly relevant nor very interesting, cause jurors' minds to wander; when an important point comes along, they may miss it.

Even though lawyers do not enjoy the script control available to producers of fictional drama, there is some choice and flexibility in the order of witnesses, documents, and other pieces of evidence. This should be a carefully thought out and well organized effort, in order to make the overall presentation as interesting as possible. Just as a conductor of popular music may have little to say about the sheet music that he and his orchestra are working with, he has much to say about the arrangement he uses and the manner in which the various musicians participate in each segment.

Similarly, there is a degree of orchestration involved in the unfolding of evidence in a trial. It is not always possible to call the witnesses in chronological order—particularly expert witnesses, who can present nightmarish scheduling problems—and when that is the case, it is essential that the jury be made to understand that they ought to pay close attention, because a later witness will highlight the importance of what they are hearing. This problem is best dealt with in a well-structured opening statement (to be described in Chapter 9), but in a long trial a reminder may be necessary. Most judges consider it appropriate for a lawyer to say, in the presence of the jury: "I would like to explain to the court that the testimony of the next witness, Mr. Jones, will be somewhat out of order; however, the importance of this evidence will be shown by the testimony of Mr. Brown, who will not be available until later in the week." This at least alerts the jury that they ought to listen to Jones even though what he is saying may not seem immediately important, and then file it away until they have heard from Brown.

When managing the trial of a lawsuit, always bear in mind that the greatest vice of appearing in court is the inconvenience it causes to the participants. Jurors who have to sit through dull areas of the presentation, witnesses who are left sitting on a bench in the corridor or in the witness room, and judges who must waste time in unwanted recesses are all victims of

shortcomings in trial management. Some are unforeseen or un-
avoidable, but most are not. A lawyer who is well prepared, well
organized, and considerate can do a great deal to ease the burden of inconvenience. In my view, this is not only a duty, but in
a close case it shows up in the final result. Juries like to vote in
favor of litigants and lawyers they respect; and if there is room
in the evidence for them to do so, they often will.

8

Dealing with Judges

I f you enter the fascinating world of trying lawsuits, you are going to form a lifetime association at the same time with a kind of person who is like no other: the trial judge. Trial judges come in many shapes, sizes, and moods, and with greatly varied backgrounds, experience, and intelligence.

Alan Dershowitz, the brilliant Harvard Law School professor who is one of the few academically affiliated people active in the trial courts, has said, in his book *The Best Defense,* that his greatest disappointment in the practice of law has been the quality of the trial judges he has encountered. Alan is a respected friend with whom I have worked on a number of important cases, and I have no doubt that his disappointment is genuine, partly because he was "spoiled," in a sense, by clerking for two of the great liberal judges in recent history: David Bazelon of the United States Circuit Court of Appeals for the District of Columbia, and Arthur Goldberg of the United States Supreme Court. In addition, Alan has handled some of the toughest, meanest cases criminal law can produce, and judges are human too. Confronted with a truly reprehensible defendant, they sometimes fail to hide the personal revulsion they feel, and can even let it creep into their rulings, which is enough to infuriate any lawyer.

My own experience, with a few unfortunate exceptions, has been quite different. I tend to like judges, and to remain constantly aware that for both traditional and personal reasons it is important to exhibit respect for the bench no matter how much one may disagree with a judge's point of view. This is not to say that it is easy to swallow unfair rulings, knowing that they may produce an adverse verdict that the client does not deserve; it is, in fact, very difficult, because appeals offer only a partial remedy for harsh treatment by judges, and then only after substantial expense and delay. Even so, you are going to have to deal on a daily basis with trial judges—all kinds of them—and very little success will come to you as a trial lawyer unless you learn how to do that early on.

Let's pause for a moment to examine just who and what a judge is in our society, and what makes him tick. Most judges are lawyers, but not all; indeed, you can be appointed to serve on the United States Supreme Court without being a lawyer, although it is likely that you would undergo intense scrutiny during your Senate confirmation hearings. Judges attain their offices either by appointment or election, and arguments rage to this day as to which is the better method. On balance, I prefer the appointive system, but I must admit that I have seen excellent judges who were elected.

A judgeship is a high office, carrying with it a good deal of power. Indeed, in the view of many, a United States District Judge is one of the most powerful individuals in the United States, often creating a greater impact through what he does than the President himself. Those who have followed elective reapportionment, desegregation, and school busing cases might be inclined to agree.

Under the appointive system, the chief executive (the President or the governor of a state) nominates a person to a judicial post, after which that person is examined by a confirming body, such as the United States Senate or a governor's council. If the appointment is approved, the person appointed is often in office to serve for life, or until a mandatory retirement age, if there is one. This provides a good deal of personal security to the judge, which is beneficial in the sense that it allows him to make rulings that may not be popular without affecting the continuity of his employment. On the negative side, it allows the judge to become a bit of a tyrant if he is so disposed, since normally he can be removed only by some sort of impeachment procedure; and impeachment is normally not possible as a political or practical matter unless the judge can be shown to have engaged in some demonstrably egregious conduct.

Elective judges are sometimes appointed in the first instance, but will be faced at some point with going through the elective process to keep their posts. Proponents of this system argue that the need periodically to win public reaffirmation keeps these judges more responsive to public feeling and opinion, and less confined to an ivory tower. Some lawyers support an elective judiciary because at election time judges must turn to lawyers for support; the lawyers feel that this probably gets them better court treatment between elections. The drawback here is that all judges are frequently confronted with making rulings that, however legally sound and proper, outrage the public. The prospect of doing one's duty in an appropriate fashion, only to be rewarded by being run out of office by an angry electorate, has led to some very bad legal rulings.

However your preference may develop, you are going to have to work with whatever judge is in charge of your case, and you must try to understand him, his background, his strong and weak points, and his personal prejudices. I began trying military courts-martial when I was barely twenty-one, and serious civilian criminal cases (murder in the first degree, rape, and bank robbery) when I was twenty-six, so I have viewed the bench from many different perspectives. In the beginning, almost all of the judges I worked with were my father's age or older; now, forty years later, they are much more likely to be contemporaries. Still, though life in the trial court becomes somewhat easier as the gray hair starts to fill out, my thoughts on the best ways to deal with judges have not changed greatly.

In accepting a judicial post, a person undergoes a rather dramatic change in lifestyle. Many also accept a reduction in income, if they have been successful lawyers. In exchange, they acquire a certain power over the lives of others and a general status of awe and respect in the community. No one in his right mind goes out of his way to offend a judge, for he never knows when he may be looking up at him in a courtroom.

But even as the public respects a judge, that same public will permit him few indulgences. He cannot go to a nightclub, take in an X-rated movie, or have a colorful love life without expecting strong public disapproval. His private life is apt to be bounded by a great many constraints, for it is required that his office be one of quiet dignity and personal restraint. For these reasons, most judges cannot be expected to evince a rollicking personality.

Most judges are very hard-working people, for their case-loads tend to be heavy. As fast as they finish one trial, which may have been exhausting, another one descends upon them without respite. Lawyers bury them with paperwork, and the less professional members of the bar assail them with arguments of little legal merit, but which are designed to impress clients who think that colorful language and a bombastic manner are the hallmarks of good representation. Being a trial judge can be a dreary and exasperating occupation, depending to a great extent upon the quality of the trial lawyers in court.

It is therefore important—because judges do talk a lot among themselves, and compare notes on which lawyers are to be trusted and respected—that you attain early on a reputation as an advocate of quality. To be held in esteem, there are several time-tested rules that you should bear in mind:

1. *Show respect for the court,* not only in the words you choose but in your manner of delivering them. If you feel that you are being treated unfairly, your remedy is to appeal, not to show your disapproval by being rude.

2. *Try to understand the judge's point of view.* You are an advocate, with a duty to plump for your client's side of the case; the judge is required to see both sides. Ask yourself, "How would I react if I had to make the *decision* on this issue, rather than my own argument?"

3. *Give the court all the help you can,* in the form of clear and reasonable legal memoranda, accommodation to its

scheduling needs, and assistance to its staff. In the military, it is often said that commissioned officers have a duty to be "officers and gentlemen." A trial lawyer has a duty to everyone, including himself and the judge he appears before, to be a "lawyer and a gentleman."

4. Always, always, but always *make sure that your word is as good as solid gold when speaking to a judge.* Courts could not function at all if they could not rely on the representations of counsel. When you make a statement to a judge, consider yourself to be under oath. Lawyers whom judges trust normally find their working environment pleasant. Lawyers who mislead a judge just once will spend years living that one incident down.

With judges, as with others alongside whom you will be working in the practice of law, first impressions are important. When you begin to make court appearances, go over your preparation repeatedly until you have it down pat, for if you are caught off guard by a question from the bench you will not have experience to draw upon in fashioning a quick and responsive answer.

And I emphasize the word *responsive.* Politicians like to skirt direct questions and turn what should have been an answer into a speech. This does not work in the courtroom. It exasperates judges to have to wrestle with counsel for a direct answer to a simple question, or even a complex question. If you don't understand what the judge is driving at, ask him to clarify his point; don't try to "wing it." Lawyers who try to dodge and duck when dealing with a trial judge are accumulating no points in the respect column.

Most judges like young trial lawyers and try to help them, provided they have done their homework. Accept such help gracefully, but without gushing your gratitude. A pleasant nod and a smile can communicate your appreciation for decent treatment from the bench, without a long statement of thanks.

I had a classmate who had been reared in one of the rougher sections of Boston, and who brought with him to law school a dialect flecked with colorful obscenities—the language of the streets. During his three years as a student he managed to refine himself considerably.

Soon after graduation, he appeared in court to defend a friend who had been caught with a small quantity of marijuana, a serious crime in Massachusetts in the early sixties. His only defense was that the police had conducted an illegal search, and that the evidence they had seized should be suppressed, or barred from use in the trial. My classmate filed a motion arguing this point, but privately told his client that the chances were slim and that a jail term seemed a distinct possibility.

The trial judge was an astute but kindly man who liked young lawyers and felt that they ought to win their first court-room cases to give them self-confidence; whenever the evidence permitted, he tried to rule in their favor. Much to my classmate's astonishment, the judge complimented him on the cogency of his legal argument and ruled that the evidence would be suppressed, leaving the prosecution no choice but to dismiss the complaint. While my classmate stood before the bench utterly speechless, the judge said: "I take it that the court's ruling meets with your approval, Mr. Vita?"

Lawyer Vita broke into a wide grin and replied with enthusiastic spontaneity, "Oh, you bet your ass I do, Your Honor . . ."

Do not expect a full explanation from the bench every time a judge makes a ruling. Standing there with a quizzical look seldom wins you very much. Frank Murray, who served as an outstanding trial judge on both the state and federal courts in Massachusetts, would often say to such unspoken queries: "This is a courtroom, not a classroom, counsel; proceed with your next question." If you are genuinely puzzled by the ruling—and you often will be in your early years—wait until the next recess and then ask politely if the judge will take a minute to explain why he ruled as he did. Most judges are happy to oblige, so long as they perceive your request to be sincere and not simply a masked attempt to argue the point all over again.

When you seek a ruling on any matter from a trial judge, be sure to state your grounds clearly and concisely, without indulging in a long harangue. If you simply say, "I object," without giving your reasons, and the judge replies, "Overruled," his ruling will be sustained on appeal if it was correct on any grounds at all. If you specify your grounds, however, in most jurisdictions the appellate court will decide whether he was correct on that ground alone, giving you a far better chance.

One of the toughest decisions a lawyer and his client may have to make in the trial of a lawsuit is whether to "waive" jury and "try the case to the court," (that is, to the judge alone) as the saying goes. Because this decision is not one that can be seen as right or wrong in the simple sense, it is a decision that the client should always make after he has been given a thorough explanation of the advantages and disadvantages of taking such a step. A number of factors must be taken into consideration.

First, consider the difficulties inherent in "merging" two distinct and powerful functions—deciding both the legal questions and the factual questions—in a single mind. In effect, the judge will be "instructing" himself as to what law he should apply before deciding what facts he ought to find to be true. Accomplishing this requires some difficult mental gymnastics.

To aggravate the difficulty, a judge sitting without jury must hear all the information offered by the lawyers in order to rule upon what is admissible evidence. Suppose that the principal evidence against your client is his own confession, which was illegally obtained from him by the police in violation of his right to have a lawyer present. To prevent the confession from being received in evidence, a hearing must be held before the judge. If he rules it out, how can he forget that a confession was made that strongly indicates your client's guilt? He will have to have a highly disciplined mind to accomplish such a feat. If a jury was involved, they would learn nothing at all about the existence of a confession, before or after it was suppressed.

Jurors are supposed to represent a cross section of the community, something a trial judge simply cannot do. He is not an average person, and the tightly controlled environment in which he must live effectively denies him access to many walks of life. His personality, or his experience, or both may leave him with a certain subconscious "mind set" for or against specific kinds of legal controversies. He may be violently opposed to sexual crimes, or he may feel that every injured person ought to collect damages, even though the party being sued is clearly not at fault. If a personal bias or prejudice is subconscious, it is very difficult for a judge to keep it from silently intruding on his rulings and his findings of fact, even though he may intend to be scrupulously objective. Although every juror in the box will likewise have certain mind sets of his own, during jury deliberations these generally either balance one another or cancel each other out.

Finally, the merger between legal rulings and fact-finding can vastly reduce the likelihood of a successful appeal if there is an adverse result at the trial. Bear in mind that an appellate court has no more power to look behind a judge's findings of witness credibility, or the inferences he has drawn from the evidence received, than would be the case had a jury made the decision. If a judge has a strong impression that a case ought to be decided in a certain way, he may try to make all trial rulings in favor of the party who is going to lose, thus leaving him nothing to complain about on appeal. Further, appellate judges often have more confidence in trial judges than they do in juries, and are less easily persuaded to upset the result.

There are distinct advantages, however, that must also be considered whenever the question of waiving a jury arises.

In terms of trial economy, the proceedings will inevitably go more quickly and cost less because of the efficiency of putting all questions to a single person. Judges can assimilate very quickly what may take a lay juror who finds himself in the strange world of litigation for the first time a long while to sort out.

Judges tend to be more consistent in their decisions than juries, and therefore more predictable. Since settlements and plea-bargains are predicated largely on the respective lawyers' predictions of what the trial result is likely to be, presenting a case to a judge alone may enhance the likelihood that the parties will get together and agree on terms that will dispose of the case short of a final result.

Finally, where there is no jury to be concerned about, mistrials are rare. A mistrial occurs whenever something happens that aborts a jury's ability to function. A witness may blurt out some inadmissible claim that is so horribly prejudicial that no instruction from the bench can cure the damage, and the jury will have to be discharged. Or several jurors may become ill or otherwise disabled—especially during a long trial—to the point where not enough alternate jurors have been provided to replace them. Or, in what is commonly called a "hung" jury, the jury may retire to deliberate, only to discover after many exhausting hours that they cannot agree upon a verdict, in which case a mistrial will have to be declared. Whatever the reason for it, a mistrial requires that the whole proceeding must start over again from scratch, and that all the time and money expended on the aborted trial has been wasted.

I am hopeful that, as time progresses, the trend toward "bench" trials will improve. In England, where trial judges come from long and distinguished experience as "barristers"—British for trial lawyers—juries are seldom used. These men are appointed for life, and their professional and ethical credentials are sufficiently impeccable that lawyers feel confident in allowing them to decide both aspects of their cases, which contributes greatly to the efficiency of the litigation process. Perhaps this is why a mere three-thousand-odd barristers are able to handle the litigation requirements for some fifty-five million British subjects, without long court backlogs.

In any event, the decision to entrust a trial judge with deciding both the facts and the law in a given case is both weighty and difficult. It should always be considered, but only after counsel has made a careful study of the judge in question—his temperament, his proclivities, and his background. While sometimes it will be feasible to put "all of the eggs in one basket," this is a step to be taken with the greatest care.

All of us who try cases for a living want to appear before trial judges who are sharp, courageous, and fair. But, quite anomalously, we may later regret our good fortune.

When the United States government prosecuted John Hinckley, Jr., for shooting President Reagan and others, it argued with great vigor that Hinckley was not insane. The jury thought otherwise, and acquitted him on the ground of insanity. Now, in order to keep Hinckley in confinement, the government argues that he *is* insane, and must be restrained.

While a good trial judge can be a joy to work with when the trial is under way, he can be very bad news if the jury makes a mistake and returns a verdict for the party that a fly on the wall would have known deserved to lose. Appellate courts, as we have seen, exist only to correct mistakes made by trial courts, and where there are none of substance, there will be no successful appeal, no second bite at the apple. Until some machinery is devised to review what juries have done, rather than just reviewing the work of trial judges, this anomaly will remain.

9

Working with a Jury

A "petit" or trial jury (as distinguished from a "grand" jury, which is an investigative body) is perhaps the ultimate audience. Generally silent and inactive throughout the show, with no license to either weep or applaud, when the final curtain is rung down they are suddenly handed—often to their astonishment—a responsibility for decisions that are frequently more complex and serious than any of them has ever confronted in his life.

Most Americans understand only vaguely what a real jury trial is all about. Having seen trials conducted by actors, they are convinced, somehow, that this is the way things really are. Nothing could be further from the truth. I have seen very few dramatic portrayals of trials in my lifetime that pay any serious attention to the actual constraints of courtroom procedure. Two excellent exceptions, *QB VII* and *Anatomy of a Murder,* are both worth studying if you can get them on videotape cassettes. Most of the rest are of the Perry Mason variety, where all of the pieces fall neatly into place, the liars all confess their mendacity in open court, and the truth becomes self-evident, leaving virtually nothing for the jury to decide.

Perhaps, as computers take on more and more human functions, the business of trials will become more precise. Very likely, however, no matter what scientific and technical advances come along, the phenomenon of trial by jury will remain very much what it is today, with all of its advantages and shortcomings. There is some hope that the current trend toward televising live trials will better educate the public to the realities of the courtroom, and that would be of some measurable help.

The jury system has a number of good and bad points and will probably always be controversial. Juries are used in those countries following the Anglo-American system of justice—principally the English-speaking countries—and are generally thought to afford the most democratic method of deciding legal controversies.

On the positive side, in many respects jurors are the best yardstick of community thought. Qualified citizens—generally, adults with no serious criminal background—are summoned in random groups, and from this number the jury box is filled, often after extensive questioning in what are called *voir dire examinations,* by the judge and the lawyers for both sides.

A jury of six or twelve people contains an admixture of different personalities, which in most cases is beneficial. Personal idiosyncrasies in a given jury tend to be dampened by the presence of the others. Bizarre thinking patterns in an individual yield to the same group pressure. Between them, they recall a great deal (but never all) of the evidence that they hear.

In a society such as ours, where personal corruption in public office threatens fairness and equality daily, juries are with rare exception not overtly corrupted. The individual biases and prejudices they deny when qualifying for jury duty are a form of corruption, to be sure, but corruption from external sources is rare. A random group whose identities are not known until a short time before they report for duty is hard to "fix," especially when there is no way of knowing which members of the group will actually be selected to sit.

Juries are society's great equalizers. In theory, at least, no man is too large or too powerful to avoid being hauled before a jury to answer for his wrongdoing. By the same token, no man is too weak or too poor to have the right to a jury trial when others seek to oppress him. Jurors punish arrogance, greed, selfishness, and a host of other vices that are not in themselves illegal. They give compensation to the unfortunate, often substituting pure sympathy for determinations of real liability. They sometimes turn aside the unfeeling strictures of the law to do justice as they see it. They operate as society's conscience, or as an echo of that conscience.

The United States Constitution provides that one is entitled to a trial by a jury of his peers. This is true only in the most general sense of the word "peers." Jurors assembled in a box seldom turn out to be a true cross section of society, for certain kinds of people are consistently missing.

Those with a criminal past are systematically excluded by the rules of almost every jurisdiction. This may seem like a good idea at first blush, but at least in criminal cases, convicted felons could probably bring great insight to a jury panel, for they understand much about street life that the average juror does not. The rich and powerful are also missing most of the time, partly because they consider jury duty a pedestrian annoyance and do all that they can to avoid it, and partly because if they are selected, one of the lawyers will get rid of them with what is called a *peremptory* challenge. A challenge *for cause* is a challenge for which a reason can be assigned, such as when a juror is related to one of the parties, or admits to having a fixed opinion about the case. These may be asserted without limit. A *peremptory* challenge is one that may be made with no reason given at all. Each lawyer is allotted a certain number of these to help him shape the jury to his liking.

The reason why strong-willed, educated, intelligent people are often removed from the jury box by the lawyers is disappointingly simple: To the fellow who believes that his case is weak, these human qualities spell "enemy." As a result, juries trying difficult cases are robbed of a most precious asset— perceptive minds. Two examples from my own experience may help to illustrate, and also drive home, a point I made earlier: that lawyers, including prosecutors, are often out to win, not to see that justice is done.

In May 1967, I defended an anesthesiologist named Carl Coppolino, in Naples, Florida, who was charged with killing his wife by injecting her with succinylcholine chloride, a synthetic form of curare, which paralyzes the muscles, including those that enable the lungs to breathe. I had defended Carl late in 1966 in Freehold, New Jersey, for allegedly doing the same thing to his lover's husband, a neighbor. The atmosphere in Naples was dripping with prejudice: New Jersey had acquitted him. The prosecution had a most tenuous case, based wholly upon some sloppy scientific experiments which had no precedent. We had conducted our own experiments, with opposite results. A great part of our evidence was expert testimony on matters of sophisticated chemistry, and we had great fears that much of it would sail over the jury's head. One of the jurors called to the box was a retired chemist from the Union Carbide Company; it was plain from his examination that he would have been able to help the other jurors a great deal, had he been allowed to sit. A prosecutor earnestly seeking a just result would have left him on the jury, for his expertise was sorely needed. The prosecutor in this case used a peremptory challenge to get rid of him, obviously fearing that he would see the holes in the state's presentation. The jury, hopelessly confused and uncertain, found Coppolino guilty of murder in the *second degree*—that is, deliberate murder *without premeditation,* a logical and literal impossibility in a poisoning case.

Had he pursued his appeals, Coppolino would probably have won a ruling that he had been legally acquitted, for poisoning can be first degree murder *only,* and of that the unwitting jury found him not guilty. Unfortunately, someone duped him into believing that, if he dropped all appeals and stopped giving the authorities a hard time, he would be granted an early parole. He wasn't.

The second example is no less maddening. When Patricia Hearst was tried for bank robbery in federal court in San Francisco in early 1976, a major part of her defense was that she had been subjected to "coercive persuasion"—often called brainwashing—by those who had kidnapped her, then accompanied her on the robbery venture some months later. Coercive persuasion is a phenomenon with which the public has had little experience; mainly, it has been a problem caused by techniques perfected by

North Koreans during the Korean War. Using these techniques, the enemy caused a number of our captured military people to make seemingly genuine confessions that they had been using germ warfare and other hideous means to violate the Geneva Convention.

Patricia Hearst had unquestionably been subjected to these techniques, which, if shown, would have gone a long way to explain why her conduct in many instances seemed to indicate that she had joined the side of her captors and had become a genuine outlaw. We were fearful that our evidence of the effects of what she had been through would be too sophisticated for the jury to grasp.

One of the jurors who qualified during the voir dire examinations and was placed in the box, subject only to peremptory challenge by either side, was a retired navy captain who had served in Korea. He was well familiar with coercive persuasion, having sat upon and convened military courts-martial that tried soldiers for treason for giving these confessions. (The military eventually learned that there was no human way to resist this technique, that the captured personnel could not fairly be blamed for their "confessions," and it stopped putting these men to trial.)

The captain, alone among the jurors selected, could have recognized that the phenomenon claimed to have caused Hearst's conduct was quite real. The prosecutors took him off the jury for reasons they chose not to explain.

There does not seem to be a remedy for this state of affairs, I am sad to report. The power to use a peremptory challenge for any purpose, however corrupt, is almost absolute. It provides an effective way to keep our most able citizens from sitting on juries, where they could make a great contribution. For these reasons, should it ever fall to your lot to defend one of society's upper crust, do not hold out much hope that he or she will find any peers on the jury. It happens occasionally, but these exceptions are rare.

The business of selecting a jury has been the subject of a good many books and articles, as well as a great many lectures at legal seminars. Experienced trial lawyers agree on some of the fundamental points of jury selection, but beyond these there is a good deal of variation in thought on the subject. Some pay considerable attention to the racial origins of a prospective juror, claiming that those of Italian, French, Spanish, or other Latin origin are more guided by emotion and thus more apt to act out of sympathy, while those of German, Polish, or Scandinavian descent are more cold and precise in their approach to human affairs. Other lawyers are more concerned with the professional and occupational status of a prospective juror. Artists, educators, and social scientists are thought to be more flexible and understanding of human foibles, while accountants and engineers are more interested in numbers and logic than in personalities.

While these broad generalizations may have some limited value, I have not paid much attention to them in my own practice. In my view, the whole business of jury selection is an approximate science at best, which has to be conducted with some consideration for the particulars of a given case and an understanding of the community from which the jury is to be drawn.

The manner in which a jury can be questioned—by the trial judge, by the lawyers, or by both—varies more from jurisdiction to jurisdiction than any other phase of trial procedure. In some states, the questions allowed are very limited, and one must decide who to pick without much information to go on. In other states, a great variety of questions are permitted, and an extensive probe of each prospect is possible. In federal courts, the questioning is usually done only by the judge; some of them do it well, and others not.

As with many other aspects of the litigation business, a lawyer's ability to perceive and understand people is a necessary asset in picking a jury. It might be helpful if we could create a master mold to take to the courtroom, and accept only those who would fit neatly into it. It is unlikely, however, that any two lawyers could agree exactly on what the mold should look like, or what its specifications ought to be. And even if we *could* construct such a mold, it is doubtful that we could ever find a human being to fit it.

A lawyer who has what he believes is a very weak case may be interested in impaneling twelve people of limited intellectual ability. Percy Foreman, a legendary criminal defense attorney from Texas, undertook the defense of Candy Mossler and her nephew, Melvin Powers, for the alleged bludgeoning murder of Candy's husband, Jacques, in Miami, Florida. The case was tried in Miami in the mid-1960s, and from press reports it seemed that the evidence was very strong against the defendants, particularly Powers. When the jury acquitted, most people were stunned. Foreman, explaining this unexpected result, indicated that he had removed those prospective jurors who were perceived to be "dangerously" intelligent, and was able to work effectively with those that remained.

If there is no mold to use in selecting trial jurors, how does one approach the matter? Well, how do you approach the everyday business of choosing roommates, or friends, or those from whom you will accept employment?

Subconsciously, we seek certain human qualities when we select those with whom we will associate in our daily affairs, and these same qualities apply to picking jurors. We want people who have a basic honesty, both with themselves and others. We want people who do not have hangups, or other personality quirks that are difficult to predict and uncomfortable to assimilate in day-to day relations. We want to be with people who have a healthy self-confidence, balanced by a modicum of humility.

We like people who are clean and neat personally—who take a certain amount of pride in the way they present themselves, without falling in love again every time they look in the mirror. We want those who respect the rights and needs of others, who have the habit of checking their impulses to act by asking, "How would I feel if that were done to me?"

We seek people who have an air of being able to look out for themselves, and at the same time an inclination toward generosity to others. We admire those who are bright and imaginative without being pompous or overbearing. We like those who have both the ability and the initiative to concentrate on a problem and think it through, but who at the same time smile easily. And most of all, perhaps, we enjoy being with those with genuine empathy for others, an ability to identify with and understand those who have problems. For seldom will you go to court with a client who does not have problems.

You should never expect to fill a jury box with twelve or more people with all the qualities listed above, for such individuals are not that common. But an old rule of thumb among trial lawyers suggests that one, two, or at most three members of a jury will lead it through its deliberations and largely control the result. For that reason, as you sift through those personalities who have been brought forward and examined, you should make an effort to rank them according to your preference, in order to use your challenges most effectively. Since we seldom see a juror who strikes us as perfect, jury selection becomes in reality a rejection process: eliminating those who are *least* desirable.

In sizing up a prospective juror, one should first take note of any background information that is furnished, such as name, address, occupation, family, or spouse's occupation. Such data at least gives a general idea of the juror's station in life: where he is "coming from," so to speak. Next, take note of the juror's appearance. How is he dressed, how careful has he been in personal grooming? Does he seem a tidy and orderly sort, or is he inclined to be slovenly? Finally, pay close attention to the responses he gives to questions put by the judge and counsel, particularly the *manner* in which he answers. Do any of the questions make him seem uncomfortable or cause an evasive reply? Is he inclined to volunteer more information than the question calls for? Does he avert his eyes when he answers? Does he appear nervous or upset? Does he seem to *want* to serve on the jury, or is he trying to avoid it?

If the case has had a great deal of pretrial publicity, a whole host of problems will be introduced into the jury selection process that do not normally affect cases that have escaped media attention. Since this topic is worthy of several chapters in its own right, I will not try to cover it in any detail. However, in such cases one must be very wary of the answers to such questions as, "Have you formed or expressed any opinion in this case? Do you think you can be fair?"

Questions of this type put a juror's integrity directly on the line, and in self-defense he will be inclined to posture as a model of objectivity with his answers. Here especially, the *manner* in which the answer is given is critical, for any uncertainty he may feel about his ability to be impartial is more apt to show up in his expression and tone of voice than in the answer itself.

I have two favorite questions for prospective jurors in difficult cases, which most judges will permit to be asked. They force the juror to think a bit, and indeed often have to be repeated before they are understood, but the answers can reveal a lot. The first, which can be used in any case, is: "If you were one of the parties in this case, would you be content to have someone in *your* frame of mind sitting on your jury?"

The second, useful only in criminal cases, is: "The judge will instruct you at the conclusion of the evidence that before you can find a defendant guilty, his guilt must be proven to you *beyond a reasonable doubt,* and that a mere probability of guilt is not enough. If after reviewing all of the evidence you believe that the defendant is *probably* guilty, but that there is still room for a doubt with a reason behind it, will you be able to vote not guilty?"

Once a jury has been selected and sworn, the show begins. The individual members of the jury should be carefully evaluated with reference to all that you have been able to learn about them, in an effort to guess who the leaders might turn out to be. Your every move throughout the trial has just one purpose—to *persuade* this group to accept your view of the case, and of what the result should be. Your manner should be pleasant without being obsequious, commanding without being haughty, and sincere at all times. A little humor is helpful when appropriate, as long as it is not overdone.

Bear always in mind that, except in rare instances, juries look up to the trial judge. He sits behind an elevated bench, wearing the black robes of the exalted, and it is he whom the jurors trust to lead them through the thicket of legal brambles into which they have been flung. If you show any touch of rudeness or sarcasm to the bench, the jurors are likely to be offended and think less of you and your case.

They are your audience, and it is your job to keep their attention. Boredom is an ever-present risk in a trial, particularly those involving stacks upon stacks of dull documents, and it is easy for minds to wander. With your manner, your tone of voice, and the order of your presentation, strive to keep their focus on what you are doing. To the extent that it is possible without making individual jurors feel self-conscious or uncomfortable, watch their reactions carefully, especially when critical witnesses are testifying. In judging credibility, most jurors are influenced as much by the *impression* a witness makes as by what he says. Often you can see in a juror's face signs of skepticism or reservation, a subconscious nod of approval, or a quizzical expression denoting poor understanding of the testimony. If you catch these signs, you may be able to help a witness clarify his statements to cure the problem.

Jurors are, for the most part, a silent group. Beyond occasional spontaneous responses, like a gasp or a chuckle, they give little indication of what they are thinking. Except in military court, jurors are seldom allowed to take notes or ask questions of their own. In short, they take what they are given, and in most trials, it seems, they feel that what they are given is less than they would like. Remember, they have learned from books, plays, motion pictures, and television that the brilliance of counsel is supposed to make the truth crystal clear before the trial is over. In an actual case, they are left with unanswered questions and direct contradictions in the evidence, which they are supposed to sort out. Your job is to give them all the help you can to see that justice is on your side of the case.

The first way that you can help your jury is in your *opening statement*—your description of what you expect the evidence to show. This is in essence a promissory note, which will be payable when you stand up to deliver your final argument at the end of the case. Therefore, you must be very careful not to overstate or exaggerate your evidence, or you could wind up with a very red face, and a jarring reminder from your opponent in *his* final argument that you failed to deliver what you had promised.

Bear in mind, as you line up the facts you wish to bring to the jury's attention and the language you intend to use to describe those facts, that an opening statement is *not* an argument. You can be interrupted by your opponent, or by the trial judge acting spontaneously, if you seek to use the language of persuasion during an opening. Each sentence you choose ought to make sense if it were preceded by the phrase, "The evidence will show that . . ." You do not argue credibility of witnesses or the genuineness of documents or other evidence in an opening. If your opponent has already made an opening statement, you may describe the evidence you expect to produce that will contradict the evidence that he has promised, so long as argumentative language is not used.

Often an opening must be given while serious questions about the eventual admissibility of certain pieces of evidence remain unresolved. Should you describe such evidence, only to have it ruled out later on, you run the risk of causing a mistrial, or at least a specific instruction from the judge that no such evidence was produced. It is better to play it safe and skirt specific descriptions of questionable evidence.

The opening ought to give the jury a good overview of the case—what the parties are disputing that the jury will ultimately be called upon to decide. As to those issues not in dispute, it is best to tell the jurors that they need not be concerned over them, that the parties are in effect in agreement. Use simple, direct language, and be as clear as you can with your message. Remember, the jury knows nothing at all about the case—unless there has been extensive media coverage—and you know a great deal about it, if you are properly prepared. Don't get bogged down in intricate detail; after all, minute points can be covered in your final argument. The mark you are shooting for is this: When you have finished describing what the evidence will and will not show, you should leave the jury thinking, "If that lawyer can prove what he says he intends to prove, he deserves to win." If you have accomplished that objective, you have probably made an effective opening statement.

When addressing a jury, look at them. This is your best chance to have them react to you directly, and thus your best chance to guess what they are thinking and feeling about the case. Try at all times to assess their receptivity to what you tell them; if necessary, vary your manner a bit and try again. Your credibility—your good faith as a lawyer, speaking to them as jurors—is of paramount importance. If they find themselves able to believe most or all of what you tell them, they will give you the verdict you seek.

10

Calling a Witness

We observed earlier that the vast bulk of *disputed* evidence in a trial involves the testimony of witnesses. To get his story before the court, a witness must go through two distinct and separate exercises. During what is called *direct examination,* he must tell his story for the benefit of the party who called him; then, during *cross-examination,* he explains its details, and how he came to know the story, to the lawyer for the opposition. Most cases won by the party who started the lawsuit—especially civil cases—are won because of the quality of the evidence adduced on direct examination.

Average citizens are ill-equipped to step directly to the witness stand and perform adequately. The environment and the methods used to adduce testimony are strange to them, and the majority feel discomfort at the thought of giving evidence. A few are downright petrified. Therefore, before you call a witness to give live testimony in a trial, you have much work to do with him.

First, back away from him and take a long, analytical look. What kind of person is he? What is the nature of his personality? Does he have any hangups that are likely to surface during his testimony? Is he nervous and upset at the prospect of being questioned in front of "all those people"? Does he show sincere respect and appreciation for the fact that he is going to be under oath, with an obligation to tell the truth as best he can? How long is the fuse on his temper? Is he likely to react defensively if he feels that he is being belittled or demeaned during cross-examination? How probable or logical is the series of observations that he will be asked to describe, and then defend?

Your ability to judge people needs to be well honed if you are to assess the strong points and weaknesses of a witness effectively before he actually takes the stand, yet it is essential that you do so. I have seen many witnesses who turned in a poor performance, not because they were not good people, not because they were trying to deceive, but simply because the lawyer who called them was not thorough enough to prepare them adequately. They seemed a little bewildered, and made mistakes, basic mistakes, about which they could easily have been forewarned. Justice must always be wounded—and in some cases fail completely—when a witness who tells the truth is not believed simply because of the *way* he has told his story. This kind of tragedy must usually be laid at the feet of the lawyer who called him.

Some personalities turn into good witnesses naturally, with very little coaching, and some will be poor witnesses no matter what you do with them. But the vast majority need and benefit from some expert pretrial help. This is time-consuming but vital, for as we've seen, there are no retakes in this business. If a truthful witness does a clumsy job of telling that truth, he is seldom given a second chance to perform (except when there is a retrial of the same case).

The public is highly suspicious of witnesses who have been coached by lawyers, for they understand the process to involve the lawyers telling the witness what he ought to say. Ethical lawyers never tell a witness what to say—the "what" is governed totally

by the witness's actual experience and the details he honestly re-
members. The *way* in which the testimony is given, however, is
necessarily and legitimately the subject of pretrial counseling.

It is even more important for the *witness* to understand that
such counseling is legitimate. If not specifically forewarned and
enlightened on this point, a great many witnesses will deny,
when asked on cross-examination, that they have discussed their
testimony with counsel. They feel that the question suggests that
their testimony is the result of collusion of some sort. Such a denial puts the witness in deep trouble, for lawyers and judges,
knowing that witnesses are not called cold to the stand, and that
there is virtually always some pretrial discussion between the
witness and the lawyer calling him, will press unmercifully
when a denial pops out. Circumstances such as these leave the
trial lawyer in a most embarrassing position, for he has an un-
swerving ethical duty to correct his own witness whenever he
knows that untruthful testimony is being adduced. Failure to
make such corrections promptly can have far-reaching and sometimes disastrous consequences, including disciplinary action.

I once defended two brothers for murder in New York. The
only issue was identification, and only one witness identified
them as having been at the scene. One brother was out of state at
the time and had a strong alibi; the other had been at home with
his family. I was satisfied (partly by lie detector tests) that neither had any involvement at all.

The identifying witness was a woman whose testimony, I
knew, had been heavily shaped by some members of the prosecution. Based on a tip, I asked her this question: "Madame, is it not
true that on the Sunday before this trial began you came to this
courtroom with the prosecutor and several police officers, and
practiced your testimony from this witness stand, including a
mock cross-examination?" She denied the event. The prosecutor,
who had orchestrated the whole affair and had indeed been
present, said nothing, even though I stared at him for a long moment after her denial.

During the defense case, I called some police officers who had
also been present, and they admitted the entire scenario. During
final argument, I took the prosecutor to task in the most severe
terms for sitting silently by when he knew his own witness was
committing perjury. If he had ever had a chance to persuade the

jury of the integrity of his case, he lost it then and there. Don't ever, ever, find yourself in a similar position!

After you have carefully explained to your witness that your talk together is perfectly ethical and proper, and that he is never to hesitate to admit that you have discussed his proposed testimony, try to get an impression of his attitude toward the case itself. If he has any bias for or against your client, you should learn it and discuss it with him, for if that bias shows through on the stand, the jury is likely to give his evidence little weight. If, on the other hand, he thinks that the lawsuit is unjustified, it will be worth a few minutes' time to explain why you, the lawyer, decided that suit was warranted and appropriate.

Give the witness some description of what issues are to be litigated, and how his testimony will bear on them—what it is that you are hoping to prove through him. At the same time, explain the contentions of the opposition and what, if any, evidence they have used or may use to refute his points. Understanding the significance of his participation this way will often assist your witness immeasurably when he is undergoing cross-examination. If he does not understand what the cross-examiner is likely to try to do to him, he may concede too easily some point that seems minor to him, but is not, or fight too tenaciously to protect some other point that is in fact obscure.

It is very important that the witness understand that you will not be allowed to use leading questions—questions phrased to suggest a desired answer—when you are examining him. You will not be allowed to say, "Now, sir, didn't you then see the green traffic light?" You must instead ask, "What did you see next?" and he must come up with the answer on his own. Indeed, this bar on the use of leading questions during direct examination is one of the principal reasons why you must go over his testimony beforehand, for otherwise he may not understand what some of your questions are seeking. It is a good idea, for obvious purposes, to ask him a number of the questions you expect to use in the same form that you expect to put them at trial. Direct examination is not like ordinary conversation, nor is it like the kind of interrogation that detectives and intelligence experts conduct. It is a tightly controlled exchange designed to explore the witness's knowledge of the subject matter at issue, without any help from the lawyer who is questioning him.

Equally important, the witness must understand that during cross-examination he *will* be asked leading questions, because the purpose is no longer to find out what he knows, but to test the accuracy with which he has described the events in question. Give him some examples of leading questions (see the next chapter), and explain that he must listen very carefully before answering. By their very nature, leading questions are designed to "lead" a witness in a direction that the other side wants, and not necessarily in the direction of the truth as the witness knows it. Though it is painstaking work, you will be wise to spend some time explaining what cross-examination is all about, what its limits are, and how you can protect the witness by interposing objections when the opposing lawyer exceeds the bounds of proper cross-examination. At the same time, when you do *not* object, he must answer. He is not allowed himself to object, and will make a very poor impression on everyone involved if he does. Encourage him to be responsive, for if he tries to duck or swerve an answer, the question will be put to him a second time, whereupon the judge will order him to answer it properly—an embarrassing experience that will damage his credibility with the jury, to be avoided if possible.

Warn him against battling with the cross-examiner, a very common mistake of inexperienced witnesses and a tactic that cannot win. Contentiousness exposes an unpleasant personality, and gives the cross-examiner a license to go after him much more aggressively without risking alienation of the jurors. Make it clear that *you* are the advocate for his side of the case, and that you will do all the battling that may be appropriate on his behalf. Also warn him that he must never, never look at you when he is being asked a question on cross-examination, unless, of course, you have risen to object. Any glancing at you will be noticed, will be interpreted as looking for a signal, and may cause the cross-examiner to insert the knife in a question like this: "Mr. Witness, I notice that you keep glancing at counsel after my questions are put to you; would you be good enough to tell us why you find that to be necessary?" There is, of course, no good answer to such a question. At worst, the trial judge may direct the witness to refrain from such a practice, and this will not be flattering.

You must go over any prior statements the witness has made very carefully, for these are the most likely source of cross-examination. Explain that, although he may change a prior statement if the truth so warrants, he is then going to have to give good reasons for having been mistaken in the first place. Review with him such evidence as may come in that contradicts his story, whether it be the testimony of another witness, a document, a photograph, or an expert opinion.

Make it clear that he should maintain an attitude and appearance of respect toward the court, the jury, and the lawyers, without appearing to be gushingly accommodating. This can turn a judge off very quickly. I once defended a self-styled gangster charged with perjury in testimony he had given before a grand jury implicating an appellate judge in a bribery incident. When the judge was called to the stand as the state's star witness, he was asked his name and address. (I will change the facts, because I'm sure he would not like a reminder of the experience.) He answered, with an inappropriate beaming smile at the jury: "I live at 325 Sycamore Street in Brookfield with my *darling* wife, Nora, and my three *beautiful* children."

I could tell at a glance that the jury had been soured by his obsequious manner. He went on to make an awful witness on cross-examination, and the jury rejected his testimony—a terrible blow to the integrity of a sitting judge, or any judge for that matter. After they acquitted the defendant, the jurors went to the clerk's office to seek a criminal complaint for perjury against the judge! Had he acted more naturally and less pretentiously, the jurors might have believed him, as I think they had fully expected to do. Sadly, many years later, this same judge was caught on videotape taking a bribe, and avoided trial and humiliation by blowing his brains out.

If, despite your best efforts, you conclude that your witness is a "wise guy" or a hopeless neurotic who is going to react adversely to almost every stimulus, strike him from your witness list if you can. A poor performance by any of your witnesses can be very damaging to your cause, and is sure to be capitalized on by the opposition in final argument. If he is absolutely essential to your case, and no one else can furnish similar evidence, then you have no choice but to take control. Point out very candidly his deficiencies. If you have the equipment (and you should have it), videotape him while you put him through a practice cross-examination and show him specifically where his conduct is objectionable. Explain that if he behaves like a fool, you can do little to protect him. He will probably be embarrassed by opposing counsel and possibly the judge, his credibility will be publicly vilified during final argument, and he risks a posttrial comment by a juror such as: "We sure couldn't believe that guy; he was awful!" As a last resort, it may be possible to intimidate him into toning down his more objectionable personality quirks. Handling difficult witnesses that you are stuck with will be one of the severest tests of your own mettle that you can expect to confront as a trial lawyer.

If your witness is an expert, there will be additional work to do, especially if he has never testified before. Expert testimony requires a two-phase exercise in direct examination. First, he must be qualified and found to be an expert by the judge before he will be allowed to offer any opinions in the case, and your opponent will have an opportunity to challenge those qualifications before the judge rules. Therefore, in your final pretrial interview you should go over your expert's curriculum vitae carefully to make sure that it lists his background and achievements correctly. Then you must go over the opinions you expect him to give, *and* their foundation and rationale, for if he is crucial to the case he will surely be cross-examined extensively over those.

Sometimes experts who know nothing about the facts of the case are allowed to answer *hypothetical* questions. In such an instance, the expert is asked to assume certain facts to be true and to offer an opinion based upon those assumptions. The jury is then told by the trial judge that if, and only if, they find to be true those facts that the expert has assumed in giving his opinion, they may consider that opinion as evidence, with whatever weight they see fit to give it; if they do not find the assumed facts to be true, they are to disregard the opinion entirely. This may seem a clumsy way of doing business, and indeed it is, but in many cases it is quite useful. An expert on automobile tires, for instance, might be asked the following:

PLAINTIFF'S COUNSEL. Sir, assume that this Acme Roadmaster tire was bought and installed on a Thursday, and on Friday, while traveling on an automobile in good running order at fifty-five miles per hour over a highway with no defects, it blew out, causing the crash here on trial; assume further that examination revealed a five-inch rip completely through the rubber and fabric of the tire, concentric in shape to the tread and at a point six inches above the tread, and that the fibers that had spanned the areas of the rip were torn, not sliced. Assuming those facts, do you have an opinion as to the cause of the rip?

A. I do.

Q. And what is that opinion?

DEFENSE COUNSEL. Objection.

THE COURT. Overruled. You may answer.

A. In my opinion, the tire failed because the double-widget machine that fabricates the tire sidewall malfunctioned, causing an overstress in the sidewall structure; when the tire heated up during normal highway travel, the structure failed, causing the tire to blow out or instantly deflate.

THE COURT. Ladies and gentlemen, you have just heard an expert render an opinion based upon some assumed facts embodied in a hypothetical question. This witness does not know whether the facts assumed are true; he was told to assume them. If, when the evidence is concluded and I have instructed you as to the law you must follow, you find that these assumed facts are indeed true, then you may consider this opinion as evidence as to the cause of the blowout. If you do not find those facts to be true, then you will be told to disregard entirely this witness's opinion. Counsel, you may continue.

In dealing with an expert, it is important to learn early on, first, everything he has written on the subject at hand, whether it be books, articles, or even speeches and learned papers; and, second, all prior instances where he has testified in a case even remotely similar. There is nothing more devastating to an expert than having something he himself has uttered used against him. If you are thoroughly familiar with these prior utterances, often a reasonable explanation can be worked out, but the courtroom is no place to learn of this problem for the first time.

Some experts are likable professionals who want to make, and do make, a real contribution to the matter on trial. Others are pompous bores with enormous but fragile egos, who become nasty and petulant if attacked. Many fall somewhere in between. Your job is to size them up carefully before they testify and to prepare them for the rigors of cross-examination—and wide latitude is usually allowed in the cross-examination of experts, so prepare them well.

When the trial is under way, it is time for the witnesses to appear and recite their recollections and (in the case of experts) opinions. Once again, first impressions are worth something. A witness who is immediately liked by the jurors will have a head start in the credibility column. If they continue to like him throughout his direct and cross-examination, they will want to believe him. It is not necessary that he be perfect. Jurors tend to identify mainly with witnesses, not lawyers, provided those witnesses seem decent and reasonable folk. It is not fatal for a witness to say, "I'm sorry, I guess I was mistaken about that," especially if the mistake is minor; indeed, such humility is probably more helpful than harmful.

The most important objective, if you can accomplish it, is to brief the witness enough about the experience that confronts him that he will feel relaxed and confident as he answers your questions. If his answers make sense, and if he is not seriously damaged on cross-examination, then his credibility will probably rise or fall on his demeanor. If he comes across as sincere but human, he ought to win the jury's confidence. And when the witnesses you call win the jury's confidence, almost inevitably you will win the case.

Incidentally, be wary of *any* witness who becomes stronger on cross-examination than she was on direct; such people are usually telling the truth, and any unfounded attack can backfire horribly.

11

An Approach to Cross-Examination

D o not begin reading this chapter unless you are well rested and in the mood to work. To absorb what is said here, even though it is essentially introductory in nature, you will need a clear head and your best concentration. Cross-examination is a most difficult concept to comprehend, for it is loaded with apparent contradictions.

But if you learn the rules and principles (and there are some, despite the kaleidoscopic nature of this unique art) and work constantly to apply them as you build your experience, you may one day be a true expert in cross-examination. As a trial lawyer, your ability to cross-examine will be the largest weapon in your arsenal, larger even than your ability to speak fluently and persuasively without notes. Should you become a true expert, you will join the ranks of a very small group, for real expertise in cross-examination is anything but abundant in the trial bar.

What is cross-examination? It is many things. It has been described as an engine of truth, and a bulwark of liberty. Some say it is the most devastating weapon man has discovered, including things nuclear. It is a nonviolent substitute for the gun and the sword.

Cross-examination is not peculiar to the trial of cases. It is used everywhere in daily life, albeit in primitive forms. You have probably used it yourself, without being aware.

Cross-examination is used in the board rooms of corporations, by executives who are trying to advance themselves through illuminating the shortcomings of others.

It is used by wives on their husbands, when lipstick is found where it ought not to be, and on their children when a deficiency is discovered in the cookie jar.

It is used by husbands on their wives, when a new wrinkle has mysteriously appeared on the left front fender of the new family car.

It is used by military leaders, when a hapless field commander is trying to explain why he had to retreat from a position he was ordered to hold.

It is used by representatives of the news media when they are questioning politicians and other public figures.

It is used in virtually every walk of life where there is human communication. It is seldom used correctly.

There is no school in this country where it is taught in any depth. It is a talent you are going to have to develop on your own, and the time to start is *now*. If, by the time you make your first appearance in court, you have mastered even the fundamentals of good cross-examination, you will tower above your colleagues, for most of them will graduate from law school with only vague notions of what cross-examination is all about, and no dexterity at all in its use.

Good cross-examination has a long list of ingredients, which will grow as you mature and ripen in the art. The primary ones, which we will be considering in our approach to this most complex exercise, are *control, speed, memory, precise articulation, logic, timing, manner,* and *termination.*

The principles of good instruction would suggest that these fundamentals be discussed one by one for best comprehension. I cannot do that, because they are so interrelated that all are in motion most of the time that the cross-examiner is at work. I will, however, endeavor to give some brief explanation of what is meant by each in the context of cross-examination.

1. *Control:* A cross-examiner must control his witness tightly, and not let him run away with long, self-serving narrative answers; he must also control the direction and pace of the questioning.

2. *Speed:* A witness telling less than the perfect truth needs time to think up and fashion his answers, time that he must not be allowed to have. Effective cross-examination must be conducted at a pace nothing short of relentless, which will give one who is fabricating his answers insufficient time to do so.

3. *Memory:* The cross-examiner must have his head stuffed with a plethora of facts and information, including every prior statement the witness has made, the testimony other related witnesses have given or are expected to give, all relevant documents and other kinds of evidence, and a clear image of the details of the scene of the event if there is one. His hands must be empty most of the time, and his eyes must be riveted on the witness. If he needs constantly to refer to notes and other written materials, he will sacrifice something essential: *speed.*

4. *Precise articulation:* Questions must be formulated swiftly, but with care. They must be clear and unambiguous, simple and not compound, in a form that is not objectionable legally, and structured to elicit a yes or no answer most of the time.

5. *Logic:* Most questions—even those intended to ridicule— must be put together within a logical framework. They may be, and often are, put out of order, or in juxtaposition to one another, but the goal should be to play the witness's total testimony off against a logical sense of what he *should* have said if he were recounting reality.

6. *Timing:* A cross-examiner must exercise excellence in timing throughout his performance. Once he has backed a witness into a corner, he must go for the jugular moments before the witness has girded himself to repel the

attack. If he can, before every break in the trial, he must leave the air heavy with doubt and suspicion about the witness's testimony, allowing this last impression to sink into the jurors' minds during the recess.

7. *Manner:* The manner in which the cross-examiner deals with a witness must be appropriate to the circumstances. One *does not* use a heavy-handed tone of voice, tinged with sarcasm, on an attractive and pleasant elderly person or child. One *does* exhibit disdain and even derision through attitude, affect, and tone of voice on a lying witness, and increasingly so as he begins to unravel.

8. *Termination:* A cross-examiner must know when to quit, on a high point and without insisting that all subjects within a witness's possible knowledge be covered exhaustively. As Alice in Wonderland was advised, "Proceed until you come to the end, then stop." Knowing when, where, and how to *stop* a cross-examination is one of the last things trial lawyers learn.

The targets of cross-examination are those same areas that were of interest to our investigator in Chapter 6, when we discussed preparation for trial. To wit: perception, memory, articulation, and candor.

What did the witness truly perceive? How well has he remembered those perceptions, and how much have they been battered by the *suggestions* of others? How well is he transposing the image in his mind into the words used to describe that image? Does he really believe what he is recounting, or is he filling in gaps with manufactured testimony? Is his central assertion itself an unmitigated lie?

Before studying how cross-examination reaches into these areas of human function, we had better start with the first *rule* of cross-examination:

RULE ONE: *Don't cross-examine.*

That's right. Disappointed? If your disappointment is acute, you will probably break this rule at the first opportunity, as most young lawyers do. The phrase "No questions, Your Honor" is the hallmark of a seasoned pro. It takes more experience, courage, and self-confidence to use this phrase than to follow the natural impulse to dive in.

Don't cross-examine a witness unless you have to. If he is the only witness to a critical issue in the trial, you may have to ask him *some* questions merely to preserve your opportunity to argue against his credibility, but if you sense that he is telling essentially the whole truth, be prepared to make your effort brief. When a witness does little more under cross-examination than repeat what he has said on direct examination, his credibility is apt to be buttressed in the minds of the jurors, simply because he has been consistent under attack. If this is the substance of your accomplishment on cross-examination, you have harmed your case rather than helped it.

Don't cross-examine unless you have thought your objective through and decided that you have something to gain. If a witness hasn't hurt you, don't cross-examine him, even if you think you can show minor points in his testimony to be inaccurate.

There are a large number of old chestnuts in the lore of cross-examination, some of which are instructive even though they may be largely fictional. To illustrate: A defendant was charged in a criminal case with maiming, a serious felony that requires proof of physical disfigurement in most jurisdictions. In this case, the victim had lost an ear; the defendant was charged with having bitten it off in the course of an altercation. The victim was a psychotic person, incompetent to testify himself. The prosecutor (who had not done his homework) therefore called to the stand the lone bystander who had been at the scene. He described seeing the fight start, and the two combatants fall to the ground. Then came the following:

> **QUESTION:** Then sir, did you see the defendant do something with reference to the left ear of the victim?
>
> **THE WITNESS:** No, actually I did not.

The prosecutor, stunned by this unexpected answer, mumbled "No further questions," and sat down, knowing that within moments the judge would dismiss the case for lack of sufficient evidence. The young defense lawyer, however, who should have been overjoyed at his unanticipated good fortune and left well enough alone, was troubled. He wanted to perform for his client, partly because he thought he should justify his fee. Furthermore, his favorite girlfriend was sitting in the front row. He rose to cross-examine.

> **QUESTION:** Now then, sir, if you didn't see my client bite off the victim's ear, why do you have the bad manners to come forward as a witness in this case?
>
> **THE WITNESS:** Because, even though I couldn't actually see your client bite the man's ear off, I *did* see him spit it out . . .

You see what I mean? *Don't!!*

RULE TWO: *Don't ask questions when you don't know the answer—the truthful answer, at least.*

In the motion picture *Anatomy of a Murder,* a young army officer played by Ben Gazzara was charged with killing a bartender in the rural Upper Peninsula of Michigan. The evidence showed that the killing took place immediately after the officer learned that the bartender had raped his wife. There were witnesses to the act, so the wily old defense lawyer, played by James Stewart, entered a plea of temporary insanity, claiming that his client had been so overwhelmed by the news of the rape of his wife that the homicide had been the result of an "irresistible impulse," a recognized form of legal insanity under Michigan law.

The last defense witness gave the prosecution a jolt. A very attractive young woman whom the prosecutor had never interviewed took the stand and said that she had been present at the scene, and had heard the bartender laugh derisively while telling the officer that his wife was little more than a slut. The prosecutor, George C. Scott, knew that this testimony might well convince the jury that the provocation for the killing had been more than adequate, and induce them to acquit. He had to discredit the witness if his case was to survive. He decided to begin his cross-examination with what he thought would be a devastating shot:

> **QUESTION:** Is it not true that you were furious at this victim for being unfaithful, because he was your *lover?*
>
> **THE WITNESS:** No, he was not my lover. He was my *father.*

When Supreme Court Justice Felix Frankfurter saw the film, he chuckled with delight over this incident. "A perfect example," he said, "of what happens when a lawyer asks a question to which he doesn't know the answer!"

Later on, you will learn that this rule has to be broken frequently, and that there are right and wrong ways to do it. Meanwhile, remember the rule.

RULE THREE: *Do not ask questions that begin with* what, when, where, why, *or* how.

Questions formulated in this manner usually invite a narrative answer, and offer the witness an opportunity to talk at length and out of your control. This rule has to be broken from time to time, too, but under very limited circumstances. Normally the time for a question beginning with one of these words is when you have a witness so badly cornered in contradictions that you don't care what his answer is.

The first principle of cross-examination is that the witness must make a *commitment* in some form before there is anything to be "crossed." The commitment necessary is a base line, or starting point of sorts, and can take a number of forms. The one most obvious and most common will be the statements the witness has made before trial, orally, in writing, or by deposition. These form his commitment to his version of what he thinks he perceived (or, if he is a liar, *claims* he perceived). His testimony on direct examination, immediately before cross-examination, forms his final commitment. Any variance between that testimony and his earlier statements usually makes fruitful grounds for exploration on "cross," as it is called.

But there are other forms of commitment as well. One may be the testimony of other witnesses who were at the same place at the same time that the claimed observations were supposedly made. Another may be some document whose authenticity the witness is in no position to deny, such as his birth certificate or record of hospitalization. Still another could be some physical reality, like the placement of certain objects in a room. Whatever it is, it should be sufficiently solid that when the witness's attention is directed to it, he cannot lightly brush it aside.

There are generally thought to be three distinct phases of cross-examination, one or two of which might be omitted under certain circumstances. They are *extraction, closing,* and *impeachment.*

When you have in your hand, or on the tip of your tongue, some material that you feel will neatly contradict something that the witness has said on direct examination, you may be tempted to charge forward and confront the witness with it, just to get the cross off to a rousing start. Be patient. In most instances there are other things to be accomplished *before* you launch your attack.

First, you will want to *extract* from the witness anything he knows that is relevant and favors your side of the case. If you question him about such matters, and he admits them readily in a good-natured way, take notice: You may have on your hands a nice person, which means that he is probably also an honest person, and thus dangerous to toy with on cross-examination.

Second, you will need to *close* a number of handy exits that the witness might try to slide through when you start to pin him down. If you wanted to capture someone, one of the best ways to do that would be to lure him to a small room, *after* you had securely locked all the doors except the one through which he was to enter; that too would have to be locked as soon as he was safely inside. This is a tedious phase of cross-examination, but quite necessary. Many lawyers skip it entirely, or touch it too lightly, because they are so anxious to leap into the impeachment phase, where the excitement is. If you are a professional cross-examiner, you will not make this mistake; if you do, you may think that you have a witness nicely cornered, only to watch him slip away with a glib but plausible explanation of what you had hoped was an airtight contradiction.

As an analogy, visualize direct examination as a series of mountain peaks sticking up out of a foggy valley. These mountain peaks are the high points of direct testimony, and on direct examination the witness will have been taken from peak to peak as he tells his story. A great deal of detail, like the terrain under the fog, will not appear. But it is there, all the same. Until the valleys of his story are mapped, the witness's *commitment* to that story is too incomplete to risk an attack. You must walk him through those valleys, covering definitively all of the small details he claims to have observed, and—just as important—all of the details known to you (as a thoroughly prepared trial lawyer) that he will admit he did *not* observe. You may feel you are boring the jury with trivia, but grit your teeth and stay with it. Move as swiftly as you can, but not so swiftly that you leave a lot of terrain unexplored. In addition to completing a necessary chore, you will be relaxing your witness. From all the movies about trials that he may have seen, he expected you to come at him with a snarling attack, perhaps. As you gently and nonchalantly press him for these small details, he will be thinking to himself: "This isn't so bad after all."

Finally, when this drudgery is behind you, you will be ready to attempt to *impeach,* or discredit, what the witness has said. Most of the balance of this chapter will focus on that undertaking.

But before any of these steps are taken, you should have formed a plan. That plan, which may have to be formulated very rapidly after the witness has completed his direct examination (if anything he has said is a surprise to you), should contemplate the following questions:

A. Has this witness really hurt my case in any way? If so, how?

B. What sort of person is the witness? Has he made a good impression on the jury up to this point? Is he rude or arrogant, or defensive in his manner? Has his story sounded credible on its face? Is he the kind of person who deserves to be confronted, or should I merely attempt to deflect his assertions and treat them as if they are largely unimportant?

C. In the statements he has made that I expect to be able to contradict, has he committed himself unequivocally, or are his statements sufficiently vague or ambiguous that he can explain my contradiction away? (If so, you have some more "closing" to do before you attack.)

A good example of proper closing occurred in the Florida trial mentioned earlier, of Candy Mossler and Melvin Powers. While the trial was under way, a surprise witness came forward and claimed that before Jacques Mossler was murdered, Melvin Powers had approached him in Alabama and asked him to kill Mossler. The witness said he would never forget the day because it was the date of his father's funeral.

On cross-examination, Percy Foreman paid little attention to anything but the *date* of the conversation. Over and over, he demanded to know whether there was *any possibility* of error over the exact day of the alleged conversation. The witness insisted that he could hardly be mistaken about the day he had buried his father. Still Foreman hammered away, until finally the trial judge said "enough."

Foreman advanced on the witness, a sheaf of very official-looking documents in his hand.

"Don't you know, sir," he said, "that on the day your father was buried, and the day before and the day after, Melvin Powers was in a hospital in Houston, Texas, undergoing surgery—as these records show?"

The witness was devastated to the point where the trial judge struck his testimony and ordered the jury to disregard everything he had said. This triumph in cross-examination—a clear example of leaving no escape doors open at the moment of confrontation—probably went a long way toward Powers's eventual acquittal. It would be nice if utter and total impeachment of this sort were possible with every lying witness, but in fact it seldom occurs.

Let's assume you have drawn from the witness all of the information favorable to your client that he can give (extraction), and have covered the details of his story so thoroughly that he is firmly committed to all that he says he perceived *and* did not perceive (closing). You are now ready to try to take his story, or—more likely—segments of that story, apart. Your ability to do that, if the witness is critical to the central issue in the case, may determine the outcome of the trial. Impeachment, when it is done, must be conducted as swiftly as possible and with care.

Before studying the various techniques used by cross-examiners to impeach witnesses, let's pause for a moment and ask: How would you go about damaging a witness's credibility if you disregard what you have read up to this point in the book and you had only your experience and common sense at your disposal? Let's assume you are defending an armed robbery case. The prosecution's only witness, and thus the only witness whose testimony might persuade the jury to convict, is the victim. He has testified that he was walking through a downtown alleyway one dark Saturday night, when a man stepped out from a doorway—a man he had never seen before—and took his wallet at gunpoint. He has pointed at your client, sitting next to you at the defense table, and said unequivocally, "That's the man who robbed me!"

You believe that your client is wholly innocent, that at the time he was at home watching television with his wife—as both have sworn—and that at the very least there is a case of mistaken identity. Your job is to show that this witness is mistaken, an effort he can be expected to resist vigorously. How will you go about it? Will you start off, as Percy Foreman did, with a question like: "Don't you know sir, that at the moment you were being robbed this defendant was miles away, at home watching television with his wife?"

It may seem that this is a logical place to start, and a proper question. Wrong on both counts. The answer you are likely to get is: "I don't care where the defendant *claims* he was, I *know* where he was. He was pointing a gun at me. I will *never* forget that face!"

That answer won't help you at all. It is one thing to have official hospital records in your hand, as Percy Foreman did, and quite another to have only the testimony of the defendant and one as obviously biased as his wife.

Back up just a moment, and let me tell you what I have done to you by giving you this hypothetical case. I have thrust you right into the toughest, meanest, most dangerous and exasperating job a trial lawyer ever has to undertake: the impeachment of an identifying witness.

You should know some things about the peculiarities of this particular task, both because I want you to learn from the exercise we are about to go through, and because if you become a trial lawyer you are inevitably, one day, going to come face to face in a courtroom with an identifying witness. There are many complexities in the whole business of one human being trying to identify another whom he has seen only once before in his life, and then under traumatic circumstances. Cross-examination of such witnesses goes into three of the target areas we have discussed—perception, memory, and candor—very thoroughly. Therefore, nasty as these cases are, an examination of one can be very instructive.

First, let's discuss what you know and have in your file about this case from your pretrial preparation. The victim,

Vaughn, first reported to the desk sergeant at Precinct One, Metropolitan Police, at 11:30 P.M. on Saturday, July 3, 1982, that ten minutes before he had been robbed at gunpoint in an alley called Allen Place. The desk sergeant referred Vaughn to Police Inspector Inman, who was on duty at the time. Inman took a signed statement from Vaughn, indicating that the assailant was about Vaughn's own height, five feet nine inches, and weight, one hundred seventy pounds. He was wearing a visored cap, dark trousers, and a light short-sleeved shirt. He was in his mid-thirties, had thinning brown hair, a fair complexion, no marks or scars, and regular features with nothing unusual about them. The lighting in the alley came from a streetlight one hundred feet away. Because the assailant was standing between Vaughn and the light, it was not possible to tell the color of the assailant's eyes.

The following Monday, at Inman's request, Vaughn returned to the police station to look over three books with pages and pages of photos of mature white males, shown head and shoulders only; there were numbers at the bottom of each picture, and Vaughn took them to be photos of men with criminal records. In the third book he saw a photo of your client, Daniels, the defendant in this case. He told Inspector Inman that this person looked quite familiar and could be the culprit, but that he, Vaughn, would have to see the man in person to be sure. Inman said he would try to arrange an opportunity for that and would be in touch. Two days later, Vaughn went back to the station and was taken to a room where six men were standing before bright lights. He was asked if he recognized any of them and, after studying them for a few minutes, pointed at Daniels and said, "That's the man who robbed me."

Daniels is forty-two years old, has blue eyes and thinning brown hair, weighs one hundred fifty-five pounds, has bushy eyebrows and an aquiline nose. His complexion is lightly pock-marked. He has a distinctively low bass voice. He is currently unemployed because of a general business recession, but normally works as a bartender. Because of his unemployment, at the time of his arrest for robbing Vaughn, Daniels had very little money in the bank and several overdue bills. His photo was in the police book because when he was thirty-seven he had an unfortunate accident with his car, in which a child pedestrian was killed. He was charged with manslaughter, and his lawyer advised him to plea-bargain. He pleaded guilty to involuntary manslaughter and received a suspended sentence.

If you decide to call Daniels as a witness, his criminal record will become admissible, which might impeach his credibility, and the jury will learn that he admitted to killing a little child. Daniels's wife, Wanda, has no criminal record, but is not very intelligent and makes only a fair witness.

When Daniels was arrested, he denied any knowledge of the robbery, insisted that he had been at home that night, and agreed to submit to the lineup without consulting a lawyer, even though he was properly advised that he had the right to do so. As required by law, a photograph (8" × 10", black and white) was taken of the lineup in which Daniels was standing when Vaughn identified him. Daniels told the police that he does not own a visored cap.

Although the photo doesn't show it, you have learned through investigation something your client didn't notice at the time: Four of the six men in the lineup were wearing blue short-sleeved shirts. The fifth man and Daniels were wearing white short-sleeved shirts, but the fifth man had a full head of dark hair.

You have skipped the extraction phase of cross-examination, because in an identification case the victim-witness typically knows nothing about the defendant, good or bad, and there is nothing to elicit. In your closing phase, you have established that between nine o'clock in the evening and the time of the robbery, Vaughn had three cocktails, but he feels that he was completely sober when he was robbed, and when he made his statement to Inspector Inman; that in talking to Inspector Inman, Vaughn used his best powers of concentration to recall and describe every detail he could about the assailant, while his memory was fresh.

Your job now is to impeach Vaughn. You will *not* destroy him, or turn him into a blithering idiot, or get him to admit that he may be in error over his identification of your client as the robber. You will, if you can, give the jury reasons to have some nagging doubts about Vaughn's declaration that your client is the guilty party. That is all you can do, and—if you have a conscientious and impartial jury—all that you *need* to do.

Let's pause for a moment and consider the matter of eyewitness identification. It is treated as a fact, even though it is in reality only an opinion. Almost every living creature has a look-alike somewhere, who would confuse his closest friends. When a witness says "that's the man," he is actually saying, "That is the *only* person in the world who robbed me, and I am *positive* that he is the person."

Of all the shortcomings in our system of criminal justice, the court's handling of identification evidence is the worst. Almost any identification, however momentarily the witness perceives the other person, is admitted in evidence. Juries take great stock in such testimony, unaware as they are that wrongful eyewitness identifications have put more innocent people behind bars than all other jury mistakes combined. Therefore, if this jury believes Vaughn, your client is going to go to jail. Daniels's only hope at this point rests on your ability to cross-examine effectively.

How should you begin this solemn and vital task of impeachment? At the beginning, that's where. It was a routine evening for brother Vaughn when suddenly a gunman was thrust into his life. Let's start off this way:

Q. Mr. Vaughn, is it fair to say that this was the first time in your entire life that you have been forced to look at the business end of a loaded firearm?

A. I would have to say yes.

Q. Would it also be fair to say that you were most concerned that the firearm might shoot at you?

A. I thought about it.

Q. You were very frightened, were you not?

A. I was concerned.

Q. Really, Mr. Vaughn, the truth is you were terrified of being shot, weren't you?

A. I was concerned about being shot.

Q. It was the first time in your entire life that you have had to look at a loaded pistol pointed at your body; do you wish to tell this jury that you were *not* terrified?

Let's pause and look at what has happened so far. You are trying to show that Vaughn's state of mind was such that he was immersed in prayerful hope that he would not be shot or killed.

He senses where you are trying to go, and does not wish to admit the terror that he felt—terror that any normal person would have experienced, including the jurors—at the moment of the robbery, for fear that people may think his mind was so preoccupied by the survival instinct that its ability to perceive and recall the identity of his attacker was impaired. He has therefore ducked a responsive answer to what your last question *assumed*—that the assailant's gun was loaded. Vaughn doesn't know it yet, but he has made a serious mistake. Let's continue:

Q. Mr. Vaughn, I believe that in your direct testimony you said that the weapon that was pointed at you was similar to one Inspector Inman showed you during your first meeting with him, is that correct?

A. I believe so, yes.

Q. And that was a .38 caliber revolver, was it not?

A. I think so.

Q. And you keep a .38 caliber revolver in your home for protection, according to state police records, isn't that so?

A. Yes, I do.

Q. And you are familiar with that weapon, aren't you?

A. Yes.

Q. And you know that a revolver has a cylindrical magazine, which enables one to see the bullets in the cylinder if the weapon is loaded, don't you?

A. That's true.

Q. But you have told us that on the night you were robbed, you did not observe whether the cylinder of the robber's gun had any bullets in it, haven't you? That's why you said you don't know if the gun was loaded, isn't it? (*The witness does not respond.*)

Q. Mr. Vaughn, did you hear my question?

A. Yes.

Q. Did you understand my question?

A. Yes, I think so.

Q. Are you unable to answer my question?

A. Could you repeat it, please?

Q. Certainly. You told us you didn't know whether or not the gun was loaded because you don't recall seeing any bullets in the cylinder, isn't that so?

A. Yes, I guess so.

Q. And that is because the lighting in Allen Place is so dark you couldn't see the bullets, isn't it, Mr. Vaughn?

We don't really care what Mr. Vaughn's answer is, do we? The point is made—for whatever reason, be it personal terror or inadequate lighting. Victim Vaughn failed to perceive something of critical importance in a weapon with which he was familiar: whether or not the gun was loaded! We have questioned the effectiveness of his *perceptions* that evening, and have shown that something of great importance was overlooked. So far so good. But Daniels is a long way from being out of the woods. We have only begun.

Q. I take it, Mr. Vaughn, that the assailant who stopped you that night caught you quite by surprise, did he not?

A. Yes, he did.

Q. But when you heard his demand, you hastened to comply with it, didn't you—gave him your wallet right away?

A. I didn't argue with him, for sure.

Q. Of course. As a matter of fact, you responded so quickly that this entire transaction took quite a bit less than a minute, correct?

A. I don't know about that—it must have been more than a minute . . .

Q. Well, let's see. Would you be good enough to look at the second hand of the courtroom clock on the wall behind the judge, and as you count off the seconds tell us how long it was from the time the robber demanded your wallet until you handed it to him?

A. (*witness studies clock*) Well, I guess it wouldn't have taken more than five or ten seconds.

Q. Thank you. And the minute he got his hands on your wallet, he took off, didn't he?

A. Yes.

Q. He was running with his back to you, wasn't he?

A. Yes, he was.

Q. So the total time during which you had an opportunity to view his face was a few seconds, wasn't it, Mr. Vaughn?

A. Something like that.

Q. And during those seconds you were more concerned for your safety than in making a study of the robber, weren't you?

A. I got a look at him.

Q. But safety was your first concern, nonetheless?

A. I was worried about it.

The whole point of this sequence is to establish the total time during which the witness had a chance to view the man he now identifies so positively, particularly since his mind was on other things. This may give the jury some cause for concern, for so fleeting an observation, under less than ideal lighting conditions, is a slender thread on which to hang a man's liberty. We continue, next trying to show the *difference* between Vaughn's description of his assailant on the night of the event and the actual appearance of the defendant, Daniels.

Q. Mr. Vaughn, at some point during the few seconds you were facing the robber, you looked him in the eye, did you not?

A. I looked at his face, yes.

Q. The face had eyes?

A. Of course it did.

Q. What color were they?

A. His back was to the light, so I couldn't tell.

Q. You are telling us that his face was not well lit?

A. I could see it, it's just that I couldn't tell the color of his eyes.

Q. For all you know they could have been brown, blue, gray or hazel, isn't that so?

A. I suppose they could.

Q. And if they were anything other than blue, then of course the robber could not have been Mr. Daniels, who has blue eyes, correct?

A. Then they must have been blue, because I know it was him.

Q. Sir, are you willing to swear to this jury that the man who robbed you had blue eyes even though you *couldn't see them* at the time?

A. I just know that face. I will never forget it.

Q. And you believe you are so sure that you have come here today willing to make assumptions, is that correct?

THE PROSECUTOR. Objection, Your Honor—argumentative.

THE COURT. Sustained.

Typically, an identifying witness will become aggressive and even hostile when discrepancies between his first description of another and the actual appearance of the defendant in open court are pointed out. But these discrepancies are primary grist for the mill of doubt, and must be demonstrated in detail.

Q. Well, Mr. Vaughn, even though you couldn't see the color of the eyes, you did see the eyebrows and sockets, didn't you?

A. Yes.

Q. And the eyes were about on a level with your own, weren't they?

A. Approximately.

Q. And because you noticed that they were on a level with your own eyes, you told Inspector Inman that same night that the robber was your own height, five feet nine, correct?

A. I said he was my height.

Q. Excuse me, Your Honor, may Mr. Daniels come forward to the witness box and approach the witness?

THE COURT. He may. (*The defendant comes forward and faces the witness.*)

Q. Now, Mr. Vaughn, would you step down from the witness box and stand about as far away from Mr. Daniels as you were from the robber when he held you at gunpoint that night? Thank you. Now Mr. Vaughn, would you tell the jury if Mr. Daniels is a man whom you would judge to be your own height, or taller?

A. About my height. A little taller, perhaps.

Q. Then if this is the same man who robbed you, why didn't you tell the inspector that the robber was a taller man?

A. I did the best I could. I didn't mean the *exact* same height.

Q. Thank you. Mr. Daniels, you may return to your seat, and Mr. Vaughn, would you resume your chair in the witness box. Now, Mr. Vaughn, you also told Inspector Inman that same night that the robber weighed about the same as yourself, didn't you—sort of the same build?

A. That was my best recollection at the time I talked with the inspector.

Q. That was less than an hour after the incident, wasn't it, when your recollection was fresh?

A. Yes, but I was nervous then.

Q. And that nervousness may have somewhat impaired the description you gave the inspector?

A. Yes, that's right.

Q. But certainly, sir, sitting with the inspector in a lighted room in the security of a police station, you had no fear for your life, did you?

A. No, I was just nervous.

Q. But surely, sir, you must have been *more* nervous during the few seconds you were being robbed than during your talk with the inspector—isn't that so?

A. I was nervous both times.

Q. But more so during the robbery, yes?

A. I might have been.

Q. And if the nervousness you felt during your interview impaired your ability to *describe* the robber, then the

nervousness you felt during the robbery itself may have
impaired your ability to *perceive* the details about the
robber—isn't *that* true?

A. A little, perhaps, but I'd know that face anywhere.

Notice that each time an identifying witness is picked up on
a discrepancy, he will attempt to bolster the weakness of his
answer by volunteering once again his original conclusion. But
as the jury sees him reassert his conclusion—"that's the man"—
in the face of some material problems, the mill of doubt is
grinding. Notice also that whereas the cross-examiner attacked
Vaughn early on with the thesis that he was too nervous while
being robbed to make good observations—which attack Vaughn
resisted—here he has trapped himself. By using his nervousness
during the Inman interview as an excuse to explain the significant difference between his height, and the robber's, versus
Daniels's, he has walked into the very trap he earlier tried to
avoid: impaired function due to nervousness. Whenever a witness
who is trying to explain himself out of a discrepancy in his testimony offers an opportunity like this one, a cross-examiner has
to pounce on it quickly. Finally, note that throughout the cross-
examination thus far, an effort has been made to invite the use of
yes and no answers, thus inching the witness along toward the
ultimate answers sought.

Q. Mr. Vaughn, did you notice when Mr. Daniels was standing directly in front of you that he has a prominent nose,
perhaps a "Roman" nose?

A. You could say that.

Q. I did say it, Mr. Vaughn—do *you* agree with me?

A. All right.

Q. You told the inspector that the robber had "regular features, with nothing unusual about them," didn't you?

A. Well, I didn't give him every detail.

Q. No, please, Mr. Vaughn, the question is, did you *say* that
to Inspector Inman during your interview?

A. If it's in my statement, that's what I said.

Q. Exactly. There is nothing in your statement about a prominent nose, is there?

A. You have the statement.

Q. Yes, sir, and now *you* have your statement. For the record, I have just handed defense exhibit C to the witness, which is his written statement to Inspector Inman at 12:45 A.M. on July 4, 1982. Now, Mr. Vaughn, would you be kind enough to examine that statement and see if you can find any reference in it to the robber's having a prominent nose?

A. (*witness examines document*) It's not here.

Q. And there is nothing there about a scarred or pockmarked face, is there?

A. No, there isn't.

Q. No mention of blue eyes, is there?

A. No, I said that earlier.

Q. So you did, so you did—I believe you explained that the lighting was poor. Is that the same reason you missed the nose and the troubled complexion, which Mr. Daniels clearly has, and you neglected to mention?

A. The lighting made it difficult.

To this point, we have made the best use of this kind of discrepancy that we can: to suggest repeatedly to the witness (and to the jury, of course) that the opportunity to observe was not good and that the resulting observation cannot be much better. Principally, this has been done by pitting the witness's very first statement against the realities of the defendant's appearance; for although a witness's first statement may not be accurate, it is probably the *most* accurate that his memory will ever furnish. Now we must set about the task of explaining how, despite these obvious discrepancies, the victim happened to single out the defendant, Daniels, as the culprit.

Q. Now, Mr. Vaughn, on Monday, July 5, you went back to the police station to look at photographs furnished to you by Inspector Inman, correct?

A. Yes, I did.

Q. The inspector explained to you that street robberies of this type are hard to solve, and that the best chance is to let the victim look at police photographs to see if he can recognize anyone, didn't he?

A. He told me something like that.

Q. Did he also tell you that you ought to be very careful in any selection you might make, because experience has shown that such identifications are often incorrect?

A. He didn't tell me that, no.

Q. In any event, you looked through two of the three books of photos he gave you without seeing anyone who looked familiar, correct?

A. That's right.

Q. And as you came to the third book of photos, you realized that this might be the last opportunity to find the culprit, didn't you?

A. Well, it was the last of the books he gave me.

Q. Exactly. And when you came to the picture that turned out to be Mr. Daniels, you thought to yourself: "This man looks more like the robber than any others I've seen," didn't you?

A. I thought he looked like the robber, but I wasn't positive.

Q. True. And that's because all you could see was his head and shoulders, correct?

A. Partly, yes.

Q. And in looking at Daniels's photo, you did not find the blue eyes to be familiar, because you hadn't seen the robber's eyes, isn't that so?

A. No, the eyes didn't seem familiar.

Q. And the curved, prominent nose that clearly shows in this side view (*shows photo to the witness*) didn't look familiar, because you thought that the robber's nose was a "regular" feature, as opposed to an "irregular" feature; isn't that also true?

A. I wasn't going by the nose, no.

Q. And of course the pockmarks on Daniels's face in the photos didn't help you, because you hadn't seen any pockmarks, had you?

A. No, not the pockmarks.

Q. Can you tell me now what it was about these photos that *did* look familiar?

A. Oh, everything else, the hair, the shape of the face, the whole picture—I recognized him.

Oops—there we go breaking the rule against asking "what" questions, and giving the witness a chance to speak in the narrative. Why did we do it? For two reasons. First, we have him pretty well "bracketed" by the features he has admitted were *not* similar: the eyes, nose, and skin. Second, since he has already admitted that the robber's face was in the shadow of the street light, he will get in trouble if he comes up with similarities *other* than what he could see in silhouette—namely, the shape of the face and the hair—and in his description of the hair, he has a definite difficulty, which we want to exploit *after* he has used it as a point of identification:

Q. Mr. Vaughn, I believe you told us on direct examination that the robber had thinning brown hair?

A. Yes, I noticed that.

Q. You have also said that he was wearing a visored cap; was the crown of that cap made of some transparent material?

A. No, no, the cap was tilted on the back of his head.

Q. Didn't the shadow caused by the light behind him falling on the uptilted visor make it difficult to see the thickness of his hair?

A. I could see it some. I got the *impression* that his hair was brown and thin.

Q. And this was an impression that formed in your mind while you were concerned about what you believed to be a loaded pistol pointing at your stomach, correct?

A. I was concerned.

The last area to be explored with the witness is that of the lineup itself, or "showup," as it is sometimes called. In view of the calamitous consequences of a mistake occurring in this procedure, a truly fair lineup should consist of two groups of at least twenty individuals each, all of whom bear *some* physical resemblance to the suspect. Unless one is on the "inside" of law enforcement, one seldom hears of the often humorous mistakes made by victims at lineups. Suffice it to say that many a police officer has been singled out in a lineup as a culprit. Nonetheless, for all its uncertainty, this form of evidence is in daily use in this and many other countries, and is a procedure with which we must live.

Recall, if you can, the details of the lineup as were earlier described. (Check back if you have to, but do try to exercise that memory a little harder if these details have slipped your mind.) We will go after Mr. Vaughn from the flank.

> **Q.** Mr. Vaughn, you have been aware of police officers in the community since you were a child, isn't that true?
>
> **A.** Yes, I suppose you could say that.
>
> **Q.** And of all the police officers you have seen in the many years that you have been aware of them, the color you would most often associate with their uniform is blue, is it not?
>
> **A.** Oh, I have seen them wear other colors.
>
> **Q.** I'm sure you have, Mr. Vaughn, but a clear majority of the ones you have seen in your lifetime were wearing blue, weren't they?
>
> **A.** I couldn't be sure of that.

At this point the cross-examiner has choices; the witness is clearly balking, afraid of a trap of some sort, for most people would readily concede that blue is the color most often associated with police dress. It would be possible to press Vaughn further on this point and perhaps back him down. My own choice would be to leave his answer in its present form, for the jurors know what it should have been, and his unwillingness to admit the point may somewhat diminish their confidence in his testimony.

Q. After you had tentatively identified the photograph for Inspector Inman, and while you were on your way to the police station a second time at the inspector's request, you expected that you were going to be asked to look at some male adults in person, isn't that correct?

A. I thought that was why I was going down there.

Q. Yes. And you also expected that the man whose photograph you had singled out would be among those you would view, didn't you?

A. Well, the inspector had told me he would try to arrange it, so, yes.

Q. And when you arrived at the police station, the inspector took you to a lighted room, did he not?

A. Yes.

Q. And when you got to that room you were confronted with six adult males standing next to each other in a row, isn't that right?

A. I believe there were six.

Q. Are you uncertain of that, Mr. Vaughn?

A. No, six seems correct.

Q. And of the six, four were wearing blue shirts, weren't they?

A. I think some of them were, I don't know exactly how many.

Q. I ask you to look at this photograph, defense exhibit E, Mr. Vaughn. Does that depict the group of men you saw that night?

A. Yes, I believe it does.

Q. Now, even though this photo is in black and white rather than color, would you agree that four of the shirts being worn by the men are of the same medium shade, while the other remaining two are much lighter?

A. It's hard to be sure . . .

Q. Mr. Vaughn, if I assure you that Inspector Inman will testify that all four of these shirts of medium shade were the same color blue, will that help you to recall?

A. Uh, I think I do remember that they were blue, at least I think that they were.

Q. Fine. Now, when you saw four men wearing blue in a police station, didn't you naturally suspect that they were police officers?

A. I could have thought that . . . I'm not sure.

Q. You had no reason to believe that the person whose photo you had selected earlier was a policeman, did you?

A. No, I had no reason to think he was a cop.

Q. Then in your own mind, after looking at the men, you may have sort of automatically eliminated from suspicion the men dressed in blue, isn't that so?

A. It's possible.

Q. Now, if you'll glance at exhibit E again, of the two other men, one has a full head of hair and the other has thinning hair, very clearly, isn't that so?

A. Yes.

Q. And, as you had told Inspector Inman right from the start, the man you were looking for had thinning brown hair, correct?

A. That's true.

Q. That would eliminate the gentleman with the full head of hair, wouldn't it?

A. I guess so.

Q. In view of these circumstances, Mr. Vaughn, isn't it possible that you selected my client from this lineup simply by *eliminating* the other five men who were in it?

A. No, I don't think so. I'm pretty sure that he's the one who robbed me.

There is little point in trying to push Mr. Vaughn much further, or to expect that he will ever concede real doubt as to his identification. His use of the phrase "pretty sure" is to be viewed as a substantial erosion of his testimony, one that most trial lawyers would be happy with. Indeed, this may be a good point on which to terminate the cross-examination, since we have covered the entire sequence from the moment of robbery through his lineup identification.

Will Daniels be convicted solely on Vaughn's testimony? He could be. Juries have done worse things. But the important matter is the result of his cross-examination, which has injected enough doubt into the mind of any intelligent and fair person to cause long hesitation before sending Daniels to jail on the uncorroborated testimony of victim Vaughn.

What is set forth above is a realistic and pragmatic cross-examination in a typical case of this sort. Society tends to take a simplistic view of trial developments, and if asked the average spectator would probably say, "Well, some parts of that were very neat, but in the end Vaughn stuck to his guns—he didn't break." The short answer is, Vaughn wasn't *expected* to "break" as such, for witnesses almost never do. The proper question for the trial lawyer to ask himself at the conclusion of cross-examination of a critical witness like Vaughn is, Did I get enough contradictions and improbable answers from the witness that in my final argument to the jury I can leave them with real doubts over the accuracy of his "opinion" that Daniels robbed him?

Because this is an exercise in training on the principles of cross-examination, we should critique it against the criteria enumerated at the beginning of this chapter.

1. *Control:* Did the cross-examiner control the witness, and thus the *flow* of the exchange? Not totally, but on a percentage basis one could say "most of the time." Go back and look at the questions, and the way they are formulated; notice the constant effort to keep the witness "reined in" by concluding each question with a gently insistent demand for a precise and narrow answer. Although Vaughn often volunteered more than he was asked, in an effort to either duck or defend himself, almost every question is leading and has the answer built into it. Almost every question is designed to elicit a yes or no answer.

2. *Speed:* While of course it is not possible to judge the speed at which the cross-examiner was working by reading a written transcript of the event, the insistent tone and the sequence of the questions discloses that a rapid pace may

have been used, giving the witness as little time to think up answers to tough questions as was humanly possible. In a real situation, a skilled and experienced trial lawyer would have kept up a rapid-fire staccato most of the time, pausing for effect only when he wanted a particular answer to sink into the jury's memory, or to cause the witness to squirm a bit as he reflected. Speed in a cross-examination of this sort translates into a form of pressure; it attempts to force the truthful and accurate answer in the witness's subconscious to pop out despite his conscious efforts to fashion answers that will better protect his stand on the issues.

3. *Memory:* From the sequence of questions, and except for the moments when the cross-examiner was handing a document or photo to the witness, it is plain that he had memorized some essential data before he went to work. He had been to the scene of the robbery, and had a mental picture of its surroundings. He was familiar with the room where the lineup identification was made and with its lighting.

   This was not a burdensome amount of data to learn and keep on file—nowhere near what would be required if Vaughn had been an expert witness testifying on a complex subject. It was not difficult material to handle, and the fact that the cross-examiner had in mind all of these facts—the ones embodied in his questions—creates further pressure on the witness to force out truthful and accurate answers.

4. *Precise articulation:* Pick a few of the questions at random and examine them. Did they zero in on a specific point each time? Were they clear and unambiguous to the point where the witness should be expected to understand them? Were they structured in such a way that a reasonable jury would feel that they deserved to be answered directly? Were they narrow and yet complete enough so that Vaughn's efforts to duck, feint, argue, and occasionally block were obvious to one truly paying attention? Was the language *simple* enough to seem forthright and direct?

I will leave it for you to decide, for it may be that your own habits and pattern of communication have a different style and verbiage, one that will work fine for you. All of these questions could have been put in different ways and yet have been quite acceptable. Think how *you* might have phrased the same thoughts, and see whether your choice of words squares with the criteria set forth above. It is important to develop your own habits in this respect as early in your career as you can, for then you will have a base to build upon.

5. *Logic:* Were the demands on Mr. Vaughn by the questions put to him made in a *logical* pursuit of facts and details that a conscientious jury ought to want to know? Were the questions relevant and pertinent? As you read them, were they the sort of questions that made you want to know the answers? Were the lines of inquiry legitimately directed to matters helpful in deciding if Vaughn should be believed? Were the contradictions explored handled in a logical sequence? If you find that each answer to the above questions is in the affirmative, then the cross-examination passes muster in the logic column. If you feel a no is warranted to any of them, let your criticism be constructive. Try to fashion better questions, eliminating the features you find objectionable.

No cross-examination is ever perfect or close to it, for there is no clear right or wrong as in mathematics. The foregoing is how I would have handled Mr. Vaughn if I had been confronted with his testimony. If you are sufficiently involved at this point that you are interested in refining any of the techniques and methods you have seen in this demonstration, then read on; it shows you have the *motivation,* at least, to be a good trial lawyer.

6. *Timing:* In order to judge whether good timing was used in handling Mr. Vaughn, go over the cross-examination section by section. Each time a new topic is raised, or a shift of scene takes place, the prior section is ended and a new one begun. Again, without having seen the exchange between witness and cross-examiner take place before your eyes, there are many details of timing that cannot be

gleaned from the printed page. Still, you will be able to note how Vaughn was led to a point, then faced with the obvious consequences of what he had just said, which entails a mixture of logic and timing. If in a given section you feel that the "pounce" came prematurely, or was too long delayed, ask yourself how it might have been done better.

7. *Manner:* Since you have not had access to the cross-examiner's demeanor or his stance vis-à-vis the witness, your ability to judge the manner he used is severely limited. What you can do is note the way questions were asked, and the words selected to ask them. You ought to perceive a manner that was polite but firm. You should note the absence of sarcasm or derisive language, which seldom have a place in the cross-examination of a witness other than one who is obviously despicable, and who is being challenged as an outright liar. Ask yourself to what extent the cross-examiner's manner kept the witness in good control, without offending anyone in the process.

8. *Termination:* This cross-examination was concluded after it was pointed out to Vaughn that process of elimination would have led him inexorably to Daniels because of the structure of the lineup, quite independently of any memory he may have had of Daniels's face. That not only was the logical conclusion of the sequence of events that were explored on cross-examination, but had Vaughn at his weakest. The best possible time to leave a witness stewing in his own juices on the witness stand is when he is weakest.

Testing this exercise against our second checklist—the human functions that cross-examination is designed to explore—we find that most of the emphasis fell to the first two: perception and memory. The witness experienced little difficulty in articulating his assertions, although he did not answer some questions responsively. We made no effort to attack his candor, since we were not trying to show that he was lying. He obviously had been robbed by someone, and his misidentification of Daniels—if it was one—was a mistake emanating in part from incautious police procedures. Any accusation that he was deliberately lying, rather than mistaken, about Daniels's participation in the robbery, would be very dangerous to make unless clear proof were available. Juries don't like to see innocent victims insulted simply because it is their misfortune to have to face cross-examination, particularly when, as here, there is bound to be an underlying sympathy for, and probably identification with, the witness.

We did probe very thoroughly his original opportunity to observe his assailant, and all of the obstacles that may have interfered with, obstructed, or distorted that perception. We discussed with him the lighting conditions, the very brief time available, and his frightened state of mind. We then touched on, in a more subtle fashion, his inability to carry a strange face, intact, in his memory bank for a few days even if he *had* had a clear perception to begin with. In both areas we made inroads, directly or indirectly, and that's what we set out to do.

At the risk of trying to sell you another book of mine, I will suggest that *The Defense Never Rests* (Stein and Day, 1971, Signet, 1972; a revised edition may be out by the time you read this) contains a number of examples of live cross-examinations, as well as some other observations that other lawyers have told me they found helpful when they were trying to understand the nature of the business. Studying the efforts recounted there and testing them against the principles we have discussed here might be a useful exercise for you. The same may be said of books written by other trial lawyers about their trials.

To illustrate the wisdom of keeping your eyes open when a trial is under way, I will reproduce one small segment from that book, from a chapter called "The Grandest Haul of All." It relates to the trial of the defendants in the so-called Great Plymouth Mail Robbery of August 1962. The trial took place more than five years later, and the government's evidence consisted entirely of a number of identifying witnesses. There were no statements by the defendants to link them to the crime, and there was no physical evidence whatsoever. One of the identifying witnesses was William Fitzgerald, who thought he had seen my client, John Kelley, near the U.S. Post Office truck containing over a million and a half dollars after it had been taken at gunpoint. The other two names that appear in the text are those of Paul Markham, who was prosecuting, and Luther Finerfrock, the chief postal investigator who was sitting in with Markham at the prosecution's table:

> The government witness, William Fitzgerald, an investigator for U.S. Civil Service Commission, claimed to have passed the moving mail truck after it had been commandeered. As he went by the truck, Fitzgerald glanced at the driver.
>
> Fitzgerald's testimony during direct examination focused on a description of the driver. When the prosecution had trouble getting responsive answers, Judge Wyzanski tried to help. Fitzgerald said the most distinctive feature he recalled was a large nose, and the judge asked him to describe it. When there was no definite answer, Judge Wyzanski asked him to draw it on a blackboard. Fitzgerald tried but wasn't much of an artist. Finally, the judge suggested that he try to find a comparable nose in the courtroom.
>
> Fitzgerald's gaze paused briefly on several people including Kelley, and finally stopped. "Mr. Markham," he said. "The nose looked like Mr. Markham's!"
>
> Soon after, when we recessed for the day, I noticed Fitzgerald writing on a piece of paper, which he put in his pocket as he left the stand.
>
> The next morning Fitzgerald continued his direct testimony. Despite the fact that he was a federal investigator in his own right, he had made no report in the immediate wake of the robbery. But a few days later, he was in an elevator in the Federal Building when a man entered from the fifth floor, where postal inspectors had their offices. Fitzgerald ascertained that the man was an inspector, gave his name, and said he was a witness to the Plymouth mail robbery. He was told he would be contacted.
>
> Almost two years passed. In June, 1964, he happened to be in the postal inspection service office and once again mentioned that he had seen part of the robbery. Shortly thereafter, he identified Kelley as the driver of the truck.
>
> Now, when Fitzgerald pointed at Jack and said, "That's the man I saw driving," I couldn't wait to start cross-examining.
>
> First I asked him why he hadn't reported his information immediately. He said he was too busy working on an investigation of his own.
>
> "I wonder," I said, "if you could describe for the jury the case that you had to investigate on your own, whose priority was such that in your own mind it supervened the importance of the largest cash robbery in the history of the United States of America."

Fitzgerald said he had been making a background investigation of a woman who had applied for the Peace Corps.

Next I asked him if he had been jotting down notes the day before. He nodded.

"Let me see the notes, please."

Fitzgerald pulled a slip of paper out of his pocket, glanced at it, and started to put it back. "I tore up yesterday's notes," he said. "These are some I made last night." Politely, I snatched them out of his hands.

"I see that at the top of this sheet you have noted the names and dates of birth of your daughters. Is that correct?"

He nodded.

"I take it that as you sat at home last night, you considered the possibility that I might cross-examine you this morning?"

"I knew you would."

"And you felt that as part of that cross-examination, I might try to demonstrate defects in your memory, right?"

Yes, he said, the thought had crossed his mind.

"And in order to guard against such a demonstration you put to paper here the names of your own daughters, in order to have a reminder in the event you should forget those names while being questioned? Is that correct?"

Unhappily, Fitzgerald said that it was. The gallery began to giggle.

"And here further down on the sheet I see you have suggested to yourself, 'Always say, to the best of my recollection.' Did you write that?"

"Oh yes, but that was because the judge here pressed me very hard when he was questioning me yesterday and I said some things I didn't really mean to say."

"I see. You were 'pressed.' Do you usually make notes to yourself under circumstances such as these?"

"Yes," he said enthusiastically. "I think it's always better to write things down."

"Indeed. I shall ask you at the conclusion of this cross-examination if you are still of the same mind."

Fitzgerald stared at the sheet of paper, and then at me. "I'm already sorry," he said. He was a man you had to like.

Nodding toward the chief prosecutor, I said, "Mr. Markham, before I put the next question, I wonder if you would be good enough to stand for a moment here before the witness box?"

Paul complied, and I went on. "Now then, would Inspector Luther Finerfrock come forward and stand next to Mr. Markham?"

Postal Inspector Finerfrock stepped up. He was a tall, gaunt, red-haired man with a generous nose.

"Now then, Mr. Fitzgerald," I said. "I seem to recall that yesterday when asked by Judge Wyzanski to point to a nose in the courtroom similar to the one you had seen on the night of the robbery, you pointed to Mr. Markham. Isn't that true?"

Fitzgerald agreed.

"And didn't you last night," I thundered, "didn't you last night write a note here, on this very piece of paper, which reads, 'Change the nose to Luther'?"

Under normal circumstances, Judge Wyzanski would never have countenanced the riot of laughter that roared back and forth across that room. But these were not normal circumstances. Judge Wyzanski had all he could do to keep from laughing himself.

I wasn't as successful as the judge.

No matter how much you learn about cross-examination, don't ever let slide an opportunity to learn more. As I have said before, if you can truly master this skill, you will stand out in the legal profession. I have tried no more with this chapter than to point you in the right direction.

12

Arguing to a Judge or Jury

T he crowning duty of a trial lawyer comes at the end of the trial, when the evidence is closed. In a few jurisdictions, the trial judge gives the jury their legal instructions before the arguments of counsel, but in the vast majority the instructions, or "charge," come last. In federal court and in many states, the party with the burden of proof—the risk of non-persuasion, remember?—is allowed to open and close the final argument, while the party defending is sandwiched in between. Under this system the closing portion by the party who opens is restricted to a rebuttal of the defender's argument; thus, if the defender chooses not to argue at all, there is nothing to rebut and the arguments are over. This, however, is rare.

In other jurisdictions, each side gets only one address to the court or jury. With a few exceptions the party with the burden gets the last (or second) word. In Minnesota, a defendant in a criminal case is permitted to argue last. Legally, Minnesota is a progressive state and is often at the head of the pack. Its rule, from an individual's point of view, is the best.

A trial lawyer's final argument—or *summation,* as it is often called—is his final opportunity to persuade a judge or jury that his claims are good ones and ought to be satisfied. Close cases are often won by effective argument, and there are very few where argument is pointless. Indeed, even when you know that the evidence has rendered your position hopeless, your client may be greatly disturbed if you say nothing at all in his behalf.

Assuming that you have taken the advice given earlier, you will have a fluent and polished ability to speak, and a sharp memory; this is the time when you bring all of your faculties to bear, to ring down the final curtain your way when you have finished your task: *to persuade!* If you have completed your earlier chores with skill and professionalism, you have but this final step to the title of advocate. Like every other phase of a trial, your summation should be carefully planned and thought through before you speak the first word.

Once again, it is time to back off—this time from the whole case. Recall the opening statements of counsel, those "promissory notes" that were given to the jury. Whose promises have been paid off with evidence, and whose are in default? No matter how well prepared a trial lawyer may be, no case goes exactly as expected, and there are variances to account for in nearly every final argument. Look at the pleadings—the complaint (or indictment) and the answer. Here is what was originally alleged; how much of his case has your opponent "proved?" Where are his weak spots, and where are yours?

Put on your neutral's hat for a moment, difficult though it may be. Suppose you were a judge or a special master (substitute judge) who had heard all of the claims and all of the evidence, and were about to decide the matter. How does the evidence look, from an overview? Which of the witnesses is solidly believable, and which is on shaky ground regarding portions of his testimony? Where does the circumstantial evidence seem to point? What about the equities on each side of the case?

In which direction does the weathervane of justice seem to be pointing?

If you can answer these questions objectively, you will have some idea of where you need to devote your final efforts. Unless the trial has been short, you cannot reasonably cover all of the evidence. You must recognize the high and strong points on both sides, and be prepared to deal with them. If there is one in the case, you must sort out and recognize the jugular vein, the Achilles' heel, the "zinger." These things cannot be overlooked, nor can they be ducked. The jury will want to hear what you have to say about them.

In a good final argument, there is emotion: I do not mean histrionics, but emotion. If the case has gotten to this stage and is yet unresolved, the parties have a lot to lose should the verdict be adverse. Some emotion is appropriate, provided it fits the circumstances. Emoting for its own sake will not win much, and may be counterproductive. But an affect that takes into account what the party you represent ought to be *feeling* at this stage of the case if he is a healthy, reasonable, decent, but anxious person will serve the argument well, provided you don't let it get out of hand. Remember, jurors are people too, and they have feelings. If you can strike a responsive chord in one or more of the jurors as you present your case to them for the last time, those jurors will *want* to see things through your eyes if conscience will permit.

Analyze the structure that has been built during the trial. If you are carrying the burden, ask whether or not you have built a building of sufficient soundness that a fair person ought to find it both stout and trustworthy? If you are defending against the burden, ask yourself the same question about your opponent's presentation. If it looks pretty sound, you have your work cut out for you.

There are many, many ways to give a good final argument. I have heard a number that vary sharply from my own style, and were excellent. Adopt a style of your own, one that is pleasing to listen to and that fits your personality. As long as you keep an eye on the basic ingredients that *every* final argument must have, any style that is effective will be acceptable.

I like to begin with a reminder that this will be my final opportunity to speak for my client, who cannot speak for himself any more than he could operate on his own gall bladder, and to ask politely for the jurors' close attention. I then like to review all of the promises made at the outset of the case, including those of the jurors during the voir dire examinations. Most important, of course, are the promises of counsel in their openings, or in any representations to the court that have been made during the trial.

Once this is done, it is helpful in most cases to remind the jury of the basic rules of the game. In a criminal case these always include the presumption of innocence, the burden of proof, and the concept of "proof beyond a reasonable doubt." It makes no difference which side of the case you may have; these basic ground rules should be discussed even though they may represent obstacles. Should you attempt to slide by them too lightly, your opponent will have a lot to say about them. Furthermore, the judge is going to instruct very carefully on these principles, and if you have ignored them while your opponent has emphasized them, it may seem to the jury that the judge is agreeing with your opponent! That you do not want.

Next, turn directly to the burden of proof and whether it has been met. Explain to the jurors that they will soon be called upon to answer that precise question, and that you would like an opportunity to point out some of the many things that they ought to consider before reaching a decision. This is the point at which you review the evidence in the light most favorable to your client, reminding the jury of what the witnesses have testified to, and suggesting which parts of each witness's testimony ought to be accepted or rejected, and why. In this phase of final argument you must rely on a combination of logic and your ability to fashion phrases that make your suggestions attractive. Almost all the devices of legitimate persuasion, from rhetorical questions to firm assertions, can be called upon, and should be.

If you size up your jurors (or the strongest of them, at least) to be people of good intelligence and sophistication, you may wish to draw heavily on understatement to accomplish your purpose. It is almost always better to induce your jury to discover the truth as you see it, rather than to leave them feeling as if you have tried to ram it down their throats. Our much-respected cousins across the Atlantic, the barristers of England, are masters of this technique, which is no surprise since Englishmen dearly love understatement. Having lectured back-to-back with a few of them, I find their command of the language both astonishing and a delight to behold. During one such encounter, a barrister and I contrived an example to illustrate the difference in approach between American and British advocates. It goes this way:

A man named Williams was arrested for a murder three weeks after it occurred, and while he loudly protested his total innocence in the matter, he was unable to furnish any information on his whereabouts that might have constituted an alibi. The case is over, and Williams testified to just this state of affairs. The prosecutor is giving his final address to the jury.

"You must *know* that Williams is a liar," thunders the American, banging his fist on the rail of the jury box. "You cannot believe that a man would be unable to come up with *any* information as to where he was just twenty-one days before he is confronted with the most serious problem of his lifetime, and therefore you cannot believe Williams!"

"I suggest to you, ladies and gentlemen," says the Englishman in firm but even tones, "that you may think it *strange* that Mr. Williams is unable to account for his whereabouts on the night of the murder. Like all reasonable people, you may find his story very difficult to accept."

Two different ways of doing the same thing, you may say, and you are quite correct. But, if you have some gray matter in the jury box, take my advice: Go English. People of intelligence do not enjoy a speaker who seems to be forever declaring the obvious. If you can lead the jurors to their *own* conclusions on what significance ought to be attached to a given piece of evidence, chances are those conclusions will take deeper root than if you serve them up and merely try to sell them.

There is a good deal of *discipline* involved in the proper functioning of jurors, because they are frequently called upon to follow rules that individually they do not like. You will recall that one of our proposed voir dire questions in a criminal case involved asking the jurors at a time whether or not each would be able, if the need arose, to vote "not guilty" because of a lingering "reasonable doubt," even though on the evidence it seemed clear that the defendant was "probably" guilty. No juror likes to do this, for when a probability of guilt appears, there is an impulse to so label the culprit and send him to his punishment. If the rules prohibit doing what impulse demands, it takes a disciplined mind to abide by them. This is one of many reasons why military juries are more apt to come out with accurate verdicts; for, in addition to being generally better educated and more intelligent than the average civilian jury, they are creatures of discipline; they are in the *habit of obeying* orders and instructions without challenging, questioning, or defying them.

Where you are dealing with a case that has received attention in the news media, there is always the risk that a juror may have heard some information that did *not* come into evidence. The possibility that this information will creep into the verdict is a legitimate concern, particularly where prejudicial but inadmissible facts have appeared in print. Near the beginning of the argument it is important to emphasize that the deliberations *must* be limited to those facts that came out in open court, and only those facts. You may mention that the trial judge in his instructions will cover this principle carefully, and that they must abide by this important rule.

Because the impressions of most laymen come from sources that ignore the realities of a trial, the expectations of most jurors exceed what is delivered to them. They expect the controversy to be solved before their very eyes, Perry Mason-style. They anticipate that by the time the evidence is closed the truth will be lying before them, in a form easily discerned. Since most trials never reach this point, the jurors are apt to be disappointed, frustrated, and sometimes even angry. They think that more witnesses should have been called, or that important questions were not put to the witnesses who did appear. Once again, the military jury is better off, because military juries can call witnesses of their own, and can submit questions to witnesses if they believe that counsel, either deliberately or through oversight, have failed to cover a point of interest adequately.

To combat this problem, it is good practice to remind the jurors that they were not impaneled to decide what really happened, or to fill in gaps in the evidence with speculation. They were sworn to answer only one question: Has the party bearing the burden of proof satisfied that burden, or has he failed to prove some essential element of his case? If he has carried his burden, he is entitled to a verdict; if not, the defense *must* prevail.

As with many other aspects of trial law, it is easier to convey the fundamentals of argument through example than by abstract description. Therefore, to illustrate some of these principles, let's use the remainder of this chapter to fashion a defense closing argument for the case from our last chapter, which we'll call *State* vs. *Daniels*. We will assume that in this jurisdiction each side gets only one opportunity to speak, and that the defense goes first. Therefore, the task of offering rebuttal to what the prosecutor—we'll call him Perkins—might have said if the case were in federal court will be omitted. In addition, because we are using the written word to illustrate the spoken word, much of the paraphrasing and redundancy that would appear in a stenographer's transcript of an actual oral argument will also be omitted—in other words, each idea will be touched only once. Assume also that one of the women on the jury has been designated as the foreperson.

Madam Foreperson, ladies and gentlemen, this is the moment for me to address you for the last time—it will be my final opportunity to speak for my client, Mr. Daniels, who is powerless to speak for himself now, when his future is on the line. When I have concluded my remarks, Mr. Perkins, the prosecutor, will give you his views; then the judge will instruct you on the law you must apply to the facts you find to be true. There will then be dumped in your laps one of the most serious responsibilities that each of you, as an American citizen, has ever had to discharge. You will decide what happens to Mr. Daniels, and right or wrong, your judgment will be cast in stone.

Before I turn to the evidence in this case, and the lack of evidence, there are some preliminary matters of great importance that I must cover with you. I am an advocate, with a cause to protect. So is my learned opponent, Mr. Perkins. You and the judge are neutrals, with a solemn duty to be fair to both sides. I am confident that the judge will carry out his duty, for he is a trained professional, selected for the quality of his wisdom and experience. He has performed this function many times before. You, on the other hand, have been required to step out of your daily lives and come to this court to perform a function with which most of you are totally unfamiliar and inexperienced.

To ask you to make this sacrifice in the first place was an imposition, in a sense; to ask, no, even *demand* that you perform your service flawlessly is an even greater imposition, and yet we can demand no less. All of us who participate in trials on a regular basis—His Honor, his staff, Mr. Perkins, and myself—cannot avoid shuddering in our bones every time we turn a case over to a jury, for we know something frightening that you do not: If you should make a mistake, there is no way on earth to correct it. To most of you, this will come as a surprise, and yet it is the cold, naked truth.

You have probably noticed that throughout the trial, no one has uttered a sound except when our very able court reporter, Ms. Roberts here, has been seated at her stenograph. She has taken down literally every word that has been spoken by the court, the lawyers, the witnesses, and even the two questions about schedule that you, Madam Foreperson, asked of the judge. But when you go into your jury room to deliberate this case, Ms. Roberts will not be going with you. None of what you say will be recorded. If you reach a verdict we will learn only what that verdict is, not how you reached it. The law conclusively presumes that you remember all of the evidence that the record contains, that you have listened carefully to the arguments of counsel, that you heard and understood every word and every concept of the court's instructions on the law, and that you correctly applied that law to the facts you found to be true. The law so conclusively presumes all these things to be true that we are not even permitted to inquire into the process that led to the verdict.

What this means, ladies and gentlemen, is that any error you may commit, however inadvertently, becomes perpetual. I know that all of you have heard of appeals, and how appellate courts sometimes reverse a verdict, or order a new trial. You may have thought that this was a source of comfort to a jury, which is asked to shoulder the immense burden of making difficult decisions where the stakes are high. I'm sorry, but that is not the case. Appeals are for judges' mistakes, if there are any, not for yours. In short, should you make a mistake and convict Mr. Daniels of this crime, there can be no appeal.

Appellate courts work only from a written record of the proceedings, and a party claiming an error so serious that reversal, or a new trial, is warranted *must* be able to point to something on that record that constitutes an error by the judge. As to your function, there is no record, as I have warned you. If the judge has allowed evidence to come before you that should have been excluded, or kept from you some evidence that you should have been allowed to hear, or if any of the instructions he is about to give you are seriously incorrect, we may ask an appellate court for relief. There are lots of appeals in criminal cases, but few succeed. Please do not have any expectation that this trial judge has committed an error, or that he will. You are duty bound to assume that your decision will be final in every sense of the word, and that if you wrongly hang a conviction around Mr. Daniels's neck, he must wear it like a yoke for the rest of his life.

The law is not unaware of the risk in attaching such permanence to your decision, a permanence it has been unwilling to attach to decisions by the judge. It has provided a safeguard to ensure that should there be an error, it will fall against the party that can afford it best: the government. If you conscientiously and scrupulously follow the rules that you are about to be given by the court, that safeguard will be activated. Should you fail to understand or appreciate them, or choose to disregard *any* of them, then *you* will put Mr. Daniels in jeopardy in a way that the law has tried very hard to prevent.

Bear in mind as I speak to you that, even though I may discuss some legal principles with you, your instructions come from the court, not from me. Should you sense any variance between what I am telling you and what the court tells you, disregard my remarks or version of the rules. By the same token, should my recollection of the facts I discuss with you vary to any degree from your own recollection, be guided by what you remember. Now let me spend just a moment explaining the safeguard I have urged you so fervently to honor and follow.

This is a nation that was conceived in a love of liberty. Indeed, you will remember the words of Patrick Henry: "Give me liberty or give me death!" The law we use to protect our citizens from any loss of that liberty is strict, strong, and designed to accomplish that protection at all costs. The law itself shudders to think that we might rob the liberty of one who had done nothing to deserve such loss.

If this were a civil case, where only property were at stake, we would be willing to cut much closer to the edge in our efforts to do justice. We use a lower standard in such cases. I will attempt to illustrate. Imagine that my upturned hands at the end of my outstretched arms are the trays suspended from the scales of justice. If this were a dispute over property, the party having the burden of proof—Mr. Perkins, in this case—would only have to fill his tray with what we call a preponderance of the credible evidence—enough to tilt the scales slightly in his favor—and he would be entitled to your verdict. You might think of that as

51 percent of the evidence, or you might think of it as Mr. Perkins having shown you that his claims were *probably true*. But that standard is for property only. This is not a civil suit by Mr. Vaughn against Mr. Daniels for the value of his property. This is a criminal lawsuit by the state against Mr. Daniels in an effort to take his liberty away from him. Slightly tilted scales are too risky. The law has decided that much greater protection than that is necessary for Mr. Daniels.

The law has given Mr. Daniels the presumption of innocence to wear like a cloak throughout this trial. He is entitled to it. The indictment charging him with a crime is no threat to that presumption at all, unless it is backed by convincing, solid proof. The law has placed the burden of proof on Mr. Perkins's shoulders. Mr. Daniels may wear his cloak of innocence without proving anything, for he has no burden at all. Finally, the most important and ultimate protection built into our law to ensure that jury mistakes never fall against the individual is the *standard* of proof Mr. Perkins must meet: It is called proof beyond a reasonable doubt, and it is a very high standard indeed. His Honor in his charge will give you its proper legal definition.

My only concern in this case is that you fully comprehend, and understand, and apply this rule. If I dwell on the point a bit, please forgive me. When I am done, I am sure that you will understand and appreciate why this is my *only* concern.

Let's look at the scales of justice once again. What must Mr. Perkins load in his tray before he is entitled to a verdict that will take Mr. Daniels's liberty away from him? Fifty-one percent will never do, says the law; indeed, percentages will no longer work. What Mr. Perkins must do is stack so much credible evidence on his side of the scales that it tips down, down, down, just as my left hand is dipping down now, down so far that not even a doubt with a reason behind it is left in the lighter tray of the scales, my tray, Mr. Daniels's tray. That is what he must do. Only when he has done that is he entitled to ask for your vote of guilty. You and you alone must hold Mr. Perkins's feet to the fire on that point, and if he has failed, you must tell him so.

To put the matter another way, since the term "beyond a reasonable doubt" is not one that you use or even think about in your everyday decisions, Mr. Perkins, through the quality of his evidence, must put each of your minds in a state where you are very, very sure—where you are utterly *convinced*—that Mr. Daniels and no other robbed Mr. Vaughn. You must be as thoroughly convinced as you would have to be in making a decision affecting *your* future the way this case will affect the future of Mr. Daniels.

Suppose now—each of you, please—that a physician told you that you had gangrene in the arm you write with, and that it would have to come off to save that gangrene from spreading and costing you not your arm but your life. People have lost their dominant arms and lived before, but none gave up easily. You would have to be convinced *beyond a reasonable doubt* by several opinions, not just one, that there were no other options before you would submit to amputation.

Suppose again—you, sir, an accomplished man with a good job and a family that has warm friends and deep roots in this community, as we learned on your examination by the judge and counsel—suppose you were offered a new job with a new company in a different city continents away, an opportunity that might improve your standard of living—or might fail. You would have to be convinced beyond a reasonable doubt that the risk was worth taking before you would quit your present job, lose your seniority and retirement rights, and deprive your family of their whole environment, would you not? Of course. The question each of you must now face is whether you would be willing to suffer amputation or total personal displacement based solely on the assurance of Mr. Vaughn that he can correctly recognize a stranger whom he saw in dim light during a few moments of personal terror.

The law does not provide for any judgment of innocence. That is never the question put to a jury. The law only wants to know whether twelve of its carefully selected citizens—carefully selected, as you were, by both sides and the court—are convinced *beyond a reasonable doubt* that another citizen has committed a criminal act against the state; the law asks you that and no more. It prohibits you expressly from asking: "Is this man guilty or innocent?" You may not ask that, nor are you permitted to answer it. You may only say: "I am, or I am not, so thoroughly convinced of this man's guilt that I have no reasonable doubt that he is guilty."

Let's turn for a moment to promises. We have made promises, all of us. The judge promised when he took office that he would treat those who appeared before him with fairness and impartiality, according to law. Mr. Perkins and I both promised you in our opening statements that the evidence would show certain things, and you are about to decide which if either of us has made good on those promises. But you made promises too, promises that I believed or you would not be sitting here now. I had challenges with which I could have removed any of you—without even giving a reason—that I did not use, because when you were questioned, Mr. Daniels and I believed your answers. We made a judgment that you were decent people, worthy of trust and belief. If we misjudged any of you, then the law itself is in trouble in this case.

Besides promising to be fair and impartial to both sides, you very specifically promised two additional things to Mr. Daniels. You promised that you were in a state of mind that was so impartial that you would be content to have *yourselves* as jurors if *you* were accused of robbing Mr. Vaughn. You also promised that even if you thought Mr. Daniels to be *probably* guilty, you would still vote "not guilty"—as the law commands you to do with all of the thunder it can muster—so long as you had any *reasonable doubt* as to that guilt. Madam Foreman and ladies and gentlemen, make good on your promises this day!

Let's turn to the evidence now, but not before I thank you for your attention to the remarks I have made so far. I know you are anxious to hear about the merits of the case, but it has been extremely important to my client—and to the law, which you serve—that you understand the framework within which you are to function. Without having discharged that duty—and it was my duty—my discussion of the evidence would make less sense than it should. You now know that I am concerned only with whether you have a reasonable doubt, and you know that as this burden of speaking for Mr. Daniels rides heavily on my conscience, I am praying that you *will not* make a mistake.

On the evidence you have heard, and under the rules the court is going to give you, no mistake should be possible. Mr. Perkins, although I respect him as a colleague and appreciate that he has been every inch a professional so far in this trial—conduct that I expect will continue—simply has not had enough solid, credible evidence to approach his burden, let alone carry it. His whole case is Mr. Vaughn, and while Mr. Vaughn is a decent fellow citizen who has been outrageously treated by *someone,* Mr. Vaughn simply cannot erase a reasonable doubt all by himself. We have sympathy for him, we have empathy for him, he did nothing to deserve what happened to him, but we cannot uproot our lives or cut off our writing arms on the bet that he has correctly identified the man who robbed him. We cannot have that much confidence in his assurances that he was not mistaken, and thus reach a point where *you* are mistaken, where Mr. Daniels must pay for your mistake for the rest of his life. Because, although it is not my place to discuss punishment with you—that is for the court and the court alone, in the calamitous event that you should somehow convict—all of you know that the crime here on trial is serious, and carries serious consequences with it.

Now then, let's go right to the guts of this prosecution—let's go down, as the great poet William Butler Yeats once said, to "the foul rag-and-bone shop of the heart." Let's get down to the realities of life and see what, if anything, has been proven beyond a reasonable doubt. In fairness, Mr. Perkins has shown to my satisfaction, and I suggest to yours as well, that Mr. Vaughn was robbed at gunpoint by *someone!*

A crime was committed, we all know that, and we need spend no further time discussing it. The sole question for you to decide is this: Are you convinced beyond any reasonable doubt that Mr. Daniels was the person who robbed Mr. Vaughn, or might it—just might it—have been someone else? After considering all of the evidence that you have to work with, which admittedly leaves a great deal to be desired, you ought to conclude not only that it *might* have been someone else, but that it *probably was.* In other words, even if this were a civil suit for money damages for the proceeds of the robbery, you ought to find that Mr. Vaughn, as entitled as he may be to relief at some point, has simply picked the wrong man!

Mr. Perkins is going to ask you, because he really has no choice since he has no corroborative evidence, to convict my client solely on the basis of the identification Mr. Vaughn claims to have made. In light of that, let's examine in detail Mr. Vaughn's performance both as a victim and as a witness. When we have finished, and no matter what Mr. Perkins tries to urge upon you in his summation—which will be a good one, because he is a very able lawyer—you will discover that you *cannot* convict Mr. Daniels, because *Mr. Vaughn himself has told you that you should not!* I know he didn't mean to tell you that, and probably doesn't realize that he did it—indeed I'm sure it was a subconscious act on his part—but he told you that nonetheless.

I heard him do it, and I know some of you heard him do it, because I glanced at the jury when it happened, and I know that at least some of you caught it. Perhaps all of you did. My glance was directed at only those sitting nearest the witness box. We will come to Mr. Vaughn's warning to the jury, inadvertent as it may have been, as we examine his testimony.

In order to evaluate Mr. Vaughn's credibility fairly, it is necessary to put yourselves in the position he was in on the night he was robbed. How would you have reacted? Would you not have been terribly frightened, facing a hostile man with a loaded pistol? Remember, Mr. Vaughn said he couldn't be sure whether it was loaded, because it was too dark to see the bullets in the cylinder. But he *never* suggested that he thought it was *not* loaded, did he? You can be very sure that he *assumed* it was loaded, and felt the terror any of us would feel when looking at the business end of a loaded pistol.

Now then, ask yourselves this question: If you were threatened in this fashion, would you calmly and coolly begin to take a physical inventory of the features of the one who was threatening your very life, or would your only priority be to give him what he wanted and get away from him? Mr. Vaughn felt just as any of you would have. He was loathe to admit the terror he felt when answering my questions on the point, but he did admit it anyway, again inadvertently: He told you that he was *still* so nervous when he was being interviewed for the first time by Inspector Inman that he may have omitted some details as to what the robber looked like. Therefore, you should be very guarded in accepting Mr. Vaughn's claim that he studied his assailant carefully enough to be able to recognize him positively now. You ought to have serious doubts about that.

Next, ask yourselves when, if ever, the victim of a street robbery will give his most accurate account of the event. It may not be very accurate at all, but it is the most accurate he will ever give. Naturally, he will give it to the first person who questions him, while the whole matter is fresh in his mind. Unless he is in a state of shock—and we know from the testimony of Inspector Inman that Mr. Vaughn was not *that* rattled—this is the best information he can ever give, uncorrupted by the power of suggestion from any external source, such as a book of photos or a lineup.

Who, then, is the man who robbed Mr. Vaughn? Well, we know *something* about him from what Mr. Vaughn initially told Inspector Inman less than fifteen minutes after the most terrifying few seconds of his entire life. He was a male, about Mr. Vaughn's own height, not two inches taller like Mr. Daniels. He was in his mid-thirties, not forty-two, like Mr. Daniels. He was about the same build as Mr. Vaughn, not slender like Mr. Daniels. He had a fair complexion with no marks or scars, no pockmark scars such as my client has. His features were regular with nothing unusual about them; Mr. Daniels has a prominent, curved line to his nose that is quite distinctive and would have been noticed if he had been present at the scene. The robber, for all we know, may have had brown eyes. Mr. Daniels's eyes are clearly blue. Mr. Daniels has a distinctive bass voice; if the robber spoke, Mr. Vaughn has no memory of it, according to his testimony on direct examination. I suggest to you that the robber probably said *something* that night, which Mr. Vaughn was too terror-struck to record in his memory. Mr. Vaughn cannot recognize my client's voice, or even tell you that it is similar to that of the man who robbed him.

On one point and one point only, ladies and gentlemen, is there any similarity at all between my client and the robber: thinning brown hair. That's all there is. And we can't really rely on that, can we, for when questioned closely on that point Mr. Vaughn admitted that the top of the head was in the shadow of the visor of the robber's cap, and all he really got was an "impression" that the hair was thinning and brown. An impression, I suggest, is a long way from a clear memory of something that was actually seen.

When you go to your deliberations, ladies and gentlemen, you will have with you defense exhibit C, Mr. Vaughn's original statement. Please carry with you the clearest picture you can of the details of my client's appearance. As you read through this statement, you will realize that Mr. Daniels doesn't fit at all the description given only minutes after the event, but is different in almost every respect. Mr. Perkins is going to have to ask you to convict on the frail notion that Daniels's being a male with thinning brown hair is enough to erase all reasonable doubt in the mind of a fair person. I will listen with great interest, as I know you will, to his explanation of how you might go about doing that.

But if Mr. Daniels did *not* rob Mr. Vaughn that night, what is he doing here, you may ask. How did Mr. Vaughn make a mistake about such a serious matter, and pick out my client? If you review the process which caused that to happen—and I do mean *caused* that to happen—it becomes quite clear why it happened.

Mr. Vaughn was given three books, and he hoped from the beginning that in one of them he would find the man who robbed him. He was angry and wanted the culprit caught and punished, which is quite understandable. Any of us might have felt the same way. When he came to the third book without having recognized anyone, Mr. Vaughn subconsciously thought that this was his last chance. If he failed to recognize anyone in this, the last book, there might be little more that the police could do. He wanted to find *someone* in that book who could be blamed. He knew that the people in that book had been in trouble with the law, and that's

why their photos were there. He felt—again, subconsciously—
that they were second-class citizens, and that putting any of
them in jail would probably be a good idea on general principles.

My client's picture was in that book because of a horrible accident, a mistake he will agonize about for the rest of his life. He
committed no malicious act of criminal intent, as had many of
the other faces in that book. He pleaded guilty to *involuntary*
manslaughter, meaning that his act was unintentional.

Mr. Vaughn was running out of opportunities. He picked a
face with thinning brown hair, even though nothing else would
fit the description he had given Inspector Inman. He said he
could not be sure, that he would need to see the whole person, but
that there was a similarity.

What happened next should never have happened. I do not
like to fault Inspector Inman, for I have known him for many
years. I like him personally, and respect him professionally. I believe him to be an honest law enforcement officer. And by reading the newspapers on a daily basis, which are full of street
crimes of every description, I know that he is overworked. But the
lineup he sent Mr. Vaughn to that night was anything but fair. I
do not suggest that it was assembled maliciously, for the purpose
of hurting Mr. Daniels, but I must complain to you that it was
assembled thoughtlessly, in such a fashion as made the selection
of Mr. Daniels inevitable.

There were, we know, six choices. We also know that Mr.
Daniels's face was fresh in Mr. Vaughn's mind, more fresh, probably, than the face of the man who had robbed him. We also know
that four of the six men wore blue shirts, which in a police station
especially is a strong suggestion that they are policemen. That left
two choices. Of these, one was quickly eliminated in Mr. Vaughn's
mind, because he had a full head of hair. That left Mr. Daniels.

Mr. Vaughn has told you that he recognized Mr. Daniels then
and there as the man who robbed him. He did not. What he should
have told you, in fairness, was that Mr. Daniels looked more like
the robber than anyone else in the lineup, and no more. That is
all he really determined that day. And that is a lot less than
Mr. Perkins promised you during his opening statement in this
case.

This, then, is how Mr. Daniels happens to be before you.
Where was he that night? He was doing exactly what many of you
were: sitting in his home watching television. Were you the victim
of the kind of mistake that has caused Mr. Daniels all this pain,
you could do no more to prove your innocence than he has done; by

showing that you were at home with your family. Mrs. Daniels has told you the same thing. Neither of them faltered at all on cross-examination. Street crimes occur at night, when innocent people are with those they love, those who are biased witnesses. I wish that Mr. Daniels had been entertaining the chief of police or a distinguished judge, but he wasn't, and neither were any of you. He has given you all that he honestly can, all that most of you would be able to give under similar circumstances. Throughout this case, his conduct has been consistent with innocence. He cooperated with the police in every respect. He declined the services of an attorney, because he thought, as many of you probably do, that you don't need a lawyer unless you've done something. He could not believe that the government would prosecute an innocent person, something you may have thought also before you saw and heard this case. He was wrong. No self-respecting lawyer would have ever willingly permitted a client to stand in the hopeless lineup that Inspector Inman put together that day, and he *should* have asked for an attorney. But he didn't, and you ought to accept that as a signal that he believed he had nothing to fear.

Now, I told you some moments ago that Mr. Vaughn sent you a signal, warning you not to convict on his testimony alone. We will discuss that now.

When Mr. Vaughn testified on direct examination, he pointed dramatically to my client and said, "That's the man." He was unequivocal. He started off the same way on cross-examination, pretending to be positive beyond the possibility of mistake.

When I pointed out to Mr. Vaughn that at the lineup he quite naturally *eliminated* everyone but my client for one reason or another, his response was this, and again I have it verbatim. He said, "I'm *pretty sure* that he's the one who robbed me." He told you he was "pretty sure." That was his signal, his admission that he is not positive. If Mr. Vaughn is only "pretty sure," how in the world can you ever be asked to be *completely* sure, with no reasonable doubt remaining? I respectfully suggest to you, ladies and gentlemen, that underneath all of the controversy Mr. Vaughn is a decent man, who suddenly realized that he had doubts. And he telegraphed those doubts to you then and there.

If he is only "pretty sure" about Mr. Daniels, he is a poor bet. Don't *bet,* ladies and gentlemen, you have no authority to do that. Just come back and tell us, with your verdict, whether or not, on all the evidence you have, there remains a reasonable doubt.

Yours is a heavy burden. Mistakes that you make cannot be corrected by any system or device available to us. They are final and permanent. If you think you might make a mistake, you must vote against the state, for that is the law's command. The law has placed Mr. Daniels's future in your hands, but it does not want you to take any chances with it.

Know as you go to your jury room, after Mr. Perkins has spoken and the judge has charged you with the law of the case, that if you recognize and report the reasonable doubt that is everywhere in this evidence, and release Mr. Daniels, when *you* are released from service in this case, and walk through that door at the back of the courtroom, justice will be walking with you. If you convict Mr. Daniels in spite of all the doubt you must feel, justice will have died in your hands this day.

Are you thinking, perhaps, that no jury would ever convict on such slender evidence? I wish you were correct. But they can, and they have. I have seen it happen on worse evidence, and watched my clients go to jail for crimes they didn't commit. Since this jury is a figment of our imaginations, yours and mine, we will never know how they would have voted. Daniels, if he was in fact innocent, paid a horrible price simply by being accused and having to stand trial. You will never know the agonies of waiting out a jury verdict until you do it with a real client hanging on the balance. Your only consolation during this anxious time, once you have taken good measure of yourself as a trial lawyer, will be the knowledge that you did your very best, and that your competence is such that with your very best, on this evidence, your client deserves to win.

If you come back to this chapter at a later time, and dissect what the jury was told in our model argument using the principles outlined earlier, you ought to find the essential ingredients. This was no perfect final argument, to be sure. It is simply the way I would have given it had the responsibility been mine. I hope the day will come when *you* can do it better.

13

What Appeals
Are All About

T his is a short chapter, for a very good reason: The law school you attend, if it is accredited, will do a very good job of teaching you appellate procedure. Indeed, most of what you learn will come from written and reported opinions of appellate courts, because virtually all law schools use the case method of education—the study of actual, decided cases that in one way or another have helped to define the law.

Because I am writing this book principally to discuss topics *not* adequately covered in the average law school curriculum, I will not go far into this one. But, so you will be familiar with them, I will discuss briefly the structure of appellate courts and their powers; and I will say a few words about the "advocacy" of appellate practice. For although quite a number of trial lawyers have no great interest in appellate work, and farm out cases on appeal, a lot of us like to handle our own, to carry the ball ourselves as far as it will go. I hope you decide to join the latter group. Even though there is no jury present, and the tone of the proceedings is quite different from that of a trial, appellate practice remains both exciting and rewarding. A trial result affects only the parties to the trial, but an appellate result affects everyone in the jurisdiction of that appellate court.

As our final argument in the Daniels case stressed, appellate judges exist only to say whether the court "below" (as it is often called) has made an error serious enough to upset the result. In all but the smallest states, and in the federal government, the appellate system is two-tiered. If either of the parties to a trial appeals the verdict, that party must file a notice of appeals in the trial court. This automatically removes the case to the lower or "intermediate" appellate court. In a federal case, for instance, the case would move from the United States District Court (the trial court) to the United States Court of Appeals in one of eleven "circuits" or regions.

The party appealing—generally the loser below, although in some cases neither party is happy with the trial result and both appeal, each asking for different kinds of relief—is called upon to file a brief, describing the case, the issues, the facts, and the arguments in support of the relief claimed—usually a reversal of the judgment or an order requiring a new trial. The other party is allowed to file his own brief in answer, and usually the first party is then allowed to file a reply brief rebutting to the opponent's answer. This is somewhat like the "open" and "close" privileges afforded the party with the burden of proof at the trial level in federal court.

When all briefs are filed, a date is set for oral argument. Some lawyers merely stand at the podium and read their briefs, or paraphrase them closely, which renders no service to the court or their clients. Oral argument is a time to give a very brief capsule of the case, to tear apart the opponent's reasoning and the cases he cited in his brief, to press your strongest points with some rhetorical flourishes, and to answer challenges from the bench about the soundness of your contentions. Appellate judges can read, and you needn't read to them. Instead, be an advocate, and persuade, persuade, persuade. Be cogent, make sure your arguments make good logical and philosophical sense, and *always* give responsive answers to questions from the court. Nothing upsets appellate judges more than a lawyer who ducks a straight answer to a simple question.

On my several visits to the United States Supreme Court—an experience, by the way, every bit as exciting and awesome as it's cracked up to be—I always enjoyed questions by Chief Justice Earl Warren. While his more scholarly colleagues pressed the technical points of an appeal, the chief justice asked simple but unexpected basic questions that often left the lawyers gaping and speechless. More than once I saw him stun a prosecutor by asking him: "I understand the legal point of your argument, but do you think what you're asking is really *fair?*" Usually, instead of an answer, he got a quizzical look back that said: "Fair? What's that got to do with anything?"

After the intermediate court has decided the case, the losing party has a right to *ask* that the case be heard by the highest court. Most of the time he will be told no. The highest court in a jurisdiction—known usually as "the court of last resort"—takes only those cases that it chooses to hear. It selects these generally because the decision will have broad application to a number of people, or because two different lower courts have come to divergent judgments on the same question, and the conflict needs to be resolved.

In a few cases, the intermediate appellate court is skipped, and the parties go directly to the highest court. A conviction for murder in the first degree, for instance, may in many states be appealed directly to the court of last resort. In federal court, if a United States district judge declares a federal statute to be unconstitutional and thus void, a direct appeal to the United States Supreme Court normally follows. When a single federal judge strikes down a law passed by Congress and ratified by the President, swift action to determine whether he acted correctly—or whether the law may remain in force because it is not unconstitutional after all—is clearly in the public interest.

You may be given the impression in law school that the law is the law, and that appellate courts are consistent in the way they interpret it. Not so. Times change, and judges change, and what was clearly the law ten years ago may no longer pass muster with those now in control of the court. For example, in 1936 the United

States Supreme Court decided that a man on trial for his life must be provided a lawyer to defend him. In 1942, the same court ruled that lawyers were *not* necessary to the defense of other kinds of crimes. In 1963, that same court said the 1942 decision was all wrong, and that everyone accused of serious crime must have a lawyer. How does this happen? Different times, different judges, that's how. In other words, don't ever get so complacent that, because the existing law is with you, you feel you cannot lose your case. You can. And the higher the court you are dealing with, the more likely it is that the precedent you have relied upon will be shattered, and that the pendulum will swing the other way.

Where does this happen most often? Which judges are most likely to change earlier decisions by the same court? Why, in the United States Supreme Court, of course, the highest court of all!

14

Computers and Their Use in the Law

W hen I wrote this book in 1981, it was my first on a personal computer; the four written before it were done on my trusty IBM Selectric typewriter, now a dinosaur of the past. Although it was apparent that the magical word-processing program had rendered the typewriter obsolete as a means of creating text, the extent to which computers in general would shrink in size and grow in capability was beyond the contemplation of all but a few visionaries like Bill Gates, founder of Microsoft, and now the richest man in America. I, proud as punch as I lugged my twenty-two-pound Osborne transportable (and later a series of Otronas) around the country, listening to the cacophony of its two 360k 5.25 disk drives grinding away almost every time I touched the keyboard, never foresaw just how invaluable computers would become to the trial of cases.

Confucius got it right many years ago when he opined that a picture was worth a thousand words, for he was talking about the transference of thoughts. As we discussed in Chapters 5 and 6, in a trial we are constantly trying to reach for the fidelity of reproduction attained routinely by motion picture photography, whether it be a strip of celluloid film, a videotape, or a magnetic (or CD-ROM) disk. The communication of thoughts through words is sadly lacking, because from the witness stand to the jury box the slippage and distortion is substantial. Just as a chain is no stronger than its weakest link, the transfer in question is no stronger than the poorest step in the process.

A witness is asked a question, which causes an image to be drawn from his memory, a picture of some scene or thing. In responding to the question, the witness will attempt to transfer the image into words through a process called *articulation*. These words are then transmitted to the jurors, who then try to reverse the process and *comprehend* these words in drawing a picture in their own minds. Ideally, the same picture that originated in the witness' mind will transfer intact to the minds of each of the twelve jurors. In reality, this almost never happens. Each juror will form a somewhat different image than his fellows, and none of them will precisely match what the witness is trying to describe.

For this reason, photographs and other graphics such as medical charts and illustrations depicting injuries have long been prized for their efficiency in bringing images to jurors' minds. We have previously touched on the principle that in dealing with the memory, *recognition* is much more effective than *recall*. Thus a witness to a complex automobile intersectional collision might struggle mightily and in vain to *recall* in words all of the details of the scene after both cars had come to rest; that same witness could easily *recognize* a photograph of that same scene, taken even as he was making his observations. Upon that declared recognition, the photograph becomes admissible and transfers the scene—intact, as it "really was"—to the mind of each juror.

The problem is, while we would all *like* to have photographs available to demonstrate each scene that is important to the presentation of our case, they are seldom available. The photo of the damaged cars at rest in our example is helpful, but not *nearly* as helpful as would have been a videotape of the accident itself, from a point where the cars were a hundred yards apart. Now, because of the rapid advancement of the CAD-CAM* computer software, it is rather commonplace to produce computer-animations of action taking place. These are figures and objects, drawn by engineers on the computer, in a sequence that will play back action in progress. The process is similar to what the police sketch artist does when the robbery victim describes the appearance of the robber. Little by little she draws from the victim's memory the details of what he thinks he saw, and forms an image on paper, adjusting each feature until he says that it is correct. Now the resulting sketch can be circulated, and the image in the victim's mind can be directly taken into the minds of those who are asked to be on the alert.

The CAD engineer does somewhat the same thing, but on a more elaborate basis. Like an expert witness, he will gather *all* of the available data pertaining to the event in question—eye-witness accounts, photos, sketches—and assimilate it. He will then construct an *animation* of the event. Once a draft is made, it will be reviewed by those who have contributed to it, and who may be asked to comment about its accuracy on the witness stand. Modifications will be made until a majority of the eyewit-nesses can agree on the depiction, and until it comports with "known" dimensions, such as the width of a street, the length of a car, the height of an individual, and any other "facts." The en-gineer then appears as an expert witness of sorts, showing the animation to the jury and explaining the bases upon which it is predicated. All of this presumes that the opposing side has had adequate notice of the animation, has reviewed it, and has pre-sented planning to enjoy the objections to the trial judge, who has ruled that all or part of the animation will be received in ev-idence. Animations recreating trauma—their prime function—can cost anywhere from a few thousand to nearly a million dollars, but often the cost is warranted. For example, in the early 1980s a Delta Air Lines' Lockheed 1011 Jumbo Jet crashed at the Dallas-Fort Worth Regional Airport in Texas. Delta, faced

* Computer-Aided Design and Computer-Aided Manufacturing.

with hundreds of millions in claims, sued the Federal Aviation Administration for negligence on the part of its Air Traffic Controllers, who, said Delta, should have recognized the "wind shear" phenomenon which actually downed the airplane, and issued a warning. At the trial,* the FAA produced a detailed animation recreating the accident, and won a favorable verdict. The trial judge later said that this animation was of substantial assistance to him in his role as the finder of fact in the case.

But there are many less costly uses for computers in litigation. In the preparation stages, dozens of programs exist for the archiving and management of incoming data; customizing programs of your own is easy enough. Computer Law Inc., a company I formed in 1986 to assist lawyers in using computers to help prepare and present their cases for and at trial, will examine the cases in question, tailor a program to permit secretaries and paralegals to input data either from the keyboard, use electronic scanning, or direct disk-to-disk transfer when the data is already in an electronic format. In this latter respect, it is of great importance to use court reporters in depositions who have either a magnetic tape or a computer disk drive built into their stenotype machines, so that transcripts of these depositions can be fed directly into an office computer program which will store and organize it.

Once this is done, the trial lawyer has a tremendous asset at hand: a quick "memory injection" to assist in recalling the evidence in the case. Until one actually begins to practice in the field of litigation, it is impossible to appreciate one of the most pervasive and frustrating difficulties in carrying on an orderly practice: scheduling! Life would be much easier if one could plan for, and get ready for a trial with some assurance that it would actually go off on the proposed date, but in forty years of trying cases, I have found this to be an unreal expectation—except in the military, where schedules are generally dependable.

There are simply too many things that can go wrong. First, and most prevalent, is the availability of the lawyers in the case. Not only is the commencement of a trial difficult to predict, but

* Held under the Federal Torts Claim Act before a federal judge with no jury; the government does not trust juries enough to permit them to decide cases brought against it.

its duration can usually only be approximated. The case of A vs. B is set for trial on Monday, February 21. On Friday, B's lawyer calls the A vs. B trial judge and informs her that the trial he is presently involved in will last another three days. Meanwhile, A has all of his witnesses under subpoena and is ready to go. But the A vs. B judge can't be expected to cool her heels for three days waiting for B's lawyer, so she calls another case, Y vs. Z. Because there is only one week left in the trial term, Y and Z did not expect to be reached for trial until the next term a month later, and thus are not ready. Given a last minute notice by the judge's clerk to be ready to select a jury first thing Monday, lawyers for Y and Z begin a crash program of preparedness, pushing aside plans for a weekend with the family, amid some not unreasonable grumbling.

I point up these discouraging—but very real—last-minute burdens not to drive good talent away from litigation, for in my view that talent is in much shorter supply than our court machinery needs and deserves. Instead, I am describing the way things *used to be* before the advent of the fast, sophisticated personal computers available today. For lawyers who will take the time to acquire good hardware and install and learn the proper software, tribulations such as those just described should smooth out considerably; indeed, there are actually some *advantages* to being forced into last minute preparation with a capable laptop at hand, assuming that the case has been thoroughly prepared and organized in the past.

Laptop computers weighing less than three pounds, but having the speed and power of a state-of-the-art office computer, are presently available, and are improving by leaps and bounds. During the past five years, my company upgraded to a new and improved laptop every six to nine months, so rapid is progress in this area. By doing this, we are able to stay at the vanguard of portable equipment, and thus be in a position to advise our clients which combination of cost and sophistication may suit their needs best.

The sheer capacity of these computers is mind-boggling. You can literally tuck many fileboxes of material into your briefcase, all on a hard disk whose capacity may range from two hundred to four hundred megabytes of storage. More important, you can ask the computer to tell you things about your case that no law clerk could ever tell you without hours of reviewing paper files.

Assume that Y is suing Z because of a motor vehicle accident
that occurred two years before. As their vehicles approached an
intersection, Z was to Y's right, but Z was confronted by a STOP
sign and Y was not. There were skid marks from which Y's pre-
accident speed can be calculated, and photos of the vehicles taken
after they came to rest and before they were moved, showing
damage to the front of Z's car and to Y's sedan in the area of the
right front door. Y suffered a broken arm, and Ms. Y, as passen-
ger, sustained a cranial injury that produced a concussive *contrecoups* injury to her brain, a phenomenon in traumatic accidents
where the brain literally "bounced" from the front of the skull
to the rear, or vice-versa. Z, on the other hand, was unhurt. Z
claims that because Y was traveling at a speed far over the
posted limit, the accident was all Y's fault. Z has made only a token offer, and obviously means to stick by his guns. A jury will
have to resolve the case.

Two eyewitnesses who saw the collision have been identified
and deposed. Both confirm that Y was speeding, but they claim
that Z did not come close to a full stop at the STOP sign. Z was
deposed, and claims that he did in fact stop. Y and Ms. Y have
been deposed, and claim that they were traveling at a reasonable
speed, and that Z did not stop. Y lost two months from work as a
machinist, and Ms. Y was unable to pursue her duties as a registered nurse for almost six months, due to unpredictable episodes
of dizziness and nausea. Both Y and Ms. Y claim damages for
lost earnings, medical bills, and conscious pain and suffering. Z
says that both are malingerers, who have greatly magnified their
true disabilities and discomfort. As the Irish are wont to say,
"The fight is on!"

Y's lawyer has his work cut out for him, and two days in
which to get "topped off" with information about the case. Before
picking his family up for their Friday trip to the shore, he swings
by the office and grabs his trusty laptop, as well as a separate
hard disk which he uses only to store information about the Y vs.
Z case. He directs an associate to arrange for the attendance of
the witnesses and to meet him at the courthouse on Monday,
with the exhibits prenumbered and the file boxes at hand. On
the way to the shore, Y's lawyer picks up an interface at a computer shop that will enable him to hook his laptop to the TV
screen for easier viewing.

The dedicated Y vs. Z hard disk connects to a port on the laptop, and operates just as it were located internally. Stored on it are the following:

1. All of the depositions of the parties, witnesses, and medical experts.

2. The police reports, which include statements by Z and both of the eyewitnesses, which were taken while Y and Ms. Y were being rushed to the hospital.

3. The photographs, which have been scanned onto the disk.

4. The pertinent medical records, which have been on the hard disk as graphics, since no computer can recognize doctors' handwriting or nurses' notes.

5. Electronic spreadsheets detailing the past lost earnings of both plaintiffs, the anticipated loss of future earnings, and the medical bills and other recoverable costs in the case.

6. All of the pleadings in the case, including the pretrial order which will govern the trial proceedings.

7. All legal memoranda, containing the cases, statutes, and arguments expected to be in contention during the course of the trial.

Thus armed, and much though he might prefer to romp on the beach with the family, Y's lawyer can settle into a comfortable corner somewhere in the cottage and begin to put together the opening statement he will give at the outset of the trial. In order to proceed logically, and if his software is properly programmed and integrated, Y may begin to query his computer as follows:

A: What are the *factual* issues to be litigated?

   (1) At what speed did Y approach the intersection?

   (2) Did Z in fact stop at the STOP sign?

   (3) How extensive were Ms. Y's injuries? (Y's fractured humerus bone is shown by x-rays, and is not disputed).

B: What are the *legal* issues in the case?

   (1) If Y and Z were *both* partially at fault, how will the doctrine of comparative negligence reduce the damages to which Y is entitled.

   (2) Since Ms. Y had suffered an unrelated and earlier brain injury, can Z use this to reduce her damages?

Having thus gotten a handle on the basics of the case, Y's lawyer decides to take a look at the evidence he will have available in his presentation, as well as that with which he will have to contend when the defense puts on its case. Since "speed" is a major issue in the case, the testimony on that point from *all* of the witnesses is important. Y's lawyer asks his computer to search *all* of the documents for any mention of the term "speed," and to bring up on screen each such instance together with three lines of print both before and after the word, so that it may be seen in context. One might expect a result somewhat like this:

  . . . and there I saw the yellow Chevrolet, which I later learned belonged to Y, out of the corner of my left eye, approaching the intersection. I noticed that it appeared to be in its proper lane, and that it was moving at a speed a little higher than I thought to be normal in the area. I have lived in a house at that intersection for eleven years now, and when the weather is nice I often sit out on the porch, just watching life go by. I did see that when Z approached the STOP . . .

p. 76, deposition of Charles Durant, 04-12-93

  . . . my oldest, who was sitting beside me. Suddenly she said "Daddy, that blue car coming toward us isn't going to stop and he might hit that yellow car . . ." and then the collision happened, just like she said. I think that the yellow car had more speed than he should have, but I don't think that blue Mercury ever really slowed very much, he just came bombin' through that intersection as if there was no STOP sign there. I heard a screech of brakes from the yellow . . .

p. 21, Deposition of Edward Foley, 08-03-93

  . . . travelling along Norcross Road just at 45 miles per hour, which was the legal limit there, when I seen this blue sedan coming from my right, which I thought was goin' to stop at the STOP sign that I knew was there, like he should, but then I saw that his speed didn't slow, like I thought it would, and I jumped on my brakes as hard as I could, and I could feel the tires beginnin' to skid some, and this other guy never touched his brakes, he just ploughed into Eleanor, and . . .

p. 141, Deposition of Harding Young, 02-18-93

Q: And then, Ms. Young, what did you then see? Tell us what you remember of what happened next.

A: I wasn't really looking out of the windshield, you know, when all of a sudden I heard Harding yell "Look at the speed that sonafabitch is goin', he'll never stop in time, hold on, honey, he's going to hit us!" Then the brakes screeched, and I saw the blue car coming at us, and I knew we were going to die there and then, and I began to pray to . . .

p. 16, Deposition of Eleanor Young, 03-28-93

. . . and the rest of what they said, these Young people, and those two guys who told the cops they were witnesses, they're all totally wrong, completely wrong. I approached the intersection, came from a slow speed to a stop at the STOP sign, looked to my left and saw this yellow car a long way off, looked to my right and started through, when this guy hit his brakes and began to vulcanize the highway, tires smoking like he was in the Daytona, then crossed . . .

p. 74, Deposition of Michael Zwal, 01-09-93

. . . as the literature shows very clearly, a contrecoups injury is a very dangerous injury and can easily be misdiagnosed and poorly treated. Fortunately, my clinic is schooled in these matters and we were able to recognize the injury. As to the speed with which a full recovery to duty may be expected, I think we have to move slowly. These kinds of damage to the brain have fooled us often in the past, and superficial signs of recovery must be accepted with caution . . .

p. 103, Deposition of G. Helmsley, M.D. 11-08-93

Whoops! How did that medical testimony get injected into a query about vehicle speed? An important lesson. Computers aren't bright, but they are methodical. If you look back to the query originally put looking for witnesses to vehicle speed, you will see that Y's lawyer unwittingly brought up a medical deposition as well, simply because of the way speed was used in the query. Not to worry. Excess information can always be shelved, or allocated to another category. Vital facts which are *missed* are a source of considerable worry. When using computers, you will not miss any information unless (1) you failed to store it properly, or (2) your call-up instructions for the information were ineffective to reach all of what you sought. Computers are wondrous instruments which are terribly unforgiving of mistakes. Nonetheless, as the example set forth above shows, a few strokes on the keyboard has given Y's lawyer an overview of all the *testimonial* evidence relating to his client's *speed,* the chief obstacle to a victory in court or an adequate settlement. Counsel will next pull up the expert's report on the significance of Y's skid marks, and what inferences may be drawn from their intensity, direction, and length.

Following that the photographs will be reviewed, then the medical records, then the spreadsheets reflecting the money damages which can be proven. With Y's lawyer's memory refreshed in each of the areas to be highlighted during the trial, it is time to turn to the delicate business of stuffing his head with facts and details.

As was suggested in Chapter 4, dealing with memory and its importance to a trial lawyer, nothing is more intimidating to a witness, even a truthful one, than a lawyer on his feet with no notes in sight, hurling questions laden with dates, times, and details which go beyond the witness' own ability to recall. He is in a quandary. He is worrying. *Clearly, this lawyer is a dangerous person with whom to disagree. With so many details in mind, he must have something to back up each and every suggestion implicit in his questions, and I probably ought to acquiesce or I will be seriously contradicted. On the other hand, he could be bluffing, trying to get me to agree with something I really don't want to say. If only I could remember . . .*

As should be plain by now, computers—especially those which are mobile—are a *tremendous* asset to an active trial lawyer. If you seriously think that trial advocacy is your calling, make it your business to become not just computer *literate,* but computer *fluent.*

15

Juries

I have said that the business of trying lawsuits is not for the faint of heart. It is a professional specialty laden with stress of many kinds, and is not to be undertaken without a full appreciation of that fact. There is no greater stress than that involved in waiting for a jury to deliberate—and then announce—its verdict.

The word *verdict* is an acronym for a Latin concept called *veritas dictum* which means—in a literal translation—"to speak the truth." And while I am convinced that with very rare exceptions American juries do their level best to speak the truth in their pronouncements, their judgments sometimes go awry. In order to be a trial lawyer, one must face the fact that over and over again one will experience waiting for a jury verdict. For every caring lawyer in any case where the stakes are high, it is a mind-squeezing, gut-wrenching, exhausting experience. In a word, it is perilously close to what hell must be!

In criminal cases especially, the tension is particularly high. The client anguishes for even the slightest form of encouragement, hoping to see a sign—any sign—which leans toward victory, and freedom. Juries often send written notes to the judge asking all kinds of questions. Frequently they ask that the testimony of one or more key witnesses be read back to them by the court reporter. Most judges refuse this request, for in a worst case scenario the entire trial record might need to be read, in effect replicating the length of the trial itself. Even when the jury's request is turned down, speculation as to the significance of the specific testimony requested starts tongues wagging and lawyers and clients guessing.

In other instances, the jury will ask for a clarification of the judge's instructions. On some occasions, especially if the "charge," as it is called, has been reduced to writing and sent into the jury room as an aid, the judge will merely direct the foreperson to the portion of the charge that needs further study; or, he may bring the jury back into open court and paraphrase what he has already said in an effort to make a particular instruction more comprehensible. Once again, the lawyers, parties and hangers-on will commence theorizing about the significance of the request, and what it may suggest about the direction in which the deliberations are drifting.

Too often, these events are cruelly misleading. The significance of a jury request may seem to sharply favor one side (Can we award *more* money than the plaintiff has requested?). The reality may be that a single, holdout juror has entrenched himself in a far-out position, and the balance of the jury wants to show him just how wrong he is by asking help from the court. The question may have no message in it whatsoever as to where the majority is leaning, and yet standing on its own it seemed to telegraph a "status" in the deliberations which stimulates ". . . that hope that beats eternal within the human breast." Heartbeats quicken on both sides, the one encouraged and the other distraught. Those in deep apprehension yearn for a signal, any signal.

A somewhat more dependable indicator of what the future may hold in the matter of a jury's verdict is the nonverbal conduct of the jurors themselves. Although in most cases a concentrated effort is made to remain stoic, and even stony-faced when filing in and out of the courtroom when deliberations are in progress, sometimes the mask slips a bit and meaningful facial expressions shine through. In a criminal case especially, a smile at the defendant or his lawyer can be taken as a good sign, *at least as to that juror!* On the other hand, the reverse is not necessarily true.

It would be too much to expect that twelve citizens (or, in many trials, six), randomly selected from different walks of life, would gravitate smoothly toward agreement on hotly contested issues; after all, if there weren't two sides to the story, there probably wouldn't have been a trial in the first place. Therefore, when jurors come back to the jury box during deliberations looking frustrated and angry, this often means no more than a disagreement in full swing, with some jurors being exasperated over the perceived truculence of their contrary fellows. This does not mean that either side is losing, but only that debate is becoming heated.

None of this detracts from the mounting anxiety of the litigants and their counsel. As long as the deliberations continue, blood pressure will remain elevated and hearts will beat faster than normal.

When the jury *does* return to announce a verdict, however, facial signals often become meaningful. When several jurors smile or nod warmly toward one side or the other, it means that those people at least believe that the side they encourage will be pleased with the result. This does not mean necessarily that they are correct; what they are giving the prevailing party may be significantly less than he or she was offered by the opponent, and thus in truth the victory belongs to the "loser." In a criminal case, however, where there are only two choices—guilty or not guilty—one or more smiles at the defense table almost invariably means an acquittal of at least the most serious charges.

But every rule has its exceptions. Many years ago I defended a middle-aged man who was one of several brothers recently identified on national television as the ruling Mafia "Family" in Boston. The charge against him, however, had nothing whatsoever to do with organized crime.

The indictment charged that he had assaulted the victim—a sixteen-year-old boy—with ". . . a dangerous weapon, to wit: a shod foot." The evidence was that the defendant had given the youth a healthy kick in the rump for insisting—after a previous warning—on having continuing intimate relations with the defendant's thirteen-year-old daughter. Historically, many fathers would have reacted with at least as much violence as was charged to the defendant. But this defendant was someone special, and the District Attorney of Suffolk County in those days was a man who never missed either a photo or a headline opportunity. Because of *who* the defendant was, the case went front page on the first day of trial. And even though my client was technically guilty of an assault, I thought the shoe being charged as a "dangerous weapon" was a bit much. I was hoping for an acquittal, or at the very least a conviction of "simple assault." There would be a strong "that kid deserved it" sympathy factor, I thought.

When the jury filed back into the courtroom with its verdict, my anxieties were comfortably dispelled, for more than half of the all-male jury was smiling unmistakably at the defense. I was shocked to my toes to hear the foreman announce "guilty."

I had misread the vital signal. The jurors *thought* that they had done us right, because of a very clever foreperson, who happened to be an executive for a large oil company, and a fanatically religious conservative. As a lone dissenter in an eleven-to-one vote for "not guilty" he had systematically turned each of his fellow jurors around by assuring them that—although no jury should appear to condone violence—he knew that the only penalty involved was a small fine! Once the verdict was recorded, the defendant was given a year in jail to think about his "self-help," and the eleven duped jurors could do nothing about it.

But this was an aberration. Recently, also in Boston, my partner Ken Fishman and I had a court appointment to defend a young man accused of two murders, which were in reality gangland-style executions. Virtually all of the five people actually involved in the shootings—three assailants and two victims—were teenagers. One of the triggermen was given an opportunity to exchange his true role for that of a "witness" by an inept policeman, and promptly did so. But because an eyewitness on the scene had seen *three* people running away, the "witness" had to arrange a substitute for himself. He named our client, who had in fact been home sick that night; but—as with most innocent people who have an alibi for a crime which occurs at 9:30 at night—his only witnesses were members of his family.

The jury that heard the case was just about the best I have ever seen from an *innocent* defendant's point of view. Of the sixteen chosen (twelve and four alternates), thirteen were women (including two lawyers and a Ph.D. psychologist) and three were men (two businessmen and a banker). Of the total, thirteen had college degrees, and the remainder a high school education. They listened very attentively to all of the evidence for seven days, and swiftly concluded that the "witness" was the true killer and that our client had been framed. This is as close to a *Perry Mason* scenario as I ever expect to come. Unfortunately, the "witness" killer was given immunity and will probably never be punished for anything.

The best jury system—at least in terms of accurate results—is that used in military courts-martial. The jurors are all—with rare exception—commissioned officers, which means that they are both well-educated and highly disciplined to follow rules, a trait most civilian juries lack. Furthermore, there are no "hung" juries in the military system. While the jury may vary in size from five to eleven members, the party with the burden of proof must convince two-thirds of those members in order to win. If more than one third vote for the defending party, the defense wins. It is a system which has worked very, very well for more than forty years, and one which I think civilian courts would be wise to adopt. A deadlocked jury, and the consequent retrial that usually follows, is in my view a colossal and unnecessary waste of time.

Discouraged lawyers and litigants—that is, those who have just lost a case they had hoped to win—have frequently complained that jury trials are too often an agonizing form of intellectual roulette. Flawed verdicts *do* occur, and they can be maddening indeed, especially after hours or days of sweating bullets in apprehension. And while it is important to accept and be prepared to live with this extraordinary form of stress, take heart: Although often for bizarre reasons, juries most often come up with a just result.

16

Going to Law School

F or most of you, the formal study of law in a law school will be a new experience, quite different from the educational experiences you have had in high school and in college. The atmosphere and environment are different, and the air has a tang in it that is like no other. You will have to reshape your mind and learn to think in a new way. Your discipline will change. So will your dialect. Law is a new language. You must learn it, but if you want to try cases you must avoid being ensnared by it: You have to stay in contact with the King's English, and not lapse into so much jargon that you sound brilliant to your fellow students and strange to everyone else.

You will have to disentangle any religious beliefs you may possess from your approach to learning the law. Though the law pays homage to the Almighty in several of its oaths and incantations, and surely judges and lawyers faced with difficult decisions often ask for divine guidance, still the law is a system of rules and principles that tries to be self-sufficient, an entity unto itself. Indeed, I'm sure that some of my atheistic colleagues would sue God if they could find him, claiming that he is liable for the tort of unexplained human suffering.

The senior professor at my law school used to wake up his new students with a bang frequently during the first semester. One of his favorites would be the question: "When in the history of the world was the first law?" Inevitably someone would raise his hand and respond: "The first law was when God told Adam not to eat the forbidden fruit; Adam broke it and got punished."

The professor's brow would wrinkle into a frown. "The graduate school of theology is just down the street," he would intone. "They do religion down there, not here. The first law was when two little guys told one big guy that if he wanted to hurt one of them he would have to fight both of them, and don't you ever forget that. The law is about the rules the three of them made, mostly by majority vote, to try to get along together."

Although we have rewritten it to a large extent in an effort to progress with the times, the foundation for our law is the common law of England, which goes back hundreds of years. Had we had the wisdom to bring the *operating standards* of the law across the North Atlantic with us when we brought the common law to America, you would probably not be reading this book. But we did not; we were a frontier society, where general practitioners were required and specialists were rare. In a small community the doctor had to perform every service, as did the lawyer. Now that the frontier is gone, we are a cosmopolitan society requiring specialization. Medicine has arranged to train and develop highly qualified specialists. The law is thinking about it, but hasn't done much yet. The barristers of England have not been replicated here as of this writing.

This same professor had another old chestnut that he used to pop on freshman classes, and it really rocked them. It's worth learning now, for it will save you a lot of agonizing when you learn that our concept of justice is more vulnerable than you may have thought. Most of us are brought up to believe that if we behave like good people, the law will be good to us, and always fair.

But the law is administered and written by human beings, and must always be flawed. Many suffer undeservedly at its hands, just as Mr. Daniels might have suffered had he been convicted for a crime he did not commit. Justice is an objective worth dedicated and sincere pursuit, but not always an attainment.

To drive this point home, my professor used to say: "At the risk of being branded a heretic and a communist, and being tarred and feathered and driven out of town, I must tell you that the God of the common law is *not* justice, as you have no doubt come to believe: The God of the common law is *consistency!* The law strives to be consistent from one day to the next, and to treat all of its constituents alike. Its promise is not 'I will give you justice.' Its promise is, 'If I put the blocks to you and treat you unfairly, I will treat your neighbor the same way!'"

He was quite right. We in the law put a high price on consistency, which is one of the reasons we are so slow to change. While medicine leaps forward whenever tests prove a new drug or technique to be beneficial, we are more interested in regularity. If you draw a will to dispose of your assets after your death, that is what we call an "ambulatory" instrument; it has no legal effect until you die, twenty years or more later. If the law of wills changed on a chronic basis, things might be distributed to your heirs in a fashion far different from what you anticipated when you had the will drafted and signed it. Lawyers like to draw their wisdom from history, to keep a steady course, to be able to predict for their clients what they may expect in a given case. Unfortunately, we follow this pattern of consistency to a fault. We change so slowly that we are often behind the times and the lives which we govern. It is one thing to abide by precedent—a principle called *stare decisis,* or "let the decision stand"—in order to protect a bunch of ambulatory wills. It is quite another to allow people to go to jail or lose their property, when they don't deserve to, because the law refuses to recognize a new scientific technique and a litigant is deprived of its use.

Appellate courts often differ, and they can be very, very wrong, particularly when they resist change. There is an old appellate opinion in Illinois that cries out at the mere thought that, by microscopic examination, an expert can say with exactitude whether a certain bullet came from a given weapon. Today, of course, we accept the body of knowledge and expert opinion that is firearms identification as readily as we accept x-rays. You are going to be disappointed by some aspects of your study of law, but those disappointments will be counterbalanced by some exhilarating excursions into real, deep wisdom. Let's hope you will be chastened by the stupid things you encounter, and inspired and motivated by the many things the law has done right.

Unless you have some special advantage when you enter law school, I would suggest that in your first semester, as you get acquainted with this "new world," you give it the best concentration you can muster. Keep your outside activities to a minimum, and bear down. If you can create the momentum to propel yourself to or near the head of the pack in the first few months, staying there will not require as great an effort. You need to make a lengthy transition into the world of law, but the day finally comes when you begin to see the big picture.

Your nightly assignments in each course will consist in large measure of "briefing" cases from your casebooks, which are textbooks containing selected judicial decisions from which you are to learn the manner in which the law works. During the first year, brief your own cases; the short-cut crowd will whisper to you about the advantages of "canned" briefs, which can be bought for a price. They are in a sense "cheat sheets," for they offer in finished form what *you* have been assigned to do: read a judicial decision, and then render a concise statement outlining the facts of the dispute, the issue or issues presented, and the holding. Since ycu are entering a world where most of what you do will be strongly influenced by what judges have said in similar cases, you need to learn how to read a case and distill its essence. If you opt for the "canned" briefs, you are cheating yourself out of some essential learning. You need to be able to analyze a case to take your exams, and if you don't learn how to do it yourself—especially, to recognize the pivotal language in a decision that makes up the holding—you are not going to find the author of the canned briefs sitting next to you in the examination room. Do your own work for the first year; if you acquire a talent to scan a case and spot its issues and holding quickly, you can use the "cans" as worksheets, provided that you read the case yourself to make sure that the author of the can has briefed the case correctly. Be advised that the authors of these cans do not always come from the top of the class.

As in almost every educational process, two things are important in law school: what you learn and file away in your memory, and how well you do in your examinations. If you were a candidate for apprenticeship in my office, I would be more interested in the former. If you are interested in starting with a large silk-stocking firm, or if you wish to clerk for a judge or be a professor, grades are paramount. If you are really absorbing your classroom material, you can get good grades simply by learning *how* to take law school examinations. I may not be able to teach you how to do that fully, but I can give you some clues.

First, get a sense of what your professors are looking for. They anticipate the day when you may be turned loose on the world with a license to practice law, a ticket anointing you with the right to counsel the lives of others. Are you going to use your maturity, judgment, professional objectivity, common sense, and legal expertise to guide these clients in the right direction, or are you going to give them bad advice? That is the central question in the mind of the person correcting your exams. Many of your examinations will pose problems requiring narrative answers that include your perception of the problem, your understanding of the facts, your knowledge of the state of the law on the points at issue, and the advice you will give, with a clear statement of the *reasons* why.

Other examinations are composed of multiple choice questions. These test a much narrower sphere of comprehension, and generally are less effective, in my judgment, than the narrative type. They allow the examinee a much more limited opportunity to show the quality of his analysis, imagination, and discretion. They are, however, much less tedious to correct, and so have crept their way into our law schools during the past three decades. The practice of law is seldom presented to the problem solver as a series of options, one of which is "right." For trial lawyers especially, the ability to crack a "multiple guess" examination is an unfaithful index.

You, however, will have to take the examinations in the form they are given, and this requires that you be adept at confronting both kinds. You will have to understand the law you have been taught, and show your ability to work with it. You will become an expert at *extrapolation,* an essential skill in legal reasoning.

To extrapolate one must take one or more similar cases, none of which is identical to the problem at hand, and draw from them in order to anticipate what a court will do with the situation *you* are handling. An example: You have a client who wants to know what a reasonable time for delivery of curtain rods would be, since his manufacturing company is trying to make delivery within the terms of the contract; but the contract is silent as to the time of delivery. Generally, whenever no time is specified in an agreement, the law imposes a "reasonable time" as a limitation. You look for a case in your jurisdiction that deals with the precise point—curtain rods—and you find none. But you look further, and you find that thirty days was found by the appellate court to be well within "reasonable time" standards for the delivery of hinges, and that four months was found to be much longer than a "reasonable time" in a case involving the delivery of doorknobs. You now have some parameters to work with. Drawing on both cases, you look to the facts, the reasoning of the court in each decision, the holding of the case, and you decide that to be on the safe side, your client ought to deliver within twenty-five days, or some judge may say the delay was excessive. You have just extrapolated the meat of two cases similar, but not identical to yours to *infer* what a court might do if confronted with your client's problem. You are in the business of predicting what courts will do, and you are guided in these predictions by extrapolating from what they have done in the past.

This way of solving problems is used in many walks of life, but is dominant in the law. The curtain rod case was comparatively easy, and the advice given was conservative: Sixty days might have been quite acceptable to most courts. As a trial lawyer, you have to deal with the *outer* parameters of what is allowable; indeed, you will often be involved in establishing them. But as we have learned in earlier chapters, one needs to know what the rules are before one sets about to figure the "right" ways to break them. If you do a good job in law school, you will learn the rules, and learn them well. Only then will you have a legitimate right to aspire to be a rule-breaker, a renegade who wants to change what exists into something better. It is the rule-breakers who keep our law from stagnating, and as a trial lawyer, breaking rules wisely will be one of your committed tasks. If you don't do it, don't wait for "them" to take care of the problem: There is no "they." When someone tells you that "they" say such and such, and therefore that's the way things are, think like a lawyer. Never mind the "they" nonsense—ask questions. What is the evidence on this point? What could I prove in court? What facts are there that a reasonable person ought to accept and believe?

You see? I told you that your thinking would have to shift, that life would be different. Now nobody can tell you anything unless they can prove it, right? Wrong. Life will go on, and people will be people, and you will have to sort them out. But when another student—a colleague—tries to persuade you of something, ask him for his evidence: the facts he can get to a jury, facts that a judge will allow into evidence—what has he really got? It can be a maddening exercise, but it is also good drill. In the law, if you shoulder the burden of proof, you can discharge that burden only with evidence. Now then, my friend, exactly what is your *evidence . . . ?*

At examination time be a crammer, a real head-stuffer. You will want to memorize the leading cases you expect to deal with, to know their names and the principles of law they stand for. In some courses you may need to memorize statutes, or code sections, by number. In responding to examination questions, you will need a working knowledge of these cornerstones, for you will be extrapolating continually in your answers. Make sure that your solutions to the problems posed are reasonable and sensible. Buried in each problem-question will be a great many issues, some of which will be obvious; others will be far more subtle. Your ability to recognize these issues is one of the primary things on which you are being tested. As a lawyer, you are not required to know all of the applicable law in a given area; you are expected to know where to look for it, and to recognize it when you see it. But until you have isolated and defined the issues, the law library will be of no help to you.

The impulse of a new law student is to be slightly pedantic and academic, and to take a positive, hard line in giving answers. Restrain yourself a bit. Check the impulse toward assertions like: "Clearly the plaintiff in this case will prevail in the Supreme Court of the United States, and should insist on complete capitulation by the other side, for they are wrong." Perhaps they are, but the Supreme Court of the United States is a long way away in terms of time and cost, and the odds are better than twenty to one that they won't hear your case anyway, no matter how right you are. Because I was actively working with practitioners when I was a student, I answered many of my examination questions by proposing a compromise, or settlement based on the risks of litigation.

A number of study aids can be useful in preparing for exams. Some students use them in lieu of doing the work itself, which is not wise. They are mere outlines, and no substitute for actually digesting the body of the decisions. But they are helpful in testing yourself to see whether you are ready, and where you have areas of weakness. One of the best is a series of law questions—very similar to examination questions—by Ballantine. Topic by topic, Ballantine covers the range of problems with which you may be confronted during the exam itself. I found it to be a dependable measuring rod of my own preparedness.

There are other aids to help you, and the senior students near the top of their class will be a good source to ask about what works best.

Be active in classroom work, and expect to get knocked around a bit in the process. Good professors continually challenge your thinking when you are expounding on a point, even when you are doing a good job of it. They will want to know not only that you recognize and understand the problem presented, but that you have some confidence in the solution you propose. If you retreat under fire, having been right in the first place will be an incomplete accomplishment. Remember, where you are going you must rely on your own judgment, that judgment must be filled out and polished by stepping boldly to the line. Mistakes there will be, for they are part of learning. Just keep track of yourself, and make sure not to repeat the same mistake. By the time you graduate, you should have made most of your mistakes, minimizing the number that are going to be made to the detriment of your clients, who have real, rather than academic, problems.

If you qualify for an invitation to be on the staff of the school's law review, by all means accept! Law review articles are respected pieces of legal writing, often cited by courts in legal opinions. They must be near-perfect in their form. The work is involved and time-consuming, but the training will benefit you substantially. Employment offers from the best law firms and companies are usually extended first to those who are on the law review. Federal judges looking for clerks—one of the best opportunities a young lawyer can ever get—prefer someone with demonstrable reasoning and writing talents, and a combination of good grades and law review experience is usually sought.

Most schools have "moot court" programs, and you should become as involved as you can in these. A moot court is one whose litigation has been dreamed up by members of the teaching staff. No real rights are at stake. Usually the issues involved are hairline in nature, which means that good arguments can be made for both sides, and there is no obvious solution. More often than not moot court exercises are appellate, which means that the facts have been settled and only questions of law are to be briefed and argued. Some schools offer trial moot court experience, but some of these programs are too superficial and shallow to give much meaningful development to budding advocates. However, do not pass them by, whatever their shortcomings, for *any* experience you can get is worth the effort. If you have good control of your English and have developed a confident, fluent speaking ability, you ought to really shine in moot court. If you find that you are *not* shining, find out why, isolate your weakness, and dive back into the appropriate chapter in this book. That is one of the reasons I suggest you keep it with you.

Of greatest importance is a recommendation I made in the early chapters: Get associated with an active law firm, one that handles litigation, on any basis you can. Work for nothing at the start if you have to. Try to arrange an introduction through someone—your professors can usually help—and offer to work on draft briefs and legal memoranda. Without being a nuisance, try to get a sense of the dynamics of the practice as it is being carried on in that office. What problems are the lawyers confronting in the cases they are handling? Think what *you* would do if those problems were dumped in your lap. Listen carefully to any talk of settlement negotiations, and how cases are evaluated; this is a band of knowledge that you are *not* going to encounter at law school.

Try to get some investigative assignments which will give you your first opportunity to deal with litigants and witnesses. Whenever you come across a piece of information, ask yourself if it can qualify as evidence. What are the grounds on which it might be admissible, and what are the grounds on which objections might be made? Keep your ears open: Lawyers talk a lot about the cases they are handling, especially those being finally prepared for an imminent trial, and you will learn a great deal by watching what they do and hearing what they say. If you find ways to help in the preparation, you will be called on with increasing frequency. A paralegal who can work effectively in the field of final preparation is a valuable aide, and that's what you must become.

In addition to your work with a firm, watch all the trials you can. Critique them as you watch. You will soon discover a wide range of competence among the lawyers on the battle lines, from very good to downright inept. Make notes of tactics and methods that seem effective—however, ask the court clerk to get you permission from the court before pulling out your notepad. Some judges do not approve of note-taking by spectators other than news reporters unless they are asked first.

Finally, in your senior year you will be wise to take a bar review course before sitting for your bar examinations. These, essentially, review all you have forgotten from the courses you have taken and acquaint you, cram course style, with the laws of the jurisdiction whose examination you will be taking. During the regular curriculum, law schools lean heavily on the law of the jurisdiction in which they are located; others do not.

Generally, two kinds of bar review courses are offered: long ones and short ones. If you have been consistently in the top 10 percent of your class, and have trained your memory well, you may be able to make do with the shorter version. If you have any doubts, play it safe and go for the longer course. Failing to pass the bar on your first attempt is an embarrassment, a psychological setback, and not very helpful to your reputation. You can learn by asking those in the class ahead of you which courses rate best, for there is some variation in the quality of the material presented. Each course normally provides a comprehensive set of notes, which are helpful when working with colleagues apart from the course itself. Do not be surprised, however, if you are advised: "Take Smith's bar review course—he gives the best presentation; but be sure to get the notes offered by the Jones course, as they are superior to Smith's."

When studying for a law exam, including the bar exam itself, working alone is not nearly as effective as working in a study group with at least one other person, up to a recommended maximum of four. These sessions usually work best when the group members are of similar aptitude and ability, question each other from notes, bar review notes, outlines, and Ballantine. Continually test one another until the answers come out right.

The one test you can't cram for effectively is the one you take *before* going to law school, known as the LSAT. This purports to be a test of legal aptitude, and law school admission committees tend to give it great weight. It is in some respects an intelligence test, but it goes into acquired knowledge and reasoning powers not examined by tests of raw intelligence. The result may have a lot to do with which law schools offer you admission, so come to it well rested and do your best.

While law school differs in many respects from other forms of education, do not get the impression that there is "mystique" involved. Mostly, it's just hard work, and if you want to be a trial lawyer I suggest you work harder than your classmates who have different aspirations. Like most other experiences involving human endeavor, you are likely to get out of your legal education pretty much what you put into it. Good luck!

17

Growing after Law School

During your senior year, you will be very busy indeed, looking forward anxiously to the time when graduation and the bar examination are behind you. But during that year you must also be planning to complete your training. You will have several options. At the head of the list I would recommend that you put clerking for a trial judge. Right after graduation is the ideal time to accept such a post if one is offered to you, for it will not break into employment of a more permanent nature. Judges usually rotate their clerks every year or two, and the experience of working for a trial judge can be invaluable.

First, you are given a box seat for his trials, with a sound opportunity to study what the lawyers are doing. You will have the vantage point of an insider, for you will have been involved, as an aide to the presiding judge, with all of the pretrial motions and much of the "discovery" material—depositions, documents, and other evidence that the advocates have amassed before the jury trial begins.

Second, you will enjoy an intimate view of a process that many experienced lawyers have never witnessed: the workings of a judge's mind as he moves to a decision. As one of his sources of legal research, your responsibilities will be substantial, and you will be able to discuss issues and precedents with him, and to learn what factors have influenced him in ruling as he does.

Third—and in view of your plans to be active in the trial court yourself, most important—you will come to learn what effective advocacy is, as seen through a judge's eyes; what approaches he finds persuasive, and what methods leave him unmoved. His critiques of the performance of the lawyers working before him will be highly informative and instructive, and will immeasurably improve your own efficacy when it is your turn to function "inside the rail," or in the bar enclosure of the court. Having seen what mistakes rankle judges most—and you will see mistakes, to be sure—you will be better equipped to avoid them yourself.

If you cannot find such a position, or if you do succeed in clerking for a year or two, the next step is an association of some kind with lawyers in the business of litigation. There are several such groups, which I would describe as follows:

Prosecutors. These are lawyers who carry the burden of proof in criminal cases, all of whom work for a government. After a comparatively short apprenticeship, young lawyers find themselves getting into action; if they manifest any extra talent—as you should, having paid special attention to getting yourself ready for trial work—promotion to greater responsibilities and more serious cases can come rapidly. When the client is an institution rather than an individual, there is less resistance to entrusting a tyro with complex litigation, simply because the client can afford to lose even when it deserves to win. Individuals are much more conservative, and are comforted to see the gray hair of an expert when they must give themselves over to someone else in a field where they are all but impotent. (If you were going in for a heart transplant, you would perhaps be less than pleased to discover that your surgeon was doing his first such operation!)

Prosecuting is good experience, and many young lawyers see it as a springboard to get into defense work in private practice. You will get a lot of experience at "putting in a case," for that will be your principal task. You will get much less experience with cross-examination, because criminal defendants do not usually call many witnesses—remember, they are not trying to prove anything, they are simply trying to raise doubts. Much of the time you will not get a chance to cross-examine the defendant himself, for he will not testify. If he *does* testify, however, you have your work cut out for you, for when a jury gets to hear the defendant, who certainly knows whether or not he is guilty, they place a great deal of weight on his credibility. If they like him, they will try to find a way to acquit him even if the evidence you have adduced is ominous.

Criminal Defense Lawyers. This is really two quite different groups, although the former will most often become the latter at some point: public defenders and private practitioners. The public defender is paid by an institution—the government—but represents individuals who cannot afford private counsel. In our society, indigent defendants probably constitute a majority of those who pass through our criminal courts. Public defense is a good position, like prosecuting, for a beginner to acquire a lot of trial experience in a short time. His chief tools are cross-examination and final argument, and he gets plenty of opportunities to sharpen his techniques and skills at both.

Public defenders handle a great many of the cases in state criminal courts, fewer in federal court. Federal criminal cases tend to be more business oriented—various kinds of fraud, tax cases, and the like—and are more apt to involve defendants who can afford to pay. These cases most often involve private practitioners. It is difficult for recent law school graduates to be retained in these cases, because frightened individuals usually want the best they can get, and in their minds that normally includes long experience. Edward Bennett Williams warned me the day after I finished the Massachusetts bar examination that one of the most difficult problems I would face in operating a private criminal defense firm would be in persuading clients to let someone other than myself handle a trial. Indeed, that prediction is still correct thirty-four years later. If you join the staff of the private practitioner with some experience, however, he can "sell" your services more easily to his clients. The fact that you have tried a number of significant cases either as a prosecutor or as a public defender will boost their confidence in your ability. Should you go this route, you will probably be asked to "second-chair" a senior defense lawyer much of the time, in addition to trying your own cases, and this is excellent experience. Until someone finds a way to teach cross-examination in the schools, you must learn it by watching others. As a group, criminal defense lawyers tend to be among the better cross-examiners in the trial bar, simply because they rely on it so much in going about the business of raising doubts.

Plaintiffs' Lawyers. One of the most active groups in the trial bar, and probably the largest single group, are the plaintiffs' lawyers. Indeed, the Association of Trial Lawyers of America was initially just that—a group of trial lawyers interested in personal injury cases. Plaintiffs' lawyers represent clients who have been injured or killed at the hands of someone who can be held responsible for the damage, and who has the ability to pay. Normally cases of this sort are handled on what is called a contingent basis; the client pays no retainer or hourly fee, and often counsel has to advance the expenses in the case. His reward comes only if there is a recovery, and then is set at an amount equal to a percentage of that recovery, usually between 25 and 40 percent. These contingent fees are often under attack as making counsel a partner in the litigation, in spurring litigation when none is warranted, and of inviting counsel to "build" or exaggerate the value of the case so that his fee will increase. The response to that claim is that the contingent fee allows those injured people who have no money to retain well-qualified counsel, for often their claims must be pressed against large companies who can afford the best trial lawyers. While both positions have merit, the contingent fee has been embedded in our custom for so long that it is likely to stay.

A beginning lawyer who takes in mostly personal injury cases is likely to suffer cash flow problems in his early years. Most settlements take at least six months, and if there must be a trial and several appeals the case can drag on for many years. Since no fees are paid until the case is finally closed—and indeed, cash will be flowing the other way, for expenses—it is best to start with a firm that already has its file cabinets bulging with cases, and work your way into your own practice after you have built up a clientele of your own. Of course, you must have a clear arrangement with the firm over the status of cases you bring in at such time as you depart; however, such arrangements are common.

Personal injury lawsuits offer good experience in all areas of trial, with the emphasis once again—since you will have the burden of proof most of the time—on "putting in" a case. Unlike the prosecutors, however, plaintiffs' lawyers gain good experience at cross-examination, especially of expert witnesses. The principal difference between criminal and civil litigation is that civil defendants usually *do* put on witnesses; and if the defendant himself does not choose to testify, the plaintiff can call him as an adverse witness and cross-examine him just as if he had been placed on the stand by his own lawyer. A capable trial lawyer who stands out in the personal injury field can expect that cases that cannot be settled will be referred to him for trial by colleagues who do not handle litigation; and, like all skilled trial lawyers except those who work for the government, he can make a very good income.

Civil Defense Lawyers. These are the advocates who handle the defense in cases brought by the plaintiffs' lawyers. They are paid by the hour or the day as a rule, although many have been known to "adjust" their fees up or down slightly depending on the kind of result they have gotten in a given case. While they do not benefit from the windfalls available in plaintiffs' work (that is, a large fee for a short trial because the injuries suffered by the client were severe), they do get paid whenever they work. Their clients are mainly insurance companies, who hire them on a regular basis, unlike the average injury victim who never sees his lawyer again—for personal injuries, at least—after his case is over. Insurance defense lawyers tend to be a more conservative crowd than those who represent plaintiffs, but their skills are often strong and their standards of professionalism and competence more carefully watched by their clients. Again, because the real client is an institution rather than an individual, young lawyers have a better chance of handling serious cases than they do on the plaintiff's side. It is a busy life, with lots of trials going on at all times, and experience builds fast. Both plaintiffs' lawyers and their defense

counterparts do a great deal of negotiating, mostly in the eso-
teric exercise of trying to put a dollar value on pain, suffering,
disability, and loss of life.

One caution, though. There is a drawback to this kind of
practice, and that is a tendency to drag out litigation that clogs
the courts. The more time a defense lawyer puts into a case, the
higher his fee. If the insurance company is in a cash bind, it will
prolong the case by authorizing inadequate settlement offers until its financial position improves. This kind of conduct brings no
credit to anyone; should you be a defense lawyer I hope you will
avoid it. If a man has been hurt and it is your client's fault (or the
fault of the insured party), he deserves to be paid a fair sum now,
not ten years from now. I hope that your personal integrity will
mean more to you than the time you can put in a file, and that
you will govern your practices accordingly.

By the same token, one of the ugly features of the law is the
so-called "nuisance" claim. Everyone knows that litigation costs
money; and frivolous claims are cheaper to settle than to fight, if
viewed on a one-by-one basis. The result, however, is that more
nuisance claims arise when the word gets around that token pay-
ments are being made. With enough of them, a lawyer can make
a living even if he never gets a client with a meritorious case.
These cases clog our courts because some lawyers will bring
them, and others are too quick to pay them. Both groups ought to
cease and desist, for such practices are an abuse of the privilege
of being a lawyer.

Military Lawyers. If you decide to serve in the armed
forces, the military is usually looking for lawyers. Should the
draft be chasing you, deferrals are usually possible if you wish
to go to law school and then enlist. The life is a good one, the pay
is adequate for one just starting out, and the experience is marvelous. I speak with a bias, for it was in the U.S. Marine Corps
that I learned to try cases when I was twenty-one years old. I
wasn't a lawyer, but they didn't have enough lawyers to cover all
their trials (called courts-martial), and the Marine Corps has
an interesting system of appointing "volunteers." I was
"volunteered," and learned a great deal about the matters addressed in this book *before* I went to law school. Today the system has changed. Courts-martial must now be tried by lawyers
who are full-fledged members of the bar of some state. But going

into the military right after graduation is still a good idea, should it fit the rest of your plans.

Military court, compared to most civilian courts, is refreshing in many respects; its procedure has been streamlined since 1951, when the Uniform Code of Military Justice became law. The pretrial discovery features are the best and most complete of any system, which sharply reduces the chances that surprise evidence will infect the trial. In addition, gaining a pervasive knowledge of the government's case enables the defense lawyer to predict the result of a trial better for his client and to advise plea negotiation if the facts warrant it.

Military juries are nearly always made up of intelligent commissioned officers with a college education. An enlisted man accused of violating the code is entitled to have one third of his jury constituted of enlisted men, but this request is seldom made. The jury consists of a minimum of five and a maximum of eleven members, and there is no requirement that its verdict be unanimous: If two thirds or more vote to convict, that is a conviction; if more than one third vote not guilty, that is an acquittal. There are no hung juries, and verdicts are usually reached swiftly. Military juries are allowed to take notes, to question witnesses, and to call witnesses of their own if they feel that counsel have omitted calling someone of importance. They also impose sentences, which is left to the judge in federal court and all but a few states. It is possible to waive jury and be tried by a judge alone, but I have had occasion to do that only once in forty years of trying courts-martial.

The training in advocacy is all in criminal cases for most military lawyers, but it is excellent training. The only drawback is that if you are weaned in military court, you are apt to feel some disappointment in the civilian system when you are discharged and shift your trial work to state and federal courts. I still try courts-martial on a regular basis, and still enjoy them more than any other trials.

Litigation Section—Large Law Firms. Most large law firms have a litigation department, and if you enjoy working for complex organizations with internal rules and policies, the training available is excellent. Most of the trials are apt to be civil, and many will be long and complex; you could wind up working on only one case for a year or two. Promotion through the ranks is apt to be slow at first, but if you have prepared yourself well for your role as a trial lawyer, as I am urging you to do, a demonstration of sound judgment and courtroom talent could accelerate your progress. As in any large organization, you *are* going to be confronted with policies, rules, procedures, and company politics; if they get under your skin, this might not be the way for you to go. But a distinguished trial record with a respected firm can be helpful should you decide to go into individual practice, for you will have learned a great deal about attracting and satisfying corporate clients who demand the best and are willing to pay for it.

Miscellaneous. There are many other litigation opportunities that do not fit conveniently into any of these groups. Every state and federal bureaucracy needs trial lawyers; many have their own litigation staffs, while others draw on the staff of the attorney general. Large companies that are frequently in litigation have their own staff lawyers, although most prefer to pass the responsibility to law firms of size and substance. There is a fair body of *administrative* litigation, before panels, commissions, arbitrators, and judges sitting without jury; while this work is less exciting than jury trials, and is often flavored with politics, the training is valuable.

In short, there are more than enough opportunities for any young lawyer who wants to try cases for his professional career. For one determined to excel, and willing to make the additional efforts we have been discussing in this book, the field is wide open and the chances for rapid advancement all but unlimited. Most respected and successful trial lawyers usually attain that status in their mid-forties and flourish for the next twenty years or so. This tendency to "bloom late" is caused by starting late; that is, most lawyers graduate from law school without any real idea of what litigation is all about, and have to begin learning things that they should have been working on before they were freshmen, or at least while they were law students. There simply are no shortcuts. There is a certain amount to be learned, and the sooner you begin, the sooner you will emerge as a full-fledged advocate ready for the responsibilities of chief trial counsel in serious, complex, and difficult cases. Gray hair may be comforting to clients, but it is not essential to sound judgment and the confidence necessary to work the front line.

I began trying cases of murder in the first degree when I was twenty-seven, and have been ever since. In looking back, I am not haunted by mistakes that I feel were caused by leaping to the fore prematurely. Of course, I had the accidental benefit of having done a great deal of legal work in the military, and of having been a trial investigator all through law school. Indeed, I cut more than a few classes to sit in on trials I had helped prepare, and benefited tremendously from the experience. You might set a goal for yourself that you will be able to act as lead trial counsel in almost any case by the time you are thirty. And don't be discouraged if recognition does not come the day you finally possess the talent. I walked into the cell of a man charged with murder in my first year of practice, after some of his friends had hired me to represent him. When I arrived, he said: "Oh, hi, kid, where's your father? He's that fancy trial lawyer they hired for me, right?" I had to let him down gently, and he was only thirty-two. Fortunately the charge was dismissed within two weeks when the state's only witness was shown to be untruthful.

Before leaving you to the labors I am urging you to undertake, I would like to pause for a few moments of straight talk. I have tried to give you an insight into the world of the trial lawyer, what he does, and how he must learn to do it if he expects to be one of the best. As I indicated at the outset, if you do become a trial lawyer you will be invested with tremendous power to affect the lives of your fellow human beings. You will often be their only hope to obtain their legal rights. Power is an exhilarating sensation, but it can also be corruptive and mean unless it is balanced with a rock-solid personal integrity. I will have done no one a service if I steer anyone into my profession who fails to bring that integrity with him. It is absolutely essential.

Always make sure that your word is good. Often you will not be able to speak because what you know was learned in confidence, but when you do speak, do so honestly. It will make life much more pleasant, and you will need a reputation for honesty to deal effectively with courts, other lawyers, and clients. The truth is easy to remember if you train your memory; I have no system for remembering stories that were made up to begin with, and you should have no need to develop such a system. Lying should be restricted to telling infants about Santa Claus and elderly people in poor health that they are looking "better."

228 To Be a Trial Lawyer

Be warned, clients often think that because lawyers know the mysterious workings of the system, they also know where its rules can be broken. Be suspicious of any fee offered you that is disproportionately high to the case you are being asked to handle. There is probably an expectation that you will get what the client wants "at all costs." You need only step over the line slightly to be in big trouble with your colleagues, and that is a misery you can well afford to avoid.

If you have the basic aptitude to become a trial lawyer, and put forth the necessary effort to learn on your own what others are not going to teach you, you will have an opportunity to satisfy all of the fundamental human needs: responsibility and the power to discharge it, recognition, respect, the knowledge that you are contributing to the quality of life, and a very comfortable amount of money. Don't, don't, *whatever* you do, wind up at the age of fifty with nothing but the money.

Appendix

Murder Cases, 1961–1994

There were 29 separate trials in courtrooms in numerous state, federal, and military courts where murder was charged. In 21 of these trials, the defendant was acquitted of everything. In 6 cases, the defendant was convicted of *one count* of murder—3 of murder in the first degree and three of murder in the second degree. In 2 of these cases, the defendant had offered—before trial—to plead guilty to manslaughter and had been turned down; in both cases the verdict was manslaughter, and so in both cases the verdict could be considered a victory, and was so treated by the client.

In the total of all of the trials, there were 153 chances to receive a verdict (or judicial finding, in the case of jury-waived cases) of guilty; thus, the 6 convictions out of 153 chances is a *rate* of 3.92%.

Irrelevant to the above summaries, in 8 cases we took on appeals that others had lost at trial, or at a lower appellate level. In each of these we prevailed, resulting in either a new trial for the defendant, or a dismissal of the charges.

*Denotes that someone else tried the case before we were retained.

Year	Case Name	State	Result	Verdicts
1961	Commonwealth v. Edgerly[1]	MA	Acquitted	1.
1961	Commonwealth v. McLain[2]	MA	No True Bill	1.
1963	Commonwealth v. Nasser[3]	MA	Murder 1 (Death) (Reversed)	0.
1964	Nasser v. Commonwealth[4]	MA	Conviction overturned	1.
1964	Commonwealth v. Shorey[5]	MA	Manslaughter	1.
1964	*Sheppard v. Maxwell (Habeas)[6]	OH (Fed)	New Trial (Mur. 2)	1.
1965	Commonwealth v. Nasser[7]	Retrial	Murder 1 (Life)	1.

[1]I walked into the Edgerly trial in February, 1961, less than three months after being admitted to practice. Chief Defense Counsel John J. Tobin (age 72) had called for polygraph evidence which he thought would be favorable. When it was not, he suffered heart problems, and was hospitalized. I (age 27) was brought in to cross-examine the polygraph operator, and went on to finish the case.

[2]Buddy McLain allegedly shot down Bernie McGlaughlin (in what was to begin a 4-year gang war with 56 victims, one of which ultimately was McLain) in Charlestown City Square on Halloween day at high noon; I came up with enough dirt on the only alleged witness (a New Jersey prostitute) to persuade the prosecutor not to indict, else he would lose the case.

[3]George Nasser had been convicted of murder at age 15, but was paroled when he was 31 as "rehabilitated." George was then charged with a new robbery-murder of a gas station attendant. The arresting officer testified that as he took George into custody he said: "Well, here we are again, George, for the same thing!" Nasser was convicted and sentenced to death.

[4]I handled the appeal by appointment, and won a new trial based on the arresting officer's "same thing" testimony.

[5]Stanton Shorey—who was being cuckolded by the town swordsman, and knew it—drove fifteen miles with a shotgun in his car, kicked in the door of his estranged wife's apartment, and blew her lover away. An offer to plead to manslaughter was rejected by the prosecution.

[6]Dr. Sam Sheppard was convicted in 1954 of Murder 2 for the slaying of his wife, who was beaten to death, in one of the most highly publicized cases in the country in this century. When I took his case in 1961, he had lost some eleven appeals, and his case was generally thought to be dead. A courageous federal judge in Dayton, Ohio, found five separate constitutional violations in his conviction and ordered him released on bail, giving Ohio 60 days in which to decide to retry him.

[7]During his second trial, George did not testify; he was convicted, and given life without parole.

Year	Case Name	State	Result	Verdicts
1966	Sheppard v. Maxwell (U.S. Sup Ct.)[8]	OH	New Trial Upheld	1.
1966	Ohio v. Sheppard[9]	OH	Acquitted	1.
1966	New Jersey v. Coppolino[10]	NJ	Acquitted	1.
1967	Commonwealth v. DeSalvo[11]	MA	Immunized	13.
1967	Florida v. Coppolino[12]	FL	Murder 2	1.
1967	Minnesota v. Mitchell[13]	MN	Manslaughter	1.
1968	*California v. Miller[14]	CA	Released	1.

[8]After Dr. Sheppard's release, the U.S. Court of Appeals reversed the order granting a new trial (2-1) and ordered him back to prison. The U.S. Supreme Court reversed the Sixth Circuit in a landmark opinion, *Sheppard v. Maxwell.* This decision was used to persuade Judge Cecil Mills to dismiss the grand jury hearing the case against O.J. Simpson in California.

[9]Dr. Sam was retried in October, 1966, and acquitted.

[10]Dr. Coppolino was indicted almost simultaneously for murders in New Jersey (his lover's husband) and Florida (his wife) caused by the injection of succinyl dicholine chloride, a synthetic form of the drug *curare,* used by Indians in the Amazon to paralyze their prey.

[11]Albert was the famous "Boston Strangler" who confessed under guardianship to murdering 13 victims. Because he was deemed incompetent to waive his rights against self-incrimination, he was effectively immunized for all the murders. He went to prison for sexual (non-homicide) crimes and was assassinated there in 1973.

[12]Carl was acquitted of first degree murder, but convicted in Naples, Florida, of "unpremeditated poisoning" (murder in the second degree), a legal impossibility on the facts of the case. He would probably have won his appeal in federal court, but a member of the clergy persuaded him to abandon his appellate efforts, on the notion that he would thereby win an early release. He didn't.

[13]Dr. John Mitchell, a chiropractor, had been deeply immersed in domestic difficulties when his wife was discovered—with all the classic signs of manual strangulation—in a house that had been set on fire. The prosecution offered Murder 2, we countered with Manslaughter as a plea bargain, which was rejected.

[14]Lucille Miller's husband died when a fire engulfed the Volkswagen "bug" he was driving. Lucille escaped. She was later arrested for setting the fire; an undercover cop was placed in her cell, pretending to be an inmate, and encouraged Lucille to talk. Lucille denied her guilt, but admitted having an affair with a local lawyer. This evidence was used against her at trial, and she was convicted. The California appellate court berated the police for their tactics, but let the conviction stand. I took over at this point (with the very able help of Harvard's Alan Dershowitz, a most respected colleague with whom I have collaborated on a number of significant cases) and got the United States Supreme Court to hear the case. After oral argument, the Court—in an extraordinary move—declined to decide the case and dismissed the *writ of certiorari* as

Year	Case Name	State	Result	Verdicts
1968	Commonwealth v. Sciara[15]	MA	Acquitted	1.
1968	Commonwealth v. Parone[16]	MA	Acquitted	1.
	Commonwealth v. Marino	MA	Acquitted	1.
1968	Ohio v. Head[17]	OH	Murder 2	1.
1968	*Commonwealth v. Brandon	VA	New trial granted	1.
1969	U.S. Army v. Cook[18] (Mannheim)	Germany	Acquitted	3.
1970	New York v. Ralph Jacobson[19]	NY	Acquitted	1.
	New York v. Danny Jacobson	NY	Acquitted	1.
1971	New York v. Phillips[20]	NY	Hung Jury (11-1 Acquit)	1.

"improvidently granted." I brought *habeas corpus* in the federal court in Los Angeles. The judge dismissed the writ on the incredible ground that the Supreme Court's action was an adverse decision terminating the case. The Ninth Circuit Court of Appeals reversed and remanded for a hearing on the merits. While this hearing was pending, Lucille was released.

[15]After the murder of a certain informant, Rudy Sciara and his two colleagues sought to collect the reward placed on the informant's head, and wound up talking to an undercover agent. Neither jury believe the agent.

[16]Sciara co-defendants, who were tried separately—twice—after Sciara's acquittal. Their first case involved a hung jury.

[17]A sad case. Walter Head, a black worker at the Fisher Body Plant in Youngstown, Ohio, was part of a striking work force. When a young Polish worker attempted to breach the picket line, he became involved in an altercation with Head and wound up dead, shot with a pistol Head had been carrying. Unfortunately for Head, the victim turned out to be a war hero.

[18]Marlon Cook was an Army corporal who had been trained in the use of a knife. When he and his twin brother were leaving the *Gasthaus* on the *Hervegstrasse* near the military base in Mannheim, six African-American soldiers descended upon them with various deadly weapons. Marlon killed three of them in thirty seconds with a switchblade, and the others ran away.

[19]The Jacobson brothers were falsely accused of executing Conrad Greaves in the parking lot of the Traveller's Inn adjacent to LaGuardia Airport. When the identifying witness was caught lying, the case fell apart.

[20]Bill was a "rogue cop" who got caught taking bribes, and turned to become a witness for the *Knapp Commission* which was investigating police corruption in New York City. He was—in my opinion, and the opinion of the polygraph examiner who cleared him—framed by the police against who he was scheduled to testify. I tried the case against the best prosecutor I have opposed in a jury trial—John F. Keenan, now a much-admired federal judge—and hung the jury favoring acquittal. Phillips was later retried by another defender against another prosecutor, and is still serving life. In my opinion he is innocent.

Year	Case Name	State	Result	Verdicts
1971	U.S. Army v. Medina[21]	GA	Acquitted	102.
1973	Illinois v. Jayne[22]	IL	Acquitted	1.
1974	New York v. Carson[23]	NY	Murder 2	1.
1976	U.S. v. Patricia Hearst[24]	CA	Immunized	1.
1977	Indiana v. White[25]	IN	Jury hung	0.
1977	Florida v. Garcia[26]	FL	Dismissed	1.

[21]Captain Ernest Medina was the commander of the invading force in the infamous "My Lai Four Massacre" in Viet Nam, in which many innocent civilians were killed. He was ultimately charged with murder of "100 unidentified Vietnamese victims," as well as the murder of a four-year-old boy and a female VC hostile (he was also charged with assault and battery with a dangerous weapon on a VC Colonel, for which he was acquitted).

[22]Silas and George Jayne—two brothers well-known in the horse business in Greater Chicago—had been trying to kill each other for years. One night—while playing chess in his basement family room—George was shot through the head with a rifle. An alleged middleman testified that Silas had hired him to arrange the murder.

[23]Sonny Carson was an African-American cult leader; a political foe was executed, and witness claimed it was on Carson's instructions.

[24]Although Patty Hearst was tried for—and convicted of—the robbery of the Hibernia National Bank in San Francisco, the ominous charge which authorities were trying to lay on her (and for which I was originally hired) involved one of the most sickening murders in U.S. history, which Patty described in her book about her experiences. Suffice it to say that during a robbery of the Carmichael Bank in Sacramento, some 20 months after she had been kidnapped and during which she was allegedly the driver of the getaway car—a pregnant woman and her 7-month fetus were blasted with a sawed-off double-barrelled shotgun. When the victim arrived D.O.A. at the emergency room of the nearest hospital, the attending doctor lifted the sheet covering the body to find himself looking into the face of his wife!

[25]Air Force Major Charles White came home one evening to find "God" staring down at him from over his fireplace; he was ordered to kill his wife, he said, and did so. During the first trial two court-appointed and two defense psychiatrists said Major White was insane. The jury hung. During the second trial *three* court-appointed and two defense psychiatrists said he was insane; one court-appointed psychiatrist said he was sane. The jury acquitted.

[26]Duped by a polygraph examiner and a police detective, Luis Garcia *confessed* to the murder of a prostitute which he had not committed. The jury hung 11-1 for acquittal. A new trial judge suppressed the confession as fraudulently obtained, which ruling was upheld on appeal. With no other evidence to offer, the prosecution had to dismiss the indictment.

Year	Case Name	State	Result	Verdicts
1978	Pennsylvania v. Fitzsimmons[27]	PA	_____	2.
1977	Indiana v. White	IN	Acquitted (Insanity)	1.
1978	Commonwealth v. Walsh	MA	Acquitted (Insanity)	1.
1982	Iowa v. Campbell[28]	IA	Manslaughter (plea)	1.
1985	Illinois v. Boyle (3 murders)[29]	IL	Acquitted	2.
			Murder	1.
1988	U.S. v. LeQuire[30]	AL	Acquitted	1.
1987	New York v. Sacco[31]	NY	Murder	1.

[27]One of the weirdest cases of all time. George Fitzsimmons, a deranged Vietnam veteran, in 1968 killed his mother and father with one karate chop each to the neck. He was acquitted (in New York) on insanity grounds, and committed to a mental hospital. After 5 years, he was deemed "recovered" and released. He promptly killed his aunt and uncle with a knife. The case was tried in Western Pennsylvania, before Judge Earl Keim sitting without jury. George told Judge Keim that he was not guilty, that "a tree did it," and that his aunt and uncle had been "just like a mother and father to me!" At the end of the case Judge Keim said: "George, you're going to spend the rest of your life locked up. I can find you 'not guilty' on this evidence, and you can go to the state hospital for the criminally insane. Or I can find you 'guilty' and you will go to state prison. You choose." George thought for a minute, and said "The movies and food are better in prison. I'll go there." Although technically he was convicted, he could have on request been acquitted.

[28]Paul Campbell was an African-American in his thirties who had spent most of his life in prison. He escaped state prison in Missouri, and while in Des Moines took up with a young white girl. At some point they argued, and— apprehensive that she might turn him in to authorities, Paul killed her with a butcher knife. He was indigent. I was appointed by Judge Luther Glanton. The evidence failed, and the jury was about to acquit when I was able to make a deal with both Missouri (he was facing thirty years there) and Iowa for a manslaughter plea, with release in five years.

[29]Barbara's in-laws were murdered by gunfire; a year later, her husband was gunned down in his garage. A co-conspirator (years later) confessed, and implicated Barbara, who had inherited a substantial amount of insurance from the decedents. She was acquitted of complicity in the deaths of the in-laws, and convicted with respect to her husband.

[30]On the eve of his trial on drug importation charges in Montgomery, Alabama, LeQuire learned that assailants had gone to the Ft. Lauderdale home of one of the witnesses against him; finding that the witness had flown to Alabama, the assailants killed his *mother* with 50 machine gun bullets. LeQuire's former wife thereafter implicated him.

[31]Frank Sacco, a man with an extensive criminal record, shot and killed a man whom he thought was going to testify against him in a criminal case. An accomplice later confessed and implicated Sacco.

Year	Case Name	State	Result	Verdicts
1989	*Tanso v. Commonwealth (App.)[32]	MA	New trial granted	2.
1990	*Orlandello v. Commonwealth	MA	New trial granted	1.
1991	*Smith v. Commonwealth	MA	Reversed (Insufficient evidence)	1.
1992	*Harbold v. Illinois (App.)[33]	IL	New trial granted	1.
1994	Commonwealth v. Tanso[34]	MA	Acquitted	2.
1994	*Crotts v. North Carolina[35]	NC	New trial granted	2.

[32]Paul Tanso, Louis Cost, and Frank DiBennedetto (all teenagers) had been convicted of executing two other teenagers at Slye Park in Boston's North End. Used against them was an uncross-examined statement by an alleged eyewitness who had fled the jurisdiction before trial. The use of this statement was held to be prejudicial error.

[33]Prosecutorial misconduct—prejudicial remarks by prosecutor in final argument. New trial granted.

[34]At the retrial, Costa and DiBennedetto were convicted; Tanso was acquitted.

[35]Mark Crotts was convicted of killing two elderly neighbors. A witness accused his lawyer from the stand of trying to bribe him. No evidence was used to contradict this assertion, and no mistrial was declared. Crotts is of marginal intelligence, and his lawyers admit that he probably did not understand his right to have mistrial. The trial judge granted Crotts' motion for a new trial.

Index